BIRDIE
BOWERS

BIRDIE BOWERS

Captain Scott's Marvel

ANNE STRATHIE

In memory of my late parents, Jack and Marion Strathie, and of my mother's much-loved younger brother, Robert Hamilton (d. 1944), who found Birdie Bowers to be an inspirational hero in difficult times.

First published 2012

The History Press
The Mill, Brimscombe Port
Stroud, Gloucestershire, GL5 2QG
www.thehistorypress.co.uk

© Anne Strathie, 2012

The right of Anne Strathie to be identified as the Author
of this work has been asserted in accordance with the
Copyrights, Designs and Patents Act 1988.

British Library Cataloguing in Publication Data.
A catalogue record for this book is available from the British Library.

ISBN 978 0 7524 6003 1

Typesetting and origination by The History Press
Printed in Great Britain

CONTENTS

MAPS

ACKNOWLEDGEMENTS

I warmly thank all those organisations and individuals who have provided everything from general encouragement to expert advice, without which I would not have completed this book nor found the process of so doing enlightening and enjoyable.

First and foremost, I thank the many museums, archives, libraries and organisations listed below and the individuals who work within them. They are the custodians of our shared heritage and continue to serve us all in financially constrained times and to remind us that, even in an electronic age, there is no substitute for seeing or reading the 'real thing'. I thank them for advice, assistance and, in many cases, for permission to quote from documents in their custody or use images from their collections.

I particularly thank the Scott Polar Research Institute, University of Cambridge (SPRI), and Heather Lane, Naomi Boneham, Lucy Martin, Shirley Sawtell and Georgina Cronin for expert help and guidance, and for permission to quote from documents and to reproduce images from SPRI's archives and Freeze-Frame collection.

I am also very grateful to Cheltenham Art Gallery & Museum (Helen Brown, Ann-Rachael Harwood); Cheltenham Library (particularly the local history section); Gloucestershire Archives and University of Gloucestershire Archives (Lorna Scott). I also thank Bexley Local Studies & Archive Centre (Sue Barclay); Bute Museum (Jean McMillan); Greenock Libraries and Museum; National Library of Scotland; National Maritime Museum; Paisley Museum (David Robertson); Plymouth Museum (Nigel Overton); Royal Geographical Society (Sarah Strong and colleagues, including for permissions); Sidmouth Library (Gill Spence and colleagues); Sidmouth Museum (Rab and Christine Barnard); The Royal Collection (Emma Stuart and colleagues);

United Kingdom Antarctic Heritage Trust. I am also very grateful to museums in other countries, in particular to Canterbury Museum, Christchurch (Baden Norris, Joanna Condon, Natalie Cadenhead, Katie Wilson) for assistance and permission to quote from documents and use images from their collections. I also thank the Alexander Turnbull Library, Wellington (Gillian Headifen, including for permissions); Auckland War Memorial Museum; the Kerry Stokes Collection, Perth (Erica Persak and Karyn Cameron, including for permissions); Museum of North Otago, Oamaru (Rowan Carroll and colleagues); New Zealand Antarctic Heritage Trust and State Library of Victoria, Melbourne (including for permissions).

My thanks also to the Authors' Foundation, whose grant was a source of both practical support and encouragement, and to the Society of Authors (administrators of the grant scheme), their staff (in particular Sarah Baxter) and members of its Gloucestershire branch.

I thank the numerous descendants of members of Scott's party, writers, historians, explorers and others who have offered guidance, information, practical assistance and encouragement, including but not limited to: Benedict Allen; Tom Avery; the Back family; Dr Paul Baker (former Rector, Waitaki High School for Boys, Oamaru); Dr Steven Blake, David Elder and fellow members of the Cheltenham Wilson centenary committee; Gill Blenkinsop; Clive Bradbury; Angie Butler; Peter Callaghan; Patrick Cordingley; Dr Ian Davis; Ivan Day; Julian Evans; Ben Fogle; Mike Goodearl; Meredith Hooper; Dr Max Jones; Roger Jones; Charles Lagerbom; Jo and Ian Laurie; Sue Limb; Mr and Mrs David McKelvie and Margaret Mackay; Kate Mosse; Adrian Raeside; Rod Rhys Jones and Ken Gibson (British Antarctic Monument Trust); Dr Stephen Ross and Dr Pearl Jacks; Michael Smith; Francis Spufford; Sue Stubenvoll (NZ Antarctic Society); Michael Tarver; Sara Wheeler; Isobel Williams; Dr David Wilson (to whom particular thanks) and Jake Wilson.

I also thank family and friends whose encouragement, support, proofreading and Antarctic-themed offerings have kept me going, including but not limited to: Jean Strathie; Roberta Deighton, Fiona Eyre, Jill Burrowes and families; Michael Bourne, the Nops, the Nuttalls, the Ridleys, Ali Rieple and other Cranfield friends; the Cairncrosses; Lin and Robert Coleman; Michael Drayton; Julia Fortes, Imogen Fortes and family; the Grays (New Zealand); Kate Howard; Tracey Jaggers; Alison Jolley; Pauline Lyons; Charlotte Mackintosh and family; Katherine McInnes; Esther Morgan; Neela Mann; Jan Oldfield and Nowton friends; Joanna Scott; St Andrew's University friends; Tivoli friends; Ann Watkin and family; Graham Webster; the late Don Weekes and Maisie Weekes; Sophie Wilson. Thanks also to Rodney Russ and all on the *Spirit of Enderby* (Ross Sea expedition, January–February 2011); Carole Angier, Allegra Huston and all at Lumb Bank (Arvon Foundation life-writing course, September 2011); and to tutors and fellow students on Open University courses.

Thank you also to staff at The History Press, in particular Lindsey Smith, Hazel Kayes and Abbie Wood, and to Simon Hamlet who gave me the opportunity to write this book.

INTRODUCTION

A few years ago I found in a cupboard a well-thumbed copy of *'Birdie' Bowers of the Antarctic*, a biography by the Reverend George Seaver, published in 1938.

Although I live in Cheltenham, home town of Edward Wilson, who famously died with Captain Scott on their return march from the South Pole in March 1912, I was not familiar with the story of Henry 'Birdie' Bowers who, aged 28, also succumbed to cold, hunger and thirst in the same blizzard-bound tent. My interest in Bowers was further aroused when I realised that my copy of Seaver's biography had been given by my mother as a Christmas present to her younger brother a few years before his death (at the same age as Bowers) in the Second World War, and when I read, in a letter of sympathy from a friend of my uncle, that the two men had regarded Bowers as an inspirational hero.

In his journal Scott described Bowers as a marvel, someone who, despite the hardships of the return journey from the Pole, remained resolutely cheerful and full of hope. Others on the expedition saw Bowers as a straightforward, tirelessly energetic young man who was eager to play his part in every aspect of the expedition. In the Antarctic Bowers was clearly in his element but my research revealed a somewhat more complex figure. Bowers was born in Scotland in 1883 to an adventurous sea captain and a considerably younger missionary teacher (who, I discovered to my surprise, had been born and raised in Cheltenham), from whom he inherited a form of Christianity rooted in a nineteenth-century schism in the Anglican Church. A traveller by upbringing and instinct, Bowers worked on a famous sailing ship which plied the trade routes between Britain and Australia, saw New York's Statue of Liberty (only twenty years after its installation) and, as an officer in the Royal Indian Marine, served the still-great British Empire in India and the Middle and Far East.

While in some ways Bowers was Victorian by upbringing and inclination, by the time he left for Antarctica he was almost ecumenical in religious outlook, was an enthusiastic photographer, had walked on the seabed in a diving suit, read H.G. Wells' futuristic fiction and dined in London's brand-new Strand Palace Hotel.

In 2011 I was fortunate enough to travel to Cape Evans and visit the hut that sheltered Scott's men from the icy winds and blizzards of the Antarctic winter. From there Bowers wrote (as he had done throughout his travels) to his mother and sisters regularly, lyrically and enthusiastically, describing his sometimes hair-raising adventures, the stunning scenery and the wildlife which was, for him, a constant source of interest and wonder. In telling Bowers' story I have tried to convey his sense of adventure and wonder at the mysteries of the universe rather than indulge in analysis informed by twenty-first-century hindsight. I have called places by the names with which he was familiar and used the measurements of weight, temperature and distance he recorded in his numerous journals and notebooks. I have also, when quoting him, retained (with minimal exceptions required for clarity) his sometimes erratic punctuation and spelling. During his short life Henry Bowers was, largely thanks to his prominent nose, given many nicknames; I have referred to him as 'Henry' (as his family always called him) until he leaves for Antarctica and 'Birdie' during the *Terra Nova* expedition.

Although I have not been to the South Pole, I have travelled far in Britain and beyond in the course of my research for this book. All along the way, both at home and abroad, I have been fortunate to receive expert assistance, guidance, kindness, generosity and friendship from many people and organisations. I thank them all and acknowledge that any errors, omissions or oversights are my own.

I hope that readers enjoy learning about the short but adventurous life of Henry Bowers as much as I have enjoyed researching and writing about it.

Anne Strathie,
Cheltenham

PROLOGUE

London, May 1910

Lieutenant Henry R. Bowers of the Royal Indian Marine had just signed on as a junior officer on Captain Robert Scott's second Antarctic expedition.[1]

This promised to be the greatest adventure of his life and he was keen to make a good impression on Scott and his second in command, Lieutenant 'Teddy' Evans. Henry knew he had been lucky, and the only one to be chosen without an interview from among 8,000 candidates. He was aware, however, that many of his shipmates were veterans of earlier Polar expeditions or Royal Navy officers and might wonder if a stocky, 5ft 4in junior RIM officer would be up to the job. But Henry had loved snow, ice and cold weather since he was a toddler in Scotland and had, at the age of 7, written to someone he mistakenly believed lived in Wilkes Land, one of the few charted areas of Antarctica:

> Dear Eskimo,
> Please write and tell me about your land. I want to go there some day.
> Your friend Henry.

Henry's letter remained unanswered but his passion for the mysterious icy continent developed. As a cadet on HMS *Worcester* he listened intently as Sir Clements Markham of the Royal Geographical Society talked about polar regions; as a young mariner, he followed newspaper reports of Scott and Shackleton's Antarctic expeditions and read the explorers' own accounts of their travails and triumphs. When, following several months of correspondence, a cable arrived in India offering Henry a place on Scott's British Antarctic expedition, he dropped everything and returned to London. Henry was dreading saying farewell to his mother and sisters but believed this expedition was a God-sent opportunity, and his destiny.

Henry's first duties in his new role were to help sort and stow the crates, cases and bundles which lined the quayside at West India Docks. He worked with a will until, as he strode across the deck of the ship one day, he failed to notice a carelessly unfastened hatch door. Caught unawares, he found himself flying through the air, plunging deep into the main hold until his descent was eventually broken by an unforgiving heap of pig-iron. He got to his feet, satisfied himself that nothing was broken, scrambled out of the hold and resumed his work. Later that day, Lieutenant Teddy Evans was heard to declare that Henry was a 'silly ass' for falling into the hold, but admitted to being impressed by his powers of recovery. Captain Scott also reportedly had his doubts about the wisdom of this particular appointment. Henry knew, however, that as soon as the *Terra Nova* set sail he would be able to show them what he was made of.

1

FAMILY ROOTS

When 7-year-old Henry Bowers wrote to his 'friend' in Wilkes Land, Antarctica, he was living in London with his widowed mother, former missionary teacher Emily Bowers, and his elder sisters, Mary and Edith. His father, Captain Alexander Bowers, had died some three years previously in Burma where he had worked as a master mariner for many years.

Henry was born in Greenock, a major centre of shipbuilding, trade and sugar-refining,[1] which lay about 20 miles down the Firth of Clyde from Glasgow, the British Empire's second city. His father, son of a Greenock shipwright (also Alexander), was born there in 1827 but had left home at the age of 13 to work on the eastern trade routes of the British Empire. He rose swiftly to the rank of captain, steered the *Geelong*[2] to victory in the China to London tea-clipper race (thus winning a substantial cash prize) and reached a new high navigation point for British ships on the Yangtse Kiang. The Captain's ships largely carried cargo but, as a staunch Christian, he regularly offered free passage to missionaries travelling along Britain's trade routes. In 1857, during the Indian Mutiny, his ship was also used as a government troopship. By 1864, Captain Bowers' reputation was such that the Glasgow-based British India Steam Navigation Company (known as BI) offered him command of a brand-new ship, the *Madras*; his first duty was to return to the Firth of Clyde to supervise his vessel's construction.

The Captain returned to his family home at Rue-End Street in the centre of Greenock, where his parents still lived. Since he had left home one of his younger twin sisters, Jane, had married a shipmaster, William Allan, and given birth to a son (also William) at the Cape of Good Hope; following William Allan's death she had married another shipmaster, James Smith.[3] Jane's twin sister Mary was still unmarried. The now-prosperous Captain decided to buy a larger home for himself and his extended family, and settled on a ten-roomed villa (yet to be built) at Battery Point, which lay a mile or so from the centre of Greenock and offered extensive views over the Firth of Clyde. The Captain christened his new home West Bank, although locals jokingly referred to it as Bowers' Folly due to its remote location and grand scale compared to the family's more modest abode in Rue-End Street.

Before West Bank was ready for occupation the Captain and the *Madras* left Greenock. During her maiden voyage she encountered a violent storm in the Bay of Bengal and was swept onto an uncharted reef.[4] No lives were lost but cargo had to be jettisoned, and while passengers praised the Captain's 'decisive and energetic' actions, his employers tried to demote him to a less responsible post. The Captain, indignant at the slur on his good name, tendered his resignation. The following year, 1866, he heard that his father had died in Greenock, leaving him as head of the family. By then he had found work, thanks to Todd, Findlay & Company, a Glasgow-based shipping company, as head of Rangoon's Dalla dockyard, headquarters of the expanding Irrawaddy Flotilla Company (in which Todd, Findlay & Co. was a shareholder).[5]

The Captain, by now also a Freemason and member of the Royal Naval Reserve, soon became an integral part of Rangoon's business community. He was asked to join a British expedition up the Irrawaddy, the aim of which was to establish the feasibility of reopening a long-dormant trade route between Burma and neighbouring China.[6] The expedition party led by Captain Edward Sladen, British Resident in Mandalay, numbered over a hundred, including representatives of the Irrawaddy Flotilla Company and other businesses, an eminent naturalist, interpreters, servants, an armed escort, and elephants loaded with British-made goods and gifts for local rulers and potential trading partners.

Before leaving Mandalay Captain Sladen obtained the King of Burma's formal approval for the expedition to enter the politically unstable border area of Upper Burma.[7] The party sailed over 300 miles up the increasingly narrow Irrawaddy to Bhamo, the last major trading post on the river; then, with the consent of local rulers, it travelled through the jungle to the frontier city known to the Burmese as Momein and to the Chinese as Tengyueh-chow. Tribesmen who had seen few Europeans before greeted them with random volleys of gunfire and invited them to join in trance-inducing and other mysterious ceremonies. When they finally reached the border country, which lay at an altitude of 6,000ft, they found fruit, vegetables and other produce growing in abundance. For six weeks they explored routes, showed their wares and promoted the benefits of trade with the British Empire. Captain Bowers recorded every detail of their journey and the countryside through which they passed; he noted that some of the native sheep resembled Scottish sheep and that some gently sloping valleys had an English character. He praised the Burmese for their industriousness, the Chinese for their aptitude for manufacture, and the Shans for their cleanliness, smart attire, and neat homes and gardens. He recorded details of places of worship and schools, and, having approvingly noted similarities between Buddhism and Christianity, came to the conclusion that British missionaries should not seek to impose Christianity on Buddhists who preferred to follow their own faith.

Following a somewhat hazardous return journey to Bhamo (during which several local guides and interpreters deserted the party), the Captain returned to Rangoon and produced a 200-page formal report on the expedition. He admitted that the British did not have a spotless record in the region – partly due to the introduction of opium – but decided that the King of Burma seemed less interested in his people's well-being than in amassing riches, indulging himself and keeping his people in thrall by propagating superstitions. The Captain made a strong case for investment in the railway lines, roads and bridges that would be required to support the reopening of the trade route to China, a development which would both serve Britain's commercial interests and provide a counter-balance to the growing influence in the region of the French, Americans and Russians.

Although his involvement in the expedition further enhanced the Captain's reputation, he received no remuneration for his participation for almost two years, during which time a fire at his house in Rangoon destroyed much of his personal property, including his precious bagpipes and Scottish books.[8] But there was considerable interest in the expedition in Britain and Captains Sladen and Bowers received invitations to speak about their findings in both England and Scotland. Captain Bowers visited his Scottish home for the first time for many years; by now, West Bank, with its high-ceilinged rooms, fine plasterwork and stained glass, was home to his 70-year-old widowed mother, his sisters Mary and Jane, and the latter's son Willie and second husband James Smith.[9]

During his visit home, the Captain addressed Glasgow's Chamber of Commerce and the Greenock Philosophical Society. He was also elected, on 27 November 1871, as a Fellow of the Royal Geographical Society in recognition of the 50ft-long chart he had made of the 1,000-mile Irrawaddy.[10] With his family continuing to expand (Jane was pregnant again and Mary was now engaged to Henry Robertson, a produce broker from Dundee[11]), the 44-year-old Captain needed more work. Through his connections he obtained an appointment as a ship's master with Patrick Henderson & Company (another Glasgow-based shareholder in the Irrawaddy Flotilla Company), which was expanding its cargo services between Glasgow and Burma. As part of his contract the Captain was required to invest in the British & Burmese Steam Navigation Company, a new company established by Henderson's to finance the construction of his ship, the *Ananda*, an arrangement which kept the Captain's financial interests aligned with those of his new employers.[12]

The Captain bade his family farewell and set sail for the East. Following early success with the *Ananda*'s new service, Henderson's commissioned two more ships – the *Shuay de Gon* and the *Peah Pekhat* – which would be owned by another new company, the Burmah Steamship Co., in which the Captain was also required to purchase shares. The Captain's three-vessel fleet offered modestly priced passenger, goods and mail services between Singapore and Penang, and to more remote areas including Perak, Penang's southern neighbour which had recently been annexed by the Indian Office.[13] Although much of his money was now tied up in the ships he commanded, the entrepreneurial Captain took the opportunity of buying some potentially lucrative timber rights in Perak.[14]

The rotund, jovial Captain, now entering his fifties, was prosperous, well-regarded within the local commercial community and had a wide social circle, including those with whom he worshipped at church on Sundays.[15] He had never married, however, so his friends were pleased when he began spending time in the company of Miss Emily Webb, a teacher at an Anglican mission school, who had recently arrived in Penang from Sidmouth in Devon.

❋ ❋ ❋

Emily Webb was born in early 1847 in Cheltenham, Gloucestershire.[16] Her father, Frederick Webb, had as a young man moved from Stroud, a centre of the Cotswolds wool industry, to Cheltenham where he worked initially as a journeyman tailor.[17] At that time Cheltenham was a thriving, expanding town with health-giving springs (given the royal seal of approval by George III in 1788), a mild climate, a wide range of 'entertainments' and good transport links to London. These features combined to make it attractive to visitors and new residents, including growing numbers of civil servants and military personnel retiring from work in India and other parts of the British Empire.[18]

By 1851, 30-year-old Frederick Webb had his own tailor's business at 3 St George's Terrace, where he lived with his London-born wife Mary Ann, 3-year-old Emily, her younger sister (also Mary Ann) and two lodgers.[19] The

Webbs were regular church-goers and their minister was the Reverend Francis Close, a famously fiery preacher from the Evangelical wing of the Anglican Church and founder of several educational establishments in Cheltenham.[20] Close had come to Cheltenham in 1824 at the behest of Charles Simeon, a leading Evangelical preacher, co-founder of the Church Missionary Society, advisor to the East India Company on recruitment of missionaries and founder of a trust which acquired church 'livings' (including Cheltenham) with a view to appointing Evangelical rather than 'high church' vicars.[21] In his sermons Close railed against the evils of horse racing and other 'entertainments' and against the Church of Rome which, in his eyes, threatened the very existence of the Evangelical wing of the Anglican Church.[22] When Close left Cheltenham in 1856 to become Dean of Carlisle, Frederick Webb joined hundreds of parishioners in signing a farewell scroll of thanks in recognition of all he had done for them and their town.[23]

Emily Webb attended Holy Trinity School for Girls, which lay a short walk from her home and adjacent to the eponymous church where Francis Close had begun his Cheltenham career.[24] By 1861, the Webbs had moved to a new, larger terraced house in nearby St George's Place, which had ample room for Frederick, Mary Ann, Emily and her two surviving younger siblings, Elizabeth and William (her sister Mary Ann had died young), a tailor's apprentice and three lodgers, two of whom were seamstresses.[25] While Emily's father might have wanted her to work in his workshop, he allowed her to continue her education at Holy Trinity School where she rose to become a 'pupil-teacher'.[26] After a few years in that role she took a Queen's scholarship examination and, with the aid of a first-class scholarship, enrolled as a student at Cheltenham's pioneering teacher training college, founded some twenty years previously by Francis Close. There, she and other young women took classes in a separate building from their male counterparts and followed a syllabus which placed more emphasis on religious and scriptural education than on school management, mathematics and sciences that featured in the men's syllabus.[27]

In December 1867, at the age of 20, Emily Webb received her diploma and accepted a post as a teacher in a church school in Sidmouth, a small seaside town in Devon. There, as in Cheltenham, she found fine Regency buildings, and a thriving Evangelical congregation based at All Saints' church, of which the vicar, Heneage Gibbes, had Cheltenham connections.[28] The progress report sent to Emily's teacher training supervisors confirmed she was well qualified, controlled her classes well and had raised the standard of sewing lessons at the school.

Emily was taken under the wing of the Radfords, a leading Sidmouth family who were involved in the governance of her school. In 1871 she acquired a handsome leather-bound copy of *The Universe, or the infinitely great and the infinitely little*, which laid out before her 'the whole panorama of nature'.[29] Meanwhile, her family continued to live and work in St George's Place, Cheltenham, where her siblings Elizabeth and William were now working in their father's line of trade.[30]

By July 1874 Emily, at the age of 27, was head of Sidmouth's parish school and ready for a new challenge. Her next move was to a mission school in the Malay States of 'Further India'. She carried with her an inscribed gold watch acknowledging her services to children's education in Sidmouth and the best wishes of the Radfords and other friends and colleagues.[31]

In her new home, over 6,000 miles from Cheltenham, Emily met Captain Alexander Bowers.

❊ ❊ ❊

On 19 July 1877, in St Andrew's Cathedral, Singapore, Alexander Bowers and Emily Webb became man and wife.[32] Despite their age difference, the couple had much in common. They shared innate intelligence, a sense of independence and adventure, a deep faith, and a dislike of religious pomp and ritual. Following his marriage, Captain Bowers continued to operate his fleet of ships and keep a weather eye on his timber and other investments. Emily accompanied him on several of his longer voyages, including to Perak where, in October 1878, she became involved in a cause célèbre of the Malay Peninsula. Captain Lloyd, an Indian government official, was hacked to death by a local gang following a disagreement with his staff over wages and an unfortunate misunderstanding regarding local social customs.[33] Mrs Lloyd was severely injured and, with the couple's still-sleeping children, narrowly escaped being burned alive when the fleeing gang set fire to their house. Captain Bowers' steamer, the *Peah Pekhat*, was summoned to assist; floor timbers from the Bowers' Perak house were used to make a coffin for Captain Lloyd and, while the Captain ferried government officials and policemen from Penang to Perak, Emily helped look after the Lloyds' frightened children.

In early 1879 Emily gave birth to a baby girl whom she and the Captain named Mary, after Emily's mother and the Captain's sister. By now the Captain's shipping business was suffering from a decline in world trade, increased competition and depressed cargo rates. To make matters worse, the *Ananda* was involved in an accident, and although the Captain had not been at the wheel at the time, his seaman's certificate was suspended for three months. Following an appeal the certificate was soon reinstated but with losses on the fleet mounting, the Captain's business partners summoned him to Scotland for a face-to-face meeting.[34]

Soon after he returned from what proved to be a tempestuous meeting, Emily gave birth to the couple's second daughter, Edith. When Emily wrote to her mother-in-law in Greenock – by now over 80 and in failing health – telling her about the baby, she hinted that the Captain's business was experiencing difficulties. Margaret Bowers responded immediately with assurances that she would not breathe a word about the Captain's problems and remained proud of her son's achievements and grateful for his generosity to his extended family.[35] The Captain's business partners were less sympathetic, however, and ordered all his three ships to be returned to Scotland to be sold. The Captain protested that a forced sale outside the fleet's sphere of operation would result in losses for them all, but his words fell on deaf ears. When he returned to Scotland, he took with him Emily and the two small daughters his family had not yet met.

By the time the Captain and his family reached Greenock, his 82-year-old mother had died.[36] His ships were sold at a loss, virtually eliminating his capital at a time when he had a young family, his sister Jane – now widowed for a second time – and her two younger children to provide for. Despite his business setbacks, Alexander Bowers' reputation remained high in Scotland and he received several offers of local employment, but his heart was in the East where he felt he had unfinished business. He entered into an agreement with his erstwhile employers BI, who agreed to build a new ship for him to operate on their behalf in the Mergui archipelago off the coast of lower Burma. The Captain had no capital to invest but BI obtained a government grant; the *Mergui*, of which the Captain would supervise the construction, would be BI's smallest seagoing vessel, nimble enough for island-hopping but sufficiently large to carry cargo and about a hundred passengers. Emily and her girls soon settled in at West Bank where Emily quickly made a circle of friends, including her neighbour Bithiah Paul, a near-contemporary with small children whose husband was a Greenock sugar-refiner.[37]

On 29 July 1883 in West Bank, Emily gave birth to a baby boy. As Alexander, the traditional Bowers family name for boys, had already been given to Jane's second son, the couple decided to name their baby in honour of his Aunt Mary's husband, who had helped the family during recent difficult times. The Captain and Emily had their son baptised at nearby St John's Episcopal Church, where he was christened Henry Robertson Bowers.[38]

2

LEARNING THE ROPES

An early studio photograph of Henry Bowers shows a sturdy toddler clad in elaborate Victorian childhood finery.

During his first two winters in Greenock, when snowdrifts blanketed the West Bank garden, Henry enjoyed romping and rolling with his father, who would regularly return from early morning walks armed with snowballs with which to pelt any members of his family who still lingered in bed.[1] Before Henry was 2 years old, the Captain returned to the East with his new ship. Under his contract with BI, the Captain received 20 per cent of the *Mergui*'s net earnings, from which he could draw 250 rupees a month, half of which was paid directly to Emily in Scotland. While this represented something of a reduction from his previous remuneration, the Captain was sure his new services would prosper and that Mergui, with its bountiful natural resources, would soon attract new settlers – and potential customers. The first leg of the *Mergui*'s maiden voyage passed without incident, but when she left the shelter of the Horn of Africa she hit one of the worst cyclones the Captain had ever experienced. As hurricane-force gusts and huge waves battered his ship, his crew lashed him to the wheel, from where he fought to save his ship, the lives of those aboard, his cargo and his livelihood. The *Mergui* eventually arrived safely at her destination, but repair work delayed the launch of the new services; when they did start, the Captain found his competitors prepared to harry his ship and block her passage in and out of harbours and between islands.

The Captain's heart, already weakened from years of hard work, began to fail.[2] In February 1887 he cabled Emily in Greenock asking her to come to Mergui. By March he was so ill that he was taken to hospital in Penang; he returned to Mergui but, according to an old friend, the once-stout Captain was now 'a small man'. By this time Emily had left Mary and Edith (now known as May and Edie) in Greenock and, with Henry in tow, was on a ship heading eastwards. Henry, a chatty toddler, soon became the ship's general mascot and firm friends with a tall Anglican bishop, with whom he would promenade around the deck. Henry also enjoyed spotting different types of seabirds but was petrified by the huge, hairy spiders which scuttled out from cabin corners in an unpredictable and, to his eyes, extremely threatening manner.

When the ship docked in Calcutta Emily received the news that her husband had died on 12 April 1887. When she arrived in Burma, she received a warm welcome and much sympathy. She heard that her husband had died peacefully at home after prayers had been said for him, and that many friends and colleagues had come to pay their last respects. Members of the Captain's close circle, in particular the Aldridges and the Foucars (who had children of an age with Emily's own), were anxious to do everything possible for Emily and her three children.[3] Emily, having already seen how tropical sunshine, mosquito bites and spiders affected Henry, declined invitations to set up home in Burma; she knew, however, that the bulk of the Captain's capital had been wiped out by his recent business ventures and that her alternatives were limited. It was the Foucars, wealthy friends with Burmese and London timber interests, who came up with a solution: they would pay the rental for a house in London where Emily could live with her three children and look after those of the Foucar children who were of an age to benefit from an English education.

On the long voyage back to Britain, Emily read obituaries and letters of sympathy praising the Captain's intrepid spirit, his vision for Mergui and Burma, his generosity and his good humour. In Greenock she mourned with her husband's family and read tributes to an esteemed, albeit often-absent, member of the town's shipping and trading community.

After a short stay at West Bank, Emily, May, Edie and Henry travelled to London, where they initially stayed in Brockley with Ferdinand Foucar's brother Alexander.[4] While there, Emily learned that her husband had left her £408 11s 2d in his will; she was not penniless, but it was only her arrangement with the Foucars that enabled her and her family to move into a sizeable house in Sidcup, along with the young Foucars. Henry, two years younger than Louis, the youngest Foucar, was very much the family 'pet', but Emily (despite being devoted to her only son) refused to spoil him and made him carry the family purse on shopping expeditions so he could learn the value of money.[5] Emily ran a Christian household: everyone sang Moody and Sankey[6] hymns round the breakfast table and the children all learned to read their Bibles, say their prayers, and be wary of 'high' Anglicans or Roman Catholics whose views differed from those of the Evangelical Anglican Bowers or the Huguenot Protestant Foucars.

Henry spent his childhood in London and the surrounding area. West Bank in Greenock had been sold and his Aunts Mary and Jane (and Jane's children) now lived in Fife at the home of Henry Robertson. Emily's elderly parents lived 100 miles away in Cheltenham.[7] But Henry's horizons soon expanded when, at a geography lesson at his first school – Miss Lonsdale's Seminary[8] – he learned about Wilkes Land in Antarctica and wrote his succinct but purposeful letter expressing a wish to visit there sometime in the future. Henry's schooling continued at Sidcup College. He was small for his age and, thanks to his now prominent nose, was soon nicknamed Polly (the parrot).[9] He preferred butterfly-collecting to classroom work or sports and spent hours roaming around fields with a friend, armed with the paraphernalia of the serious collector. In an effort to convert others to his hobby he organised a 'society' with a self-penned magazine which was transcribed by his long-suffering sisters. He persevered with his schoolwork, however, and won a form prize, and his headmaster commented on his report that whatever Henry decided to do he would do well. Before leaving Sidcup Henry confided to a friend (but not to Emily) that he wanted to become a mariner like his father.

After Emily, her children and charges moved to Streatham, Henry attended Streatham High School for Boys where, according to his reports, he was a conscientious scholar with a genuine interest in learning. He learned shorthand, received a prize for Euclid and, despite his short legs, won a quarter-mile race and a coveted place in the school's cricket eleven.[10] Now known as Beakie, he learned to be teased and to tease others, including his sister May (now a trainee teacher); he wrote her a letter addressed to 'My dearest Duchy Darling Cherub May', which was liberally scattered with deliberate spelling mistakes, crossings out and slang references to an intra-family loan of '10 bob', which he warned her not to lend to 'every young calf who is wanting chink'.[11] Although Henry was doing well at school, when Emily found a picture of a sailing ship pinned to his bedroom wall she bowed to the inevitable, presented him with her precious copy of *The Universe* and submitted an application for him to join the Thames Nautical Training College.[12]

On 16 September 1897, 14-year-old Henry Bowers boarded the training ship HMS *Worcester*, a retired battleship moored at Greenhithe on the Thames.[13] After a brief period as Gilly-loo-lah Bird, he became known as Kinky-boke, a slang reference to his 'bent nose'. In the classroom he filled exercise books with copious notes on navigational theory and nautical astronomy, and on general subjects such as grammar, French, religion and geography.[14] The latter subject included lessons on 'Peoples of the world', during which he copied down notes on his own race:

Aryans or Indo-European people (c.650 million of the world's estimated population of 1,500 million): Increasing ever in civilization, in intilectual [*sic*] power from age to age this race has become the dominant one in the world … supplanting many inferior races and re-peopling wide areas like America and Australia. The chief characteristics of this family are – white skin, oval face, arched nose, high forhead [*sic*] and the teeth in the upper jaw perpendicular to those in the lower jaw.

He also learned that Christianity, 'the religion of Jesus Christ', was practised by 'almost all the Aryan races' and had 450 million adherents (including 'converts') who outnumbered Buddhists, Hindus, Mohammedans and 'Heathens, etc.' He learned that an empire was 'a collection of states … all subject of one sovereign who is called an Emperor' and that colonies were 'territories in foreign lands, either directly dependent or subordinate to a parent state'. The pages of his atlas showed him that Britain's Empire, coloured pink for easy identification, included Canada, India, Further India, South Africa, Australia, New Zealand and numerous smaller outposts.

In order to remember everything he wanted to tell his mother and sisters about, Henry began keeping his first journal:

Sang 'Hearts of Oak' at new cadets' singing … Took the Theory Prize – *Story of our Planet* – and Scripture Prize – *Life of John Davis*.[15] … Pillow-fight – splendid fun – got one or two nasty ones. … Carruthers and I explored the Fore Peak, also the Tank-room. Climbed through a small hole in the bulkhead: got right aft under Mr. Golding's store-room. Hid a candle and matches down there, went often. Tried to enter Magazine – could not. Found two 28 lb shot, brought them out at the end of term and put them in our chests. Made up our minds if possible to break into Magazine next term. I bring lantern, Carruthers brings tools.

In the event, the planned break-in was thwarted, but sporting activities kept him busy: 'Went in for Paper-chases – grand sport. Ran with Carruthers – couldn't keep up with him after a bit – kept running and got into an awful state … Thought I should have dropped several times – was almost too giddy to stand when I stopped.'

HMS *Worcester's* captain-superintendent, David Wilson-Barker, aware that Emily Bowers was a widow, took a fatherly interest in Henry's schoolwork and hobbies. The captain, himself a keen butterfly-collector, showed Henry how to breed butterflies from caterpillars and took him to see a friend's particularly fine collection. He also taught Henry how to preserve bird specimens and demonstrated the rudiments of photography so he could record interesting 'finds'. While on the *Worcester*, Henry's interest in the polar regions was reignited through talks given by Sir Clements Markham, a member of the *Worcester*'s governing committee and president of the Royal Geographical Society.[16] During his visits to the ship, Markham regaled Henry and his fellow cadets with tales of his South American and Arctic adventures and details of plans for a British Antarctic expedition for which he was already raising support.[17]

Henry, still small for his age, was sometimes picked on by larger cadets, who for amusement would scrub his prominent nose until it was red and raw. Following such incidents an unhappy Henry sought reassurance from Carruthers that his nose was no bigger than average but was simply (as even Henry conceded) the 'wrong shape'. But with Henry, anxieties soon passed as he became absorbed in the next 'prank' or in his daily Bible reading, which he did for fifteen minutes each evening while other cadets played rowdily around him. In the classroom Henry's powers of concentration served him well and he developed what the captain described as a 'quiet sense of duty', demonstrated when he rescued a fellow cadet – a non-swimmer who had fallen into deep water and was struggling until Henry (not yet a particularly good swimmer himself) jumped in and held him afloat until help arrived.[18]

In July 1899, just before his 16th birthday, Henry left the *Worcester* with a 'First Class Extra' in Scholastic and Seamanship subjects (a rare combination), a third-place award in the Queen's Gold Medal (for boys expected to make outstanding sailors), an award for good conduct and a presentation Bible. He was now ready to go to sea.[19]

3

SAILING THE SEVEN SEAS

I n autumn 1899 Henry embarked on a four-year apprenticeship, under sail,
with Aitken, Lilburn & Co., Glasgow-based owners of a fleet of long-haul
ships. Before leaving home, he submitted an application to join the Royal
Naval Reserve which would, if successful, bring him a step closer to his goal of
joining the 'Senior Service'.

Henry, along with Eric Graham, one of his best friends from the *Worcester*,
joined the *Loch Torridon*, a 2,000-ton Clyde-built, steel-hulled, four-masted sailing barque. Captain Robert Pattman, a hard-bitten veteran of the jute trade,
had been in charge of her since 1882 and had a reputation for fast sailing times,
particularly on routes to and from Australia.[1] In December 1899 Henry began
his first letter-cum-diary for Emily:[2]

Dearest Mother

We have now been a month at sea, and I must begin my letter to you,
although there will be no chance of posting it until we reach Adelaide … but
I shall just go on and on when there is anything to write about, and make one
letter of it.

After saying Good-bye to you at the station I felt pretty miserable, but
Louis [Foucar] met me at Fenchurch Street Station and accompanied me on
board … Eric was on the ship before me and I was jolly glad to see him. We
share a cabin together … [we] learn navigation, when we are not working
with the men, i.e. scrubbing, cleaning, painting, serving out water, etc., etc.
… the work never stops day or night. The other two apprentices are from
Scotland, they are older and bigger than we are, but Eric and I soon found
that our training on the *Worcester* gave us a tremendous pull over them in
seamanship … we sailed past the *Worcester* and dipped to her and wondered

what we were in for. When we got past the North Foreland, a stiff gale got up against us in the Channel … I was so horribly seasick, I won't say any more about it, it was awful, I had no idea it could be as bad as that, however I know all about it now and thank goodness I don't suppose I shall ever have it again.

As winds filled the *Loch Torridon's* sails and whipped her along at full speed, Henry was glad to be on such a fine ship. He had already learned, however, that Captain Pattman was considerably less fatherly than Captain Wilson-Barker:

You know of course that a Captain is always called 'The old man' although of course he is not old. Father would be called the 'old man' too, when he was Master of his own ship at 19! … our 'old man' is very much feared by everyone, and I may say heartily disliked by most. He has a kind of steel grey eye, which seems to have the power of withering those that come up against him, also nothing escapes him. He is always quarrelling with the Mates, if they venture to disagree with him, and he is very stern with the crew. … All the same he is a splendid seaman (of the old school, of course), a man who knows every inch of his ship and one you can depend upon to give the right order under any circumstances. You will be thinking he is a bit of a tartar, and so he is, but I will say he is just on the whole, and it would be useless for a man to be 'soft' at sea, with these different nationalities which make up a crew, it would be fatal; there is one thing sure, no one will ever get the upper hand of him.

On their first Atlantic crossing Henry and Eric discovered that going aloft in a full swell was very different from climbing the mast of the *Worcester* while she was moored at Greenhithe. As the *Loch Torridon* approached Brazil, however, the winds suddenly dropped and the heat became intense. Henry gazed in fascination on the phosphorescent sea, which sparkled with 'millions of tiny luminous jelly fish' and from which flying fish occasionally leapt onto the ship's deck. As he gazed on inky night skies he could pick out the Southern Cross, which he had learned about during his HMS *Worcester* studies. He and Eric were expected to spend any spare time 'mugging' for examinations, which Eric hated but which Henry knew he needed to pass in order to progress in his career.

On Christmas Day 1899 Henry wrote wistfully:

My first Christmas Day at sea. I suppose I shall have many. It seemed strange not to be able to wish you a Merry Christmas. The only thing like home was a jolly good dinner with the Captain and Mates, but he soon got up and left us to it. Otherwise it was a day of hard work and dirty weather.

The 'dirty weather' precluded a landing at the legendary volcanic island of Tristan da Cunha, which Henry had hoped to visit, but he enjoyed identifying the Mutton Birds, Cape Hens and 'Mother Carey's Chickens' ('like swallows in their markings – very pretty')[3] that swooped around the ship. He took photographs on a camera presented to him by Captain Wilson-Barker of a huge white albatross, its massive wings outstretched in full flight. Henry decided to start an ornithological collection, despite initially finding it distressing to see an albatross being 'dragged aboard flapping and screeching'. After his first attempts to catch birds were unsuccessful, the captain gave him some bird parts so he could start his own collection through exchanges ('such as a head for a leg') with other crewmembers.

When the *Loch Torridon* finally docked in Adelaide, Henry signed his lengthy epistle to Emily, completed his unloading duties and rushed ashore to see if he had any mail from home. In port he and Eric had to help overhaul the ship; on their first few evenings they enjoyed a cooling dip in the river after a hot day's work but ceased the practice when three sharks were spotted approaching the ship.

Henry enjoyed life in Adelaide.[4] He attended church on Sundays ('rather high') and he and Eric explored the city's lush hinterland where Henry chased butterflies and the friends purchased a basketful of apples for a few coins. In port they met up with several 'Old Worcesters' who had, to Henry's annoyance, forgotten his surname but remembered his unflattering nickname Kinky-boke. Adelaide was currently in the grip of patriotic fervour, with *Soldiers of the Queen* being sung regularly in honour of those fighting the Boers in South Africa. When Henry learned that the brave soldiers included his captain's son and the brothers of two of his crewmates, he expressed the hope that the British army would soon 'knock Cronje up' and deliver victory.

The *Loch Torridon's* next port of call was Melbourne, which Henry found to be a 'splendid city'. It also appealed to several of the *Loch Torridon's* crew, who immediately jumped ship, and to Captain Pattman, who suddenly and mysteriously became a perfect host to friends, acquaintances and business associates whom he invited to his cabin for a duty-free whisky.[5] The captain's newfound bonhomie even extended to Henry, Eric and the other apprentices, whom he invited to join him on a visit to the home of his 'dear friends' the Brearleys, who lived in Kew, a suburb of Melbourne. Henry was very taken with 'the true Colonial hospitality' and enjoyed a 'ripping time':

We were just right for numbers and the girls were awfully nice and very pretty. The mother is a real mother, and just wanted us to enjoy ourselves ... They made us at home from the first … We played tennis in their garden, and stayed to supper. … we are invited to come as often as we can, spend Sundays, etc.

Of the pretty Brearley daughters, Henry particularly took to Miss Nancy. As he left Melbourne, he was already looking forward to the following year's visit, noting that Miss Nancy and her sisters were too young to be married before he returned.

As the *Loch Torridon* headed back to Britain, Henry began preparing his bird collection to show to Emily and his sisters; he was particularly proud of a dead albatross with a wingspan in excess of 6ft, which he felt would 'look well upon the walls'. On the way home the ship crossed the northern end of the Southern Ocean ('very cold, with heavy squalls of hail and sleet'), rounded Cape Horn (where Henry spotted his first Cape Crow) and passed the Falkland Islands (where he saw a rare black albatross). Near the equator it became so hot that one of the sailors became hysterical and had to be doused with water. Henry resorted to sleeping on deck and, with little to do on a becalmed sailing ship, devoted his limited energy to reading *Christendom Astray*, one of the books Emily had sent him.[6] In late July 1900, more than eight months after leaving Britain, the *Loch Torridon* entered the Thames, passed the *Worcester* and docked in London.

Henry celebrated his 17th birthday with his family, enjoyed two months' shore leave and rejoined his ship in October. On 1 November 1900, the first anniversary of his signing his apprenticeship indentures, he wrote to Emily in reflective mood:[7]

The Captain called us into the cabin, congratulated us, shook hands all round, and invited us to supper, which made a pleasant change, certainly. When I think of this past year, and what I was a year ago, I could smile at the difference. I was a boy then, and now I am a man, not only in my work … but also in my thoughts. Coming back home, after the first voyage, I realised what a lot it meant to me to have you all to look forward to, some chaps haven't got a real home, and I can't imagine anything more rotten. I know, too, that life has been full of difficulties for you, but the day is coming when I am going to make up everything to you, you can depend upon that, dearest, you will yet be jolly glad you have had a son, although he has cost you a lot! I think about all these things, especially when I am alone on a watch at night, and things come nearer to one. It is wonderful being at sea on a calm, starry night, picking out all the constellations and stars that one knows and getting to know new ones. I am allowed to take the wheel now, and steered her until dawn, by Canopus last night.[8]

Henry's second Christmas at sea was celebrated in 'the usual way', albeit in midsummer weather with a concert on the half-deck. After a stormy passage the *Loch Torridon* docked in Adelaide, where the pattern of desertions and long, hot days of hard work by a depleted crew repeated itself. When the news arrived from England that Queen Victoria had died on 22 January 1901, church bells tolled, gun salutes were fired, flags were lowered to half-mast and black-clad crowds flocked to special church services.[9] The period of official mourning did not prevent Henry from enjoying outings with Louis Foucar and several 'Old Worcesters', including an expedition to the zoo.

In Melbourne he visited the Brearleys and found Miss Nancy (as yet unmarried) and her sisters 'just as nice as ever'. As he enjoyed tennis parties and a 'topping' ball, however, he noticed that Eric's good looks seemed to 'weigh a lot with the girls'. Henry's appetite for food (a longer-standing preoccupation than girls) was well-satisfied during his visits to Kew and he was delighted with the Brearleys' parting gifts of jam, cakes and produce.

The three-month return voyage to London was a now routine matter of flooded quarters, storm-drenched clothing and seabird collecting. Henry was happy to see his family again but disappointed when his gift of preserved bird specimens (two with wingspans over 7ft) failed to generate much enthusiasm and several decaying bird parts were consigned to the fire.[10] But an invitation to HMS *Worcester*'s sports day gave him the opportunity to present some of his trophies to fellow ornithologist Captain Wilson-Barker – and to carry off the trophy in an 'Old Worcesters' race.[11] At dinner that evening with other 'Old Worcesters', Henry met Lieutenant Albert Armitage, a 36-year-old Scottish merchant seaman who had been to the Arctic and recently been appointed second in command and navigator to the forthcoming British Antarctic expedition led by Captain Robert Scott, RN – an appointment, Henry learned, which owed something to the influence of Sir Clements Markham. The expedition ship, the *Discovery*, would be leaving England during the summer, would sail to New Zealand and then on to McMurdo Sound, at the southern end of the Ross Sea, before the sea-ice closed in.[12] That evening Henry also met 'Old Worcester' Lieutenant Teddy Evans, who was, despite being only three years older than Henry, already climbing the ranks of the Royal Navy.[13]

While at home during August Henry read newspaper reports of the official departure of the *Discovery* from Cowes in the presence of King Edward VII. He also almost ended his naval career through one of his 'pranks'. He scaled a roof in order to startle a visiting friend by peering through a skylight and, while laughing at his victim's surprise, lost his grip and tumbled down two storeys onto a conservatory roof. He damaged his arms and shoulders so badly that professional massage was required; he also found that when he rejoined the *Loch Torridon* he felt seasick even within the confines of the English Channel. Captain Pattman made no comment, however, and read out a letter from the Meteorological Office praising a set of navigational observations Henry had made on the previous voyage. Henry was now third mate, which involved additional duties; he had been worried that Eric and the other apprentices might resent his early promotion, so was relieved when Eric, whose family was comfortably off, assured him he understood Henry's need to 'get on' in financial terms.

As the *Loch Torridon* entered calmer equatorial waters, Henry, although still feeling queasy, began to appreciate his surroundings and the 'inexpressibly magnificent' sunsets which reflected in the sea 'like glass beneath us'. But soon calm waters gave way to ferocious South Atlantic storms: 'We were up aloft … the Captain was bellowing to everyone at once, and when I got down a tremendous sea came over us, soaking us and somehow I got such a mouthful of it that I nearly choked.'

As they sailed through damp mist and driving rain, Henry heard unfamiliar bird cries; suspecting they might be penguins, he wondered if he might be about to cross the Antarctic Circle.[14] Henry was disappointed when the *Loch Torridon* veered northwards and headed for Kangaroo Island, off Adelaide, where he spent his third Christmas away from home. In port the first mate, who had suffered from the captain's wrath for much of the outward voyage, deserted; when the second mate fell ill Henry, technically next in the chain of command, began worrying that some of the older seamen might not take orders from a relatively inexperienced apprentice.[15] In the end, however, the only additional duty Captain Pattman delegated to Henry was to secure the release from gaol of the ship's cook who had been imprisoned for onshore misdemeanours.[16]

Henry enjoyed another stay in Adelaide, with regular hours of sleep, daily swims and sorties into the countryside where he could take photographs of the scenery and local wildlife.[17] By the time the *Loch Torridon* left Adelaide, however, the weather had turned cold and miserable, he was itching from numerous mosquito bites and finding the poor behaviour of hastily recruited replacement crewmembers equally annoying. Henry's work commitments had prevented him from attending a match in the England-Australia test series in which England had recently scored a win – about which his old friend Alfred Aldridge (who had recently moved to Australia) warned him that the Australians were not being particularly sporting. He was also disappointed that he would not be visiting Melbourne – and the Brearleys – on this trip.[18]

On the voyage home, more serious anxieties began troubling Henry: 'This life at sea, so dependent on nature, and so lonely, makes one think. I seemed to get into a quagmire of doubts and disbeliefs. Why should we have so many disappointments, when life was hard enough without them? Everything seems a hopeless problem.' One night on deck, however, his outlook suddenly changed:

> … when things were at their blackest, it seemed to me that Christ came to me and showed me why we are here, and what the purpose of life really is. It is to make a great decision – to choose between the material and the spiritual, and if we choose the spiritual … it will run like a silver thread through the material. It is very difficult to express in words what I suddenly saw so plainly, and it is sometimes difficult to recapture it myself. I know, too, that my powerful ambitions to get on in this world will conflict with that pure light that I saw for a moment, but I can never forget that I did realize, in a flash, that nothing that happens to our bodies really matters.

When the *Loch Torridon* rounded Cape Horn and encountered a series of violent storms, Henry had little time for spiritual reflection. Ferocious winds whipped sails to shreds, mountainous seas swamped the decks and a spectacular hail and lightning storm damaged vital items of equipment. When Henry was knocked down by waves and submerged for several minutes, he feared for his life and his ship's fate, but Captain Pattman 'kept his head' and proved 'every inch a seaman'. Before reaching England the seas became calmer and Henry could work on running repairs and resume his studies for his forthcoming second mate's examination.

Henry arrived back in London on his 19th birthday and made his way to Wallington, where Emily had moved in his absence.[19] Over the summer he met Tryon Campbell Bayard, an 'Old Worcester', whose family, like the Foucars, were of Huguenot origin and had Burma connections.[20] He also received a letter confirming his appointment as a midshipman in the Royal Naval Reserve and completed an application to join the Royal Indian Marine (RIM), a service which ranked between the merchant marine and Royal Navy in status.

On Henry's next voyage with the *Loch Torridon*, favourable winds propelled her to Adelaide in time for Henry's best Christmas since going to sea.[21] Just after New Year 1903 he was promoted to second mate and received a salary increase which allowed him to make a 'sensible addition' to family finances. In Australia, with no visit to Melbourne in the offing, he and Eric consoled themselves with an onshore outing with two young ladies, the photographs of which led to warnings from Emily and teasing from May. In early June

1903 the *Loch Torridon* arrived in San Francisco following one of her fastest-recorded runs from Australia, one which ranked, according to one newspaper, with 'those flying whirls of which ancient shellbacks love to yarn'.[22] A pile of letters awaited Henry in port – and more arrived while they serviced the ship and waited for Captain Pattman to procure sufficient cargo to cover the costs of the long journey back to England.

The news was not all good. A letter from his new friend Tryon Campbell Bayard reported that, according to one of Henry's sisters, Emily had been 'upset' and 'very poorly' during Henry's prolonged absence. In an effort to help, Tryon had cycled over to Emily's new home in Anerley (to where Emily had moved in Henry's absence) to tell her that he had read in a newspaper that the *Loch Torridon* had arrived safely in America.[23] Emily's numerous letters to Henry suggested that she was indeed in an anxious state.[24] She was glad he had passed his second mate's examination and was climbing 'the ladder', but worried he would forget that worldly achievements were a result of God's goodness rather than one's own efforts. While she looked forward to seeing pictures of San Francisco (which she understood to be a beautiful city), she hoped he would not fall prey to the numerous vices of city life. On the latter count Henry assured her he spent much of his time with Eric and had recently been confirmed by the Anglican bishop of San Francisco – unfortunately there was less he could do to help her financial worries.

Emily's arrangement with the Foucars had kept the Bowers housed, clothed and educated for several years following her husband's death. As Louis Foucar and his elder siblings completed their education, their places were taken by younger Foucars and the children of other expatriates who wanted to educate their offspring in London. Over the years, however, as Emily's ties with Burma weakened, the supply of scholar-lodgers eventually dried up and Emily, who only had a few illiquid investments in Penang, was struggling to make ends meet. Recently, she confessed, she had been relying on the generosity of old friends (in particular Miss Radford from Sidmouth) and any contributions which May, Edie or Henry could make; her recent move from a house in Wallington to a small flat in Anerley had been prompted by the need to reduce her outgoings.[25] She asked Henry to send money to clear a bill he had incurred on his last home leave and admitted she could not afford to attend a dog show with May. The latter had recently acquired two much-loved canine companions but Emily was worried that May's unhappiness with her work (as a teacher of French) was affecting her health. Emily had, despite her financial concerns, made plans for the two of them to take a modest break in Scotland where they would stay with Bithiah Paul in Greenock and with the Captain's sisters in Fife. More cheerfully, Emily told Henry that his RNR handbook had arrived, that she had enjoyed reading his news from Australia and was looking forward to having him home in time for Christmas. Knowing of his interest in the Antarctic, she enclosed with one letter some newspaper reports about Captain Scott's expedition.

As Captain Pattman struggled to obtain a cargo to finance the return journey of the ship, Henry was relieved to receive a considerably more cheerful letter from Emily in Scotland. She addressed it to her 'own dear laddie' and regaled him with news of Greenock friends and excursions to Loch Lomond, Loch Goil and the island of Bute, a popular Firth of Clyde holiday resort.[26] Despite occasional rain ('no new thing here'), Emily was thoroughly enjoying herself and her friend Bithiah was trying to persuade her to move back to Scotland. Although Emily felt the sea air and opportunities for hill-walking would benefit May's health, she was unsure as to whether suitable teaching work would be available, but as May was now considering working abroad for a while (France, Germany and Canada had all been mentioned) it might be Edie who moved north, in which case nursing work would be the issue. During her stay Emily had been offered rent-free lodgings on Bute (which would solve any problems regarding 'ways and means'), but she assured Henry that no final decision would be made until a full family conference was held.

By the time the *Loch Torridon* left San Francisco, almost six months had elapsed since her triumphant arrival in America. As she tossed on stormy seas off Patagonia, Henry mourned the prospect of another Christmas away from home, and when off-duty occupied himself with editing, illustrating and writing items for the *Loch Torridon Xmas Magazine 1903*. 'How to entertain on other people's money (without going to jail)' satirised Captain Pattman's lavish entertaining in Australia, while other contributions referred to his irascible temper and his duty-free 'slop chest' of tobacco and alcohol (which he resold at exorbitant prices). 'Why I did not get near the Pole' mocked Eric's failure to meet deadlines and Henry's fascination with Antarctica. Henry also contributed cartoon Egyptian cryptograms[27] and a poem, 'Christmas off Patagonia, 1903', which exhorted readers to forget raging storms and petty differences and remember loved ones at home and the Heavenly King born on Christmas morning. The New Year came and went, and in March 1904 the *Loch Torridon* finally docked in Liverpool. Henry, released from his apprenticeship indentures, took leave of his ship and shipmates and shook hands with Captain Pattman who had, despite their numerous differences of opinion over the years, provided him with surprisingly favourable references.

Now on the brink of promotion to first mate and a member of the Royal Naval Reserve, Henry was eager to be home with his family and to find out if there was any news regarding his application to the RIM.

4

ENTERING NEW WORLDS

etween April and July 1904 Henry took part in two four-week drill exercises with the Royal Naval Reserve.[1] There was still no news regarding the fate of his application to join the Royal Indian Marine and he knew he must find other work so that he could make a contribution to family finances.

Over the summer he visited Greenock and stayed with Emily's friend Bithiah Paul (whose son James was Henry's longest-standing friend) and found work with the Lyle Shipping Company, owners of the 'Cape' fleet.[2] He knew experience under steam would add another string to his bow but became downcast when he found that his first mate's sailing certificate only entitled him to serve as a third mate under steam, and wondered whether he should have spent less time planning ahead and left more to divine providence.[3]

Henry soon decided, however, that his captain on the *Cape Breton* was 'decent enough, and not too high and mighty' and enjoyed his first visit to New York – of which May was very envious.[4] He admired the huge Brooklyn suspension bridge (completed in the year of his birth), over which cars crossed to and from New York City (for a toll of 5 cents) alongside tracks for trains and tramcars and walkways for pedestrians. He was also impressed by the Statue of Liberty, with its visitors' balcony that ran around the huge bronze torch in the statue's gigantic hand. He read in the newspapers about the presidential election campaign, in which the incumbent, Teddy Roosevelt, was under attack for making concessions to ex-slaves, and decided he admired Roosevelt's stand and hoped he would be re-elected.[5]

Despite his reduced pay, Henry found he was easily making ends meet and promised Emily her first dividend from her 'male investment'; he also took out an insurance policy on his life which would, he assured Emily, leave her well-provided for should he be unlucky enough to perish at sea. As May, Edie and Henry began to contribute to the family finances, Emily arranged for a trust deed to be drawn up which would ensure that any property they lived in or owned, and any capital they accrued, would, in the case of something happening to one of them, automatically go to the others.[6]

The *Cape Breton*'s next stop was Australia where Henry found Brisbane to be 'a jolly pretty little place, with palm trees and houses set on piles'.[7] The prospect of a shore outing in Sydney with his erstwhile shipmate Eric prompted him to tell Emily that he was not ready to settle down or become 'spliced' for some time to come. At their next stop, the Philippines, Henry found the weather oppressively hot and local cultivation methods not conducive to his enjoyment of raw vegetables. He had heard nothing about his application to the RIM so was pleased to receive a letter from Captain Wilson-Barker confirming that he was doing everything possible to promote Henry's application. Henry's mentor also assured him that his prospects in the merchant marine looked excellent and encouraged him to 'keep up' his natural history as it would prove useful in 'out-of-the-way places'.[8]

As the *Cape Breton* left the Philippines she passed the Russian fleet, which, with its black-liveried 'gruesome engines of death', reminded Henry of a funeral procession.[9] As Henry sailed along the coast of the Malay Peninsula he wondered whether the 'Bowers Reef' he had spotted on a chart had been named for his father. He missed having Eric for company and was spending a lot of time alone with his thoughts; although barely a year had passed since his confirmation in San Francisco, he found himself suffering periodic attacks of religious doubt. He had recently read Charles Darwin's *Descent of Man* but remained sure that God had created the inherently inexplicable and apparently chaotic world. On the other hand, he sometimes felt as if his worldly ambitions robbed him of enjoyment of the present and 'the peace that passeth all understanding', and that his Evangelical Anglican faith was under siege from atheists, agnostics, those of other faiths, Roman Catholics and even 'high' Anglicans.

Back in Britain, life was also uncertain for May and Emily. Old friends from Burma, the Balthazars, had suggested May could follow in Emily's footsteps and become a teacher in the East. When they proposed that Emily could join May there, she protested that she was now too old to go 'knocking around the world'. After some deliberation Emily decided to move to Scotland; by early 1905 she was ensconced, rent-free, in a little cottage near the seashore at Port Bannatyne in Bute. A few months later she learned she would be receiving a legacy from a generous spinster friend. While Henry was delighted at his mother's good fortune, he was worried she might not remember to give her new address to the RIM's London office. His fears were justified as, at his next port of call, Colombo, he received two letters: one was from Emily telling him to cable the RIM office in London immediately; the other was from Captain Wilson-Barker explaining that a set of RIM documentation dispatched months previously had been returned unopened 'through a wrong address being left at the India Office'.[10]

Thanks to the captain's prompt action and his having secured references for Henry from Sir Clements Markham and Sir Thomas Sutherland, chairman of the Peninsular & Orient Shipping Company, all was now well. Henry responded immediately: 'I should like to say how very much obliged to you I feel for the trouble that you have taken on my behalf. I am sure that I am indebted to you enough already as regards the Royal Naval Reserve and the various other things that you have done for me since I went to the Worcester.'[11] Emily was contrite about her oversight, particularly as everyone regarded Henry's appointment as a sub-lieutenant in the RIM as the 'chance of a lifetime' and a stepping stone into the Royal Navy; she assured him that the legacy coming her way would cover any payments required by the RIM.[12]

On Henry's last voyage on the *Cape Breton*, a crewmate who had been unwell but still able to work suddenly collapsed and died. The funeral service performed by his captain with the aid of Henry's prayer book (apparently the sole copy on board) reminded Henry of the fragility of man's existence and made him glad he believed in life after death: 'To see that lifeless parcel, under the Union Jack, which had so recently been as alive as any of us, made me think of the littleness of our life, here to-day, gone to-morrow, forgotten the day after – by most.'[13] When the *Cape Breton* reached New York, Henry was discharged from his duties, obtained a passage to Britain on a passenger ship and was waved away from America by his well-travelled friend, Louis Foucar. As Henry crossed the Atlantic in crowded steerage-class accommodation, he realised how much luckier he was than some of his travelling companions, once-hopeful Central Europeans who had been refused entry to America and were now returning to their native lands.

Before joining the RIM Henry spent a few weeks in Bute, passing the time with family and friends, swimming daily, walking on the hills around the Firth of Clyde and playing tennis with whichever of his sisters was at home. Emily dispatched the sizeable payment required to secure his future in the RIM; despite family 'ways and means' having recently been supplemented by a legacy from his aunt, Mary Robertson, Henry felt guilty about the amount involved and hoped his mother and sisters felt it was in a good cause.

In early October he left Bute to join other RIM personnel in Southampton. He passed through London so he accepted Captain Wilson-Barker's invitation to lunch on the *Worcester*, which gave him a chance to thank his mentor in person for his recent efforts on Henry's behalf. When he arrived he found that the other lunch guests included Sir Clements Markham, whom he was keen to thank for his reference.[14] Sir Clements was full of tales of the recently returned British Antarctic expedition and the exploits of his protégé, Captain Robert Scott, and of 'Old Worcester' Albert Armitage. Henry also heard that Teddy Evans, whom he had met on the *Worcester* with Armitage, had served as second officer on the *Morning*, one of the two relief ships which had freed Scott's *Discovery* from the Ross Sea icepack. During the lunch Captain Wilson-Barker told Sir Clements that Henry was someone who, in his view, had the potential to lead a future Antarctic expedition.

Before leaving London, Henry took May (who had not yet moved to Bute) on a farewell outing. The next day, on the train to Southampton, he scribbled a hasty postcard wishing her 'good-bye for 4 years' and promising to write from Suez. At Southampton, Louis Foucar appeared to wave Henry off to a part of the Empire they both half-knew from childhood memories and their parents' tales.[15]

As soon as Henry boarded the transport ship *Plassy* ('a dream of nautical luxury'), he realised he was entering another world.[16] Her decks thronged with British government civil servants and senior army and naval officers (virtually all English) returning to duties in India and 'Further India'. Senior officers were so 'rigged up' in their gold-trimmed dress uniforms that Henry and his RIM cabin-mates, in their more modest attire, were regularly taken by army officers' wives for *Plassy* crewmembers. Without duties to fulfil Henry found the days at sea dragged, but filled his time playing deck-cricket or strolling round the deck with cabin-mates or 'Old Worcesters' he came across. In the evenings he grappled with the intricacies of chess and attended concerts which sometimes included displays of reels and piping by Scottish officers from Sandhurst ('Scotch to the bone' despite lacking discernable Scottish accents). Food and drink were in abundance and Henry was soon teasing his cabin-mates – self-declared teetotallers – about their lapses from their abstinence vows. The *Plassy* was also equipped with the latest in hot showers and marble baths; Henry enjoyed bathing daily before dressing for dinner in full RIM dress uniform – a process which was sometimes interrupted by the regular displays of onboard patriotism:

Whenever the band winds up they play the National Anthem ... everybody wearing the King's uniform has to salute, or if without a cap on, stand to attention. It is rather an amusing sight, the deck covered with chairs and people in every attitude of repose, or engrossed in books, etc. Suddenly the well-known tune starts and like the dead men in the prophet's vision, every-body leaps to attention. It is a sight to remember, and so used do you get to it that I stood to attention in my bath, the other day.

Henry left the *Plassy* in Bombay where his branch of the RIM was based. As his vessel, the troopship *Dufferin*, was not yet in port he was temporarily billeted on the *Dalhousie* – which to his delight had its own pet gazelle. The *Dufferin*, while lacking a pet gazelle, was one of the largest and newest ships in the RIM fleet, furnished with 'electric lights, fans & every convenience'. When Henry entered his cabin, however, he noticed cobwebs in the corners; he summoned his 'boy' who removed them and cleaned all the curtains and loose furnishings, leaving Henry to make himself at home. All was well until:

> ... out rushed a mouse – I thought ... [but] you may guess what it was. If it was a Cobra I should have been cool but a spider!!! Well I returned as grace-fully as I dared to my boy's presence, & told him to kill it. He missed it but out it came right up to me – then there was a mess on the deck. I did it as quickly as I could – oh it makes me shudder to think of it – I would face anything in heaven or Earth rather than a spider like that! ... I have had the room washed and scoured in every corner, watched it done – and yet I shall always dread sleeping there. I shall most certainly sleep on deck as long as I can.

Spiders notwithstanding, Henry knew that apart from the Royal Navy he could not have done better. He would soon be able to start repaying Emily's 'investment' in him, but in the meantime was grateful for May's pre-payday 'subs'. Henry, now known as Bosun Bill (his first nickname not to allude to his nose), launched himself into his duties and the onshore Bombay social whirl. He joined the Gymkhana Club[17] ('a very good thing to belong to'), exer-cised, took donkey rides, and played tennis and football – all of which helped offset the effects of the *Dufferin*'s regular and elaborate twelve-course formal dinners. He endured dances during which his captain would haul him by the arm 'to the slaughter' and introduce him to 'charming youthful mammas'. On such occasions Henry noticed how at ease other young officers seemed to be and realised that his own (self-admitted) lack of maturity and social graces probably made him, in some people's eyes at least, 'a sort of conundrum'.[18]

He found his new captain and fellow officers to be 'very decent all round' but found RIM seamen (particularly 'slackers' or those who seemed over-servile) to be no better than their merchant marine counterparts. He established that he might reach the well-remunerated rank of commander by the age of 36 (compared to 40 in the merchant marine), particularly if he was selected to attend courses at the Naval College in Greenwich.

During Henry's first months aboard the *Dufferin* she ferried troops to Calcutta, carried Lord Curzon (the departing Viceroy of India) to the Suez Canal and 'His Excellency the Governor' to Karachi. Following rumours of trouble in Somalia she also made several forays into the Arabian Sea. Between voyages Henry met up several times with Louis Foucar and attended social functions, including a dance hosted by the deputy director of the RIM. Eager to avoid the dance floor itself, he wandered round the official residence, gardens, orchards and tennis courts and found himself impressed by the benefits which accrued to those who reached the RIM's upper echelons. To counterbalance visions of such material splendour, Henry visited the YMCA and joined in communal prayers and familiar Moody and Sankey hymns. With regular mail services and frequent visits to RIM offices, Henry found it relatively easy to keep abreast of family news. In Bute Emily had made friends with fellow newcomers to the island, the Maxwells, 'nice people' whose new house, Caerlaverock, had a ground-floor flat which might just suit Emily. May was currently being pursued by a young man of whose merits Henry was uncertain, and was now so unhappy in her London teaching work that she was seriously considering a move to Scotland or further afield. Edie, following a brief and unhappy period working in a mental asylum, had now applied for a post at Simpson's Memorial Hospital in Edinburgh.

Henry supplemented letters home with picture-postcards of Bombay's sights, including the 'Scotch' church, local wildlife (crocodiles and vultures) and locals dressed in native costume.[19] While eager for news from Bute, he had little interest in the Liberal Party's 'momentous' 1906 landslide election victory and felt that 'the little island off the coast of France seems little indeed'. After attending the unveiling of a new statue of Queen Victoria in Karachi, in the presence of the Prince of Wales, Henry decided that while the king seemed 'a jolly old buster', his loyalty was more to his country than the monarchy per se.[20] As the *Dufferin* ferried troops to and from Egypt, South Africa, the Seychelles, Ceylon[21] and Mauritius, Henry dispatched picture-postcards of local sights, flora and fauna. When off-duty in Mauritius he and some shipmates climbed the island's highest mountain – and managed, on their descent in the dark, to cover themselves with cactus prickles. During Bombay's monsoon season rain fell sixteen hours a day; as Henry sweated 'like billio' he thought wistfully of temperate Bute, where Emily was now settled in the ground-floor flat in Caerlaverock.

As his first year in the RIM drew to a close, Henry was involved in a troop-carrying mission to Rangoon which showed him, as his father before him, how treacherous the Bay of Bengal could be:

> About 3 a.m. the sea was running high … when suddenly, out of the darkness was seen a huge wave, simply towering over the others, coming towards us. The wave preceding the monster was pretty well over the average, and on it the ship of course rose like a cork, plunging down into the hollow, where … before she had a chance to rise, the big chap was on top of her – water, iron, wood, men, sheep, goats, dog, tanks, ropes and general wreckage being floated aft in one confused medley. … all awning, booms and stanchions went like matchwood and the iron funnels … joined the happy stream as if they had been paper, lead sheeting was ripped off the deck like you would peel an orange and any such trifles such as heavy iron ventilators and teak-wood ladders, disappeared altogether.[22]

Although Henry did not fear 'a sudden departure from one's mortal husk', he was glad when the sea calmed and turned pea green, a sure sign that the Irrawaddy delta and 'land of pagodas' were near. From Rangoon he sent Emily picture-postcards of a Shan in native costume and the Shwedagon Pagoda, which he knew she and the Captain had visited together. On the travel front, Emily was currently considering a trip abroad (her first since the Captain's death) as May had finally resigned from her London teaching job and wanted to go to Europe. Emily also sent Henry some Evangelical magazines and cuttings which made him realise that worldly ambitions loomed too large in his mind at present and that he must adhere to the vows he had made following his conversion and during his confirmation in San Francisco.

Henry had recently been promoted to the responsible post of mate of the deck and was also studying for his first Hindustani examination (a prerequisite for promotion and further allowances). While he would have been happy to stay on the *Dufferin* – particularly as she might be going to China, another of his father's old haunts – he was pleased to learn that he was to be transferred to the *Sladen*, a paddle-driven gunboat based on the Irrawaddy.

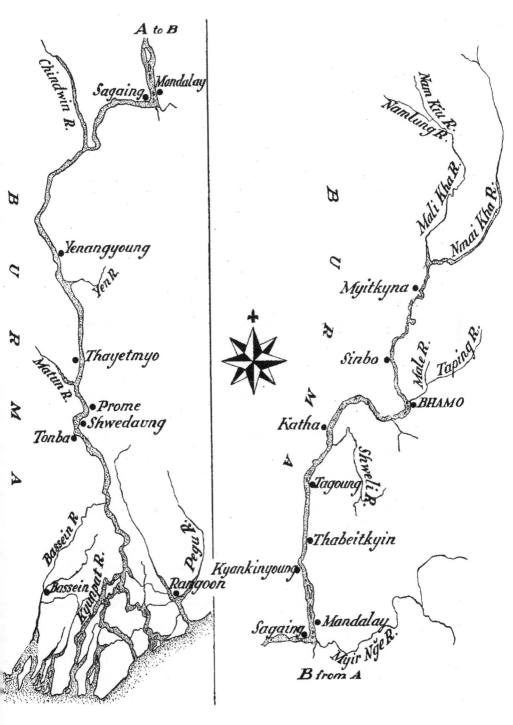

Map 1 The Irrawaddy, Burma (now Myanmar). *Unknown artist* © *private*

5

IN CAPTAIN BOWERS'
FOOTSTEPS

In January 1907 Henry returned to Burma to start duty on the *Sladen*, a shallow-draught steamship named after Captain Sladen who had led the expedition in which Captain Bowers had taken part.

In Mandalay Henry saw the places his father had known, described and sketched: hundreds of pagodas, the famous Golden Kyoung, the massive Mingoon Bell and the Royal Lakes. While Henry was sad to see the state of decay of many buildings he found that, like his father, he liked and admired the people of Burma. He also agreed with his father that the Irrawaddy's reputation of being difficult to navigate was overstated and was not greatly impressed by his new commanding officer, Captain Henley, who appeared 'all at sea on the river'.[1] As HRH the Duke of Connaught and his entourage were due to join the *Sladen* for a journey up the Irrawaddy's upper reaches, Henry began filling pages of his notebook with endless lists of tasks to be done, from running repairs to special 'surveys' of linen and cutlery.[2] During the voyage itself he realised he still had something to learn about handling his vessel on the unpredictable Irrawaddy:

> The river has a sharp bend across the other side, which causes the tide to run, when ebbing, almost at right angles to the main stream ... we were at once swirled off by the tide at a tremendous rate ... I saw her take another swerve to Port and then realized a smash was inevitable. I at once rushed amidships ... we were going full speed astern ... I simply prayed that she would not hit, but I knew that nothing could prevent it. ... I trotted up on top & started giving orders in my most casual manner, as though a collision was an every-day occurrence with us.[3]

Happily for Henry, the duke was happy to disembark and entertain his guests to lunch on shore.

The *Sladen*'s next distinguished passenger was His Honour Sir Herbert Thirkell-White, Lieutenant Governor of Burma. Henry enjoyed eating with the official party and meeting local 'big-wigs', but did not immediately take to Sir Herbert – who had recognised him as the son of Captain Bowers of the Sladen expedition – or indeed his wife: 'I really think a lady who smokes is as objectionable – to my mind – as a Suffragette. It takes away all a man's ideal in a woman to see her act the same as he does. The woman of my fancy is as <u>unlike</u> a man as it is possible to be.' During Sir Herbert's tour Henry met employees of the Irrawaddy Flotilla Company (which had expanded considerably since his father's day), including a Mr Wingate of Greenock who, despite working in Burma for almost thirty years, had retained his 'Greenockian' accent.[4] Regarding his own career, Henry discovered that Sir Herbert's private secretary earned significantly more than him for a job which appeared less demanding than Henry's own. Despite his misgivings about his captain's navigational skills, Henry was pleased to discover that Henley was a vicar's son and 'most punctilious at Church going'; in terms of his own beliefs, Henry had recently concluded that he no longer believed in the concept of a literally 'Blazing Hell'.

During his free time Henry took his bicycle and headed off into the countryside, including the areas around Bhamo and the Burma-China border area, which his father had explored:

In Bhamo everything was very curious indeed, the Burmans being quite in the minority and replaced by Shans, Kachins and Chinese. ... The Hill tribes are friendly but a little uncertain, and there being numerous caravans and miles of jungle to pass through, I thought it just as well to take a Service revolver, and a dozen rounds ... [which] I did not need however. ... As the light increased it was simply magnificent. Later I came to a low flat rice plain interspersed with streams, the bridges over some being broken, which necessitated up-bike and ford it. ... There were enormous teak trees that made one giddy to look up at, and dense bamboo clumps ... There is an enormous amount of big game in Burmah, tigers, elephants, bison, etc. It is all shut up in these forests, though ... I proceeded up and up, meeting numerous armed Shans, whom I stopped and tried to buy one of their curious swords. They were most good-natured, and very curious altogether; none of them would sell their weapons, though one thought a lot over 5 Rupees I offered him. ... I reached the summit and fell exhausted under a tree ... to watch all the strange jungle creatures in the trees.[5]

On his return journey, Henry suffered a puncture, tested his brakes to the limits on some vertiginous slopes and noticed some sparkling sand on a streambed:

> A short inspection soon showed me that it was interspersed with *gold*. So I took a few handfuls back. It is certainly gold, and were I not in the Service I might prospect. As it is I have kept *chup* [quiet], but … I have since heard that gold is *supposed* to be in those hills, and that some people are searching for it. No doubt they will have discovered my 'claim' long ago.

Henry was trying to stay on the physical and spiritual 'straight and narrow' by keeping fit, limiting his intake of food and reading his new Diaglott Bible, a gift from Edie.[6] He felt gratified when Captain Henley left him in temporary charge of the *Sladen*, particularly as he was beginning to realise that promotion in the RIM was rather a lottery. Despite his natural tendency to plan ahead, he decided to draw the line at maintaining a list (as others did) of superiors rumoured to be ailing or approaching retirement.

As Henry sweltered and battled mosquitoes ('unmentionable for pertinacity & efficiency in penetrating the human frame'), spiders ('great hairy legs') and ants ('go indiscriminately into shoes, trousers, coats and singlets'), he found Emily and May's postcard of the Swiss Alps particularly appealing: 'The snow takes my eye more than anything though. I don't recollect having seen any now since I was off Cape Horn. Snow! How I would wallow in it if I could! If ever you find me preferring heat to cold, please hit me with the nearest thing to hand.'[7] Of an evening he would cool himself by paddling in a skiff among stilted bamboo houses and timber rafts from where locals gazed at the 'white creature in the boat'. He also visited the 900ft-deep Gokteik Gorge where waterfalls with 'rainbows all down them' gushed into raging torrents at the foot of the chasm.[8] When he returned to show his 'boy' these marvels, they met the man who had built a series of makeshift bridges across the foot of the gorge:

> He showed me where one could cross the river … It was a plank about a foot under water in a narrow place with the water running over it like a mill sluice. Really, if I had not seen this chap go over it I should, I fear, never had dared … but I was not going to see a land-lubber do it alone, so I went across … as if I had done it a dozen times. We then had to jump from rock to rock like chamois; it was *quite* exciting, however.

Henry's explorations and excursions ate into time allocated for his Hindustani studies, but he found a local teacher who spoke fluent English and assisted him through the linguistic maze. On the day of his exam Henry dressed in full uniform and reported at Mandalay's fort where he was ushered into the court martial room. There, under the supervision of a bored, fidgeting invigilator, he wrestled with the exam paper (and hoards of flies) for three hours. His teacher assured him that the paper had been a difficult one so Henry was not particularly optimistic.[9]

Meanwhile, Emily and May had returned from Switzerland via Paris. Although Henry considered the French capital to be a morally decadent city, he was pleased to receive their postcards and was interested to know what they thought about plans to build a tunnel under the Channel.[10] In terms of other current affairs, Henry was still against women's suffrage ('if men would only be <u>men</u> nowadays the women would not need to clamour for the vote') and, nearer to his current home, was concerned about rumours of insurgency in Burma, demands for home rule for India and plans to transport troops and government personnel in India by rail rather than on RIM vessels.[11] Regarding Britain, Henry felt proud of his country's achievements and was loyal to the place he regarded as 'the very best place on God's earth', one for which he was prepared to fight should the need arise. In June he received two telegrams: one announced that he had failed his Hindustani exam; the other declared that he was being placed in temporary command of RIMS *Bhamo*, a shallow-draught gunboat which operated on the uppermost 300 miles of the Irrawaddy. According to RIM lore, the *Bhamo* was difficult to handle but Henry was pleasantly surprised:

> Here I am squatted at my table, a helmsman alongside me, a clear stretch of river ahead, and a good ship under me, punching against a tremendous current at about 8 or 9 knots over the grounds, with all her fancy mechanism and expensive engines and other trifles dependent on my little red nob! ... How many fellows in the service would not give anything for such a chance ...[12]

Henry had read in his father's report on the Sladen expedition that local people had flocked on board or knelt on the riverbank at their first sight of a steamer; now, almost forty years later, the *Bhamo* was a familiar sight to most people and the Captain's generation were known as 'old busters'.[13] Although the unpredictable currents of the Irrawaddy occasionally gave Henry 'hideous anxiety & some horrible scares', he found his crew of lascars to be hardworking and intelligent, particularly the ship's pilot who could be trusted to steer the ship at night.[14] To his pleasant surprise, Henry remained in charge of the *Bhamo* for several months, during which time his speedy dexterity on river manoeuvres earned him the nickname Comet.

He found his 'palatial' cabin made a comfortable study for revising for his second Hindustani exam and reading the Evangelical magazines Emily still sent him.[15] Henry was by now, he told May, developing his own form of Christianity:

> I am sure you realize as I do the hopeless fallacy of all the religious 'forms' and 'creeds'. Personally, I continue to go to whatever Christian church is handy simply to worship God in my own way, but do not identify myself with any beyond the fact I am a Christian (would I could say I were a better one) – I wish for no further identity ... no denomination.[16]

In conversation with the commodore of the Irrawaddy Flotilla Company, Captain Ballantine, Henry learned that his father was regarded as a 'pioneer of British influence & commerce' in Burma and a 'jolly clever far-seeing man' whose business ethics and commercial dealings were more 'above board' than those of many of his contemporaries.[17] On 29 July 1907 Henry celebrated his 24th birthday and his continuing captaincy of the *Bhamo*. Mail from 'the Better Country' included news of Louis Foucar's engagement and a postcard of the recently launched Cunard liner, the *Lusitania*, which Henry thought looked a 'whopper'.[18] He was, however, distressed to learn that May sometimes found his letters difficult to decipher and resolved to make more of an effort in that department.[19] He was, he told her, becoming disillusioned with aspects of 'Empire culture' following an encounter with a government official who had introduced his child by a local woman as 'my little bit of sin'.

In August Henry received the results of his first-level Hindustani exam – this time he had passed with flying colours, a result which would mean additional allowances and a foot on the next rung of the promotional ladder. But when Henry read the newspaper cuttings Emily had sent him about the departure of Shackleton's *Nimrod* for the Antarctic, he admitted where his heart lay: 'Ever since I went within 3 degrees of the Antarctic Circle, I looked due South. I have thought – as I thought then – that's my mark – the Southern Continent. Reading Capt. Scott's books on the 'Discovery' made me as keen as mustard. Perhaps my chance will come later.'

In the meantime, Henry's role as acting captain of the *Bhamo* kept him so busy that his weight dropped from the 12 stone it had been on the *Sladen* and he found he could again fit easily into his tight-fitting RIM formal uniforms. His appetite for promotion did not diminish, however, particularly when he learned how much senior RIM and Irrawaddy Flotilla Company officers earned.[20] He was already studying for his next Hindustani examination and would, he had been pleased to learn, be in command of the *Bhamo* until the end of the year – despite, as he admitted to May, some navigational near-misses:

> There is no doubt that for river work she is just the thing, sound, fairly fast, light & not so very hard to handle if you use your intelligence & take wind, current, etc., into consideration. ... I had no idea she had such a reputation. The Harbour Masters here are in no end of a funk of her. I cannot understand it. When I arrived I dashed right through the harbour full speed – as then you have full control of her – & took up my moorings without any assistance. When I reported myself to Capt Hooper he said 'What, you dared to come in without a Harbour Master, don't you know the rules?' ... The Harbour Master said 'She's simply unmanageable. I will never shift her again if there is any wind at all.' I simply laughed ...[21]

In the same letter he regaled May with gossip about various ladies, including a Mrs Vines and others who seemed to enjoy Henry's company and took a keen interest in his weight loss and social life. A colleague had accused Henry of having been 'keen' on Mrs Vines but Henry assured May that, although he liked her type ('not too tall – very fair'), this was not the case. He concluded his letter with loving greetings to her and Emily which, apparently forgetting May's recent complaints about the illegibility of his letters, he scrawled crosswise over the first page of his missive.[22]

From Rangoon Henry made a 1,600-mile, 140-hour round trip by train to an army station in the mountains to sit his next Hindustani examination. When he returned with the *Bhamo* to Mandalay he found a pile of telegrams waiting for him with copious instructions for the forthcoming visit of the new Viceroy of India, some of which made him wonder if 'His Excellency', Lord Minto, was aware of the difficulty of procuring fresh cream and other delicacies in Upper Burma.[23] By now Henry was looking forward to a lengthy period of home leave and was saving as much of his salary and allowances as possible; with another Hindustani exam under his belt he was hoping for further promotion, but, as he told May, he felt torn between his natural ambition and his commitment to Christ:

> My body is <u>not</u> a living sacrifice, my talents are not all for the Master's use. My ambitions are not altogether untinted with the shades of this world. ... My present object is to stand, be as upright as possible under modern circumstances, overcome myself (a very hard job), and become a thorough master of my profession. ... At present I am called to be a sailor, & as such

I must remain till I am shown unmistakably that the time has come for me to do something else.

When May, well aware that Henry's idea of 'something else' included Antarctic expeditions, wrote criticising 'foolhardy' and 'vainglorious' explorers, Henry was indignant:

> Would you call all the Brave Men who made reasonable attempts to reach the Poles fools? Or would you even malign them to the extent of saying that they did it all for vainglory or self aggrandisement? I think not. How can anyone on conjecture say it will be no use to mankind to penetrate North or South to the Pole? ... Besides, apart from all the magnetic or meteorological interest, is it nothing to a nation to produce men willing to undergo hardships and privation with practically no gain to themselves? ... a country which can produce men to set their backs on the modern effeminate tendencies & make an effort with an object requiring hard work & privations still has some backbone in it. That is my view of a polar expedition – something to accomplish that only a manly man could dare to tackle ...[24]

Although far from Bute, Henry sided with those demanding home rule for Scotland. He felt that 'Britain is governed, financed & practically run by Scotsmen & yet in England it is not recognised', but noted that Scots (who ran almost all the large British shipping companies) seemed to 'show up best in England or abroad' rather than in their native land where they sometimes seemed 'narrow'. Despite his love for Scotland Henry abhorred (although not for reasons of temperance) its national beverage. He dreaded the RIM's annual St Andrew's Day celebrations at which, that year, the viceroy ('a nice old chap at close quarters') had been in attendance. Whisky had been compulsory ('sodas were allowed under protest') but Henry had managed to secrete a small bottle of hock of a similar colour in a floral table arrangement and 'thereby passed as a Scotsman!'[25]

At another dinner held in the viceroy's honour, Henry learned that his father had developed a soft spot for the town of Bhamo and had named several things after it – including a racehorse which had won the Rangoon Derby. He also found out that it had been thanks to Sir Herbert Thirkell-White that Henry's command on the *Bhamo* had been extended to almost eight months.[26] With his ninth Christmas away from home approaching, Henry wondered if Emily, May and Edie would be spending theirs at Caerlaverock with their neighbours – and now friends – the Maxwells, and offering 'the Bowers hospitality' to friends and callers.[27] In Rangoon he found a church and a Seaman's Institute where the Christmas services were more to his liking than those at the cathedral. As the endless round of dinners, receptions and other celebrations began to pall, Henry longed for the quiet upper reaches of the Irrawaddy where he could shoot game and stock up the *Bhamo's* larder.

In January 1908 Henry transported the men and mules of the 27th Mountain Battery, the 91st Punjabis and the 25th Mule Corps, and, on one potentially career-enhancing occasion, played host to the director of the RIM.[28] When his command of the *Bhamo* finally ended he was transferred to the *Minto*, the RIM's Rangoon station ship, as navigation officer under Captain Balfour, a hard worker who expected the same level of commitment from his men. He put Henry in charge of all the navigational equipment and records, and asked him to take soundings along the Burmese coast and around the beautiful Coco Islands in the Bay of Bengal – where Henry enjoyed swimming daily among the coral reefs.[29] On her next trip out the *Minto* helped refloat the *Ivydene*, a British ship which had foundered on a reef ('a good day's work and saved £50,000'). Henry also had time for studying for his next – and he hoped final – Hindustani examination and discovering more about the tropical waters and their inhabitants:

> ... you can see down 15 or 20 feet like bluey glass. ... One of my favourite dodges is to dive down, catch hold of a rock or chunk of coral, and sit or lie there with my eyes open as long as I can hold breath ... [and] glance at crabs and tropical fish of all colours ... we have great competitions in bringing up specimens from the bottom from considerable depths. When we meet it is almost irresistible to laugh, and then you at once dissolve into a cloud of bubbles and make for the surface. ... We stopped at Oyster Island, where I had a glorious swim, and spent an hour or more, chipping oysters off the rocks, which were sent aboard for dinner in triumph! Still I cannot eat them off the rocks – Ugh! they wriggle in your mouth! The only way I like them is fried in bread-crumbs.[30]

When Henry passed his 'Higher Standard' Hindustani examination the path to promotion to lieutenant was open. Although he vowed never to attempt to learn another language, he was becoming more religiously tolerant, not only to a High Church Anglican fellow officer, but also in terms of his regret at having failed to fully understand Islam and the apparent parallels between Allah and his God.[31] May sent him more cuttings about Shackleton's expedition; by now Henry's thoughts were also turning to Scotland, where he would be spending his forthcoming eight months' home leave – which he had organised so he would both miss the forthcoming monsoon season and be able to celebrate Christmas in Bute.[32] Henry left the *Minto* in Rangoon and booked a passage on the *Pentacota*, which was sailing for London via Madras and Ceylon. When he discovered the ship was owned by his father's former employers, BI, he considered making himself known, but decided against it given that the Captain's relationship with the company had sometimes been stormy.[33] His name on the list of reservations had not, however, gone unnoticed:

> [The marine superintendent] said, 'I hear that you are off in the *Pentacota*.' I said 'yes'. He said 'Well! had I known you were an RIM officer I would have arranged a 1st class berth for you – all full up now.' Then he added – 'By the bye, are you any relation to Captain Bowers?' I said I was his son. 'Well! if I had only known that before.' He bustled off to the Chief of the Embarkation Dept., but it was too late, all I. and II. berths were full, and I was one in a berth of 4.

Although Henry's passage was less comfortable than it might have been, he was glad not to be indebted to the company which had, he felt, sometimes treated his father badly.

In early July, following several weeks of inactivity which did nothing for his weight, Henry arrived in 'dear old London' and checked into the Charing Cross Hotel. He dropped a line to Emily letting her know that he had arrived safely and that, after a 'prowl around', including to Greenwich to check on progress regarding RIM training courses, he would be with her by the weekend.[34] Henry was home again and looking forward to seeing the new Bowers' family home in Bute.

SCOTLAND, DANGEROUS WATERS
AND A BEAUTIFUL ISLAND

Henry was reunited with Emily in Greenock, where they spent a night with Bithiah Paul before taking the morning ferry across to Bute.[1]

Emily's new home on the ground floor of Caerlaverock was comfortably spacious with large windows to the rear, which offered magnificent views over the Kyles of Bute and the mouth of Loch Striven to the hills and mountains beyond.[2] For the next few months Henry had no formal duties, no ships to steer, no crew to manage and no dignitaries to look after. He enjoyed Emily's cooking and home baking and being able to gulp down pints of fresh water which ran clear from a tap. Now he could talk to Emily and his sisters face to face about anything and everything, and discuss any contentious matters without worrying about misunderstandings which might occur due to letters crossing in the post.

Henry thrived in Scotland's temperate summer weather; he rose with the lark, swam for miles before breakfast and exercised vigorously with dumb-bells or Indian clubs. With his short, stocky frame and sunburned fair skin Henry was beginning to look more like his father; now, with promotion imminent, he looked forward to being able to support Emily as Captain Bowers once had. He loved the Scottish outdoors and persuaded his sisters and others to join him on morning swims and long walks on the Kyles of Bute's rocky beaches, round nearby lochs or across heather-clad moors. Henry and his family visited the Highlands where Henry, during the course of a week, made three ascents of Ben Nevis and ensured he was the highest person in Britain by shinning up a flagpole at the top of the mountain. In Bute he partnered May (one of the island's best female tennis players) to victory in a mixed-doubles tournament. Between bouts of physical activity he spent time with old friends in Greenock and made new friends on Bute, including Emily's upstairs neighbours, the Maxwells, May's friends from the tennis club and fellow worshippers at St Ninian's church in Port Bannatyne.[3] He also struck up a friendship with the Reverend Peter Dewar, whom he rowed across a mile of turbulent sea on a stormy night so the elderly minister could visit a parishioner on Bute's neighbouring island.

At home Henry was always, as he had been as a boy, cheerful and full of fun and rarely 'low' or troubled as he sometimes seemed in his letters. As winter approached and the days shortened he would spend hours pursuing his interest in biblical and ancient history by reading about the Great Pyramid; on clear, dark nights he honed his navigational skills by rattling off the names of the stars and their distances from the earth to his patient, shivering sisters. When he discussed his past and future career he admitted that his progress so far had been thanks to a combination of his own efforts and 'chance', whether in the shape of Captain Wilson-Barker, Sir Clements Markham and Sir Herbert Thirkell-White, or a divine hand through which 'big changes are ordered'. At a party on Bute he was persuaded to have his palm read to see what the future held in store for him; when the amateur clairvoyant, having looked at his hand, announced she had 'nothing to tell', Henry asked her what she meant. She simply admitted to being baffled as to how he was still there at all, a pronouncement which Henry treated as a great joke.

Happily for Henry, snow fell early on Bute that year. As Christmas – his favourite season of the year – approached, he launched himself into decorating the rooms at Caerlaverock and, when that was done to his satisfaction, assisting neighbours to adorn their houses. Christmas 1908 was a happy time for Henry and his family, but only too soon it was time for him to start packing. On his last night he and May sat up late, 'yarning' and discussing plans for the future.[4] The following day the Bowers family took the ferry from Rothesay to Greenock where Emily, May and Edie waved Henry off on his long journey to London and to the East.

As Henry passed through the Suez Canal on the transport ship *Rohilla*, he wrote the first of many picture-postcards: 'Here we are at this beastly old canal again – it is cool so far, but anticipation of what is beyond is not nice. ... Some chaps have gone to Cairo – not enough time for me. ... I don't know which of these is the great Pyramid of Cheops but fancy it is the furthest one ...'[5]

With his social life on the *Rohilla* being less frenetic than that on the *Plassy*, Henry had time to reassemble his bicycle, attend onboard Sunday services and discuss the current state of the Anglican Church with the ship's parson ('quite a good chap & strictly evangelical').[6] None of the unattached young lady passengers took his fancy but he was pleased to note that some 'peculiar fellows' had managed to persuade 'nice girls' to be their wives. At Bombay he boarded the troopship *Dufferin*, which carried him to Burma:

> What a crowd of recollections for me hang around Burma, and its great port! Although I have no love for Rangoon itself, I could not help feeling a little responsive just now as I spotted Syriam and the Shwe Dagon Pagodas glittering in the sun, to say nothing of the ruined Davot Pagoda at the mouth of the Bassein Creek – the gate of the Irrawaddy! So well do I know this river now – every house almost, and every tree.[7]

As Henry looked back on recent happy times in Scotland – the longest period he had spent with Emily for many years – he realised how much his mother worried about him, whether he was scaling Scotland's highest mountain or sailing on distant oceans and rivers. He wrote, encouraging her not to fret but admitted that his gender precluded him from fully understanding the depth of her maternal concerns. In Rangoon Henry, now a full lieutenant, learned that he was to join the *Fox*, an armed cruiser currently on patrol duty in the Gulf of Oman and round the mouth of the Persian Gulf:

> As we rounded one of the huge bare cliffs of Muscat harbour we suddenly came upon the wily *Fox* lying in a cove ... Everybody aboard is much enamoured of the Captain, Allan [*sic*] T. Hunt.[8] He is a tall thin man, bearded, with a long straight nose and a full-rigged uncynical smile. ... a ripper, and enters into everything we do.[9] He comes and boxes with us on the Quarter Deck and also does fencing and bayonet practice. ... We are in a part of the world as unlike the Clyde as it is possible to imagine. Hills there are certainly, but absolutely bare and sun-baked. ... The weather is remarkably cool, not to say chilling in the early morning, and one is always glad of a blanket sleeping on deck. July, August and September are supposed to be insupportable and all the ships except ours and the three R.N. gunboats manned by lascars are withdrawn ... The *Fox* has never entered the straits north of the Gulf of Oman. We are not in *the* Gulf, i.e. the Persian Gulf.[10]

Two days later, however, the *Fox* and Henry (now nicknamed Nosie) were in the Persian Gulf. Captain Hunt and his crew's main duty was to prevent arms and ammunition (largely manufactured in the French protectorate of Oman) from being smuggled in *dhows* and by caravan to Afghanistan and Balochistan, where they could be used by border tribesmen against British forces guarding India's North-West Frontier.[11] Henry explained his duties:

> On the Oman or Arabian side we can do nothing. Any dhow can be full of arms provided she keeps within the 4-mile limit, outside that we can nab her. These dhows all come via Muscat, some from as far as Aden. ... In the day we cruise about & chase every sail we see, make them heave to & examine them ... We heard that the Afghan dealers had ordered all gun-running to be suspended till better times, which will mean as soon as the *Fox* goes. After April they cannot send them up-country as there is no water for the caravans.

During Henry's first *dhow*-hunting 'season' the British Resident in Bandar Abbas (on the north-east coast of the Persian Gulf) summoned the *Fox* for assistance after Persian nationalists occupied the town. Although no blood had yet been spilled, the situation was delicate:

> A Persian Man-o'-War ... is due tomorrow and may want to bombard the town. Our own action depends on which side the British Govt. decides to take. Personally, I hope we won't have to bombard them as I am in sympathy with the rebels, who want a Constitution.

When the shah's only warship appeared offshore, the nationalists opened fire from the town; after the *Fox* trained her searchlights on the town things calmed down for a while, but as night fell both sides 'bust off again'. For the first time in his life Henry went to sleep 'in sound of men killing each other', although he admitted it had not kept him awake for long. Next day the shah's warship withdrew, leaving Bandar Abbas in nationalist hands and the majority of the shah's naval officers on the side of the nationalists. The *Fox* docked in Bandar Abbas where Captain Hunt and his crew were greeted warmly and shown around the nationalist blockade, where 'every man was armed like a stage brigand'.[12]

In port, Henry read news cables announcing that Shackleton's attempt to reach the South Pole had failed due to adverse weather conditions and a shortage of food; he still thought 'the S. Polar show was splendid' and longed for more details about the expedition. Thanks to an increased salary and few spending opportunities in the Gulf, Henry could send a contribution towards May's 'holiday fund' and look forward to repaying some of Emily's 'investment' in him. With a continuing eye to future promotion and extra allowances, he was now pressing to be sent on a training course in Greenwich and had, despite his vow to eschew further foreign languages, begun to learn Persian.[13]

Henry had recently received distressing news about a RIM fellow officer (whom he had known from the *Dufferin* and recently met in Karachi) who had apparently killed himself following a court martial and dismissal from the service. Henry's spirits were lifted, as ever, by the wonders of nature, in this case one of the Gulf's worst recorded storms:

> We were all up on the Quarter-deck admiring a magnificent electric storm, one of the finest I have seen. ... lightning of a most vivid character, forking everywhere. ... everything was as black as pitch ... Awnings were blown to ribbons, our wireless gear came crashing down ... a very big sea got up in no time ... everybody had to have two or more men holding on to him or some of us would certainly have been overboard. ... I must say I enjoyed it from first to last.[14]

With postal services between the Gulf and Britain somewhat erratic, Henry was pleased to receive from Emily a bundle of cuttings about the *Nimrod* expedition, from which he gleaned that Shackleton, on 9 January 1909, had planted the Union Jack at 88° 23' South, a 'Furthest South' less than 100 geographical miles from the Pole. Henry would have loved to have been there but told Emily (only half in jest) that he hoped Shackleton and other explorers might now 'leave the South Pole itself alone for a bit' so he had a chance to get there.[15] In answer to her claim that he currently placed too much emphasis on promotion and monetary advancement, he agreed that he was often 'blinded to the things eternal in the rush and strenuousness of life', but assured her he knew his advance owed as much to divine providence as to his own efforts, and asked her: 'What are "chances" but definite opportunities? What is luck and circumstance but unseen arrangement?'[16]

After Bushire (which lay up the eastern Gulf coast from Bandar Abbas) fell to Persian nationalists, the *Fox* was dispatched to protect British interests in the town. When Captain Hunt went ashore with a set of mysterious 'Confidential Code books', Henry was left in charge of the ship, and it was not long before he was called to action when a launch laden with contraband arms and ammunition was seen leaving Bushire at speed. Henry grabbed his pistol and, along with a few members of the *Fox*'s crew, jumped into a steam-driven cutter and gave chase:

> My crew were entirely unarmed ... I headed to cut her off but soon found she was ... as fast as we were, with a start of 3 good miles. ... I never saw a little boat whizz like [ours] did then under the utmost pressure. ... We at last

drew nearer ... It was nearly 8p.m. ... too dark to see much, but she was full of men and armed ... I think the darkness saved us as [the smugglers] had no idea I had not an armed guard hiding in the boat. I kept the men down as much as possible and then, pointing my pistol at a man, who luckily was the Captain – said I would fix him off if I heard a trigger click. ... The man alongside me said, 'Sir, they are all armed.' Had they had the pluck and known our few numbers, they could have fixed the lot of us. [We] were aboard with a flying leap and the sight of us in the dark, and my pistol, which I took good care to let the light of a skylight shine on, fixed them off. ... the sailor with me pointed the pistol-case at them, seeing the light did not shine on it.[17]

Henry and his crew bluffed the smugglers into laying down their weapons, transferred all the contraband arms and ammunition onto their cutter and headed back through the inky blackness towards the welcome beam of the *Fox's* searchlights. Back offshore from Bushire, they learned that nationalists had seized the shah's warship, which Henry referred to as 'the Persian Ex-Navy'; they were dispatched to board the warship and persuade the nationalists not to bombard Bushire.

After a successful mission the *Fox* docked in Bushire and Henry joined the shore party as second in command. He was billeted at the Custom House, near the British Residence, where light duties – such as looking after 'chaps from the British firms and banks, etc., who drop in at odd times & lap up whisky' – left ample time for water sports, including water polo which generally degenerated into a ducking match.[18] By the time the *Fox* left Persia for India at the end of May, the weather was oppressively hot. She was restocked in Bombay, where Henry caught up with the latest RIM news and gossip, then headed eastwards through a south-westerly monsoon that inspired Henry to write to May on the subject of his feelings about the sea:

It was pure selfishness when I went to sea, but ... from the time I was first able to think for myself on general subjects, no idea of anything else had ever crossed my mind. I do not wish to defend my action, but whenever I thought of Mother I used to say to myself 'No! I can't do it.' Even after I went to the *Worcester* I used to lie awake at night and vow I would never go to sea ... One thing I have always felt grateful to Mother for is that she did not attempt to dissuade me from the last thing she wanted me to do.[19]

As Henry was unlikely to have sufficient leave to allow him to return to Britain in the immediate future, May and Emily now decided to spend several months in Switzerland and other countries in Europe. Thousands of miles away Henry was on his way to Ceylon, the island of 'spicy breezes' where the *Fox* moored at Trincomalee, a 'spot to be dreamt about'[20] on the east coast of the island:

> The harbour is invisible from seaward … When you get there, however, you turn round a wooded island and a big place like a lake opens up. Out of this several lochs run, most of which are absolutely hidden until their mouth is reached. There are numerous wooded islands and all the shores are wooded, terminating in beaches in places … everyone would be invisible from seaward.

Without nationalist insurrections, *dhow*-chasing or dignitaries to deal with, Henry had time for bike rides, swimming, crocodile hunting and tennis – which helped compensate for a painful tooth abscess and an abundance of spiders. He and several *Fox* colleagues joined some army officers and volunteers for training manoeuvres at a Royal Navy hill station; the exercises were strenuous but with the *dhow*-chasing season approaching and the *Fox* on permanent twenty-four-hour alert, Henry was glad to improve his fitness and marksmanship.[21] There were the inevitable dinners with 'big-wigs' but he managed to fit in some butterfly-hunting and reading, including H.G. Wells' *War in the Air* (sent by May), which he found to be 'horribly descriptive' of possible future aerial battles and barbaric societies.[22] Wordsworth's poetry provided more soothing bedtime reading, although he always kept 'one eye aloft for spiders' after one fell on his bed.

In the remote hill station mail was infrequent so Henry was pleasantly surprised to receive a letter from Glasgow; Captain Pattman of the *Loch Torridon* now showed considerable interest in Henry's career – and Henry admitted, with hindsight, that his erstwhile mentor-adversary was a fine 'trainer of boys'.[23] In the newspapers Henry read with interest about Ernest Shackleton's triumphant return to England and about concerns regarding Germany's ambitions. He decided, however, that there was 'no good raving about Germany [as] no power of man yet prevented an energetic nation's development'.[24] On his side of the world the whole East seemed to be 'bubbling' politically and, more parochially, he was concerned that the current logjam of young RIM lieutenants awaiting promotion might mean him languishing at his current rank for several years. He immediately cheered up, however, when he heard from Captain Hunt that there was the possibility of him staying on the *Fox* for a further six months and that he was also due two weeks' local leave.

The next morning Henry left Colombo before dawn with his bicycle 'well loaded up, a frame satchel amidships and an iron support aft for a meagre roll of bedding and a butterfly net'.[25] He pedalled northwards along the coast for 50 miles until he reached Chilaw, where he spent the night near the beach; the next morning he awoke feeling stiff and cycled north towards Puttalam at a more leisurely pace. He spent a night beside a sheltered lagoon and decided to ignore warnings not to venture further north unless armed (which he was not) due to reported sightings of wild elephants, bears and leopards in the area. He stopped beside the Kala Oya river for a cooling swim, but the sight of a crocodile 'drifting slowly down like a log of wood' convinced him to head east and inland for a late breakfast at the rest house at Mihintale – where he found nothing wilder than butterflies, monkeys, stoats and squirrels, and took the opportunity to visit a ruined temple:

> It was a gloomy sort of spot, overhung with thick trees and weird indeed, when after about a half mile I saw a vast stone staircase ascending into equally dense forest … Up this I trudged and came on human habitations – a number of priests' huts in fact, with the ruined Dagoba or Temple on the hill above. … When I reached the top (about 1,000 ft. up) the view repaid me hands down. … I could see the sea to the East and West with the thickly wooded plains all round … The great Dagobas at Anuradhapura above stuck up out of the green sea. It was quite a sight to remember.

The next day he visited Anuradhapura itself and was amazed by the size of the dagobas[26] erected in Buddha's honour over 1,000 years previously and by the beautiful statues of Buddha, which reminded him of those in Burma. After detours for butterfly-hunting and to visit Tirappane's beautiful lake and flower gardens, Henry spent the night in Sigiriya before tackling the famous 'lion rock':

> It is a wonderful place, simply precipitous all round and overhanging mostly – just like a boulder resting on a plain. It was an ancient fortress and religious centre and certainly deserved the former designation, as a more impossible place to scale one could hardly imagine. Without artificial aid nothing without wings would hope to tackle it – barring perhaps lizards. … On the top of the rock alone, there were about 6 baths of considerable size. The walls and remains of the Citadel and temples are overgrown ruins and all that remains of this monument to early Buddhist energy is a mound surmounted by a pole. The whole is 500 ft. high and seems higher viewed from the platform of the plains. The high land to the southward looks very near and almost would make a cyclist's heart fail to contemplate the ascents

necessary. I have set myself to do it though and I would not belong to the family of Bowers if I did not attempt the apparently impossible. I could hardly be in better all-round condition for something strenuous, than I am at present anyhow.

After an uphill ride through paddy fields and tea and rubber plantations, Henry allowed himself a day's butterfly-hunting in Nalande, which proved to be 'excellent sport' and resulted in the capture of numerous 'very lively and pretty wily' specimens. He also encountered a spider that had spun its web right across a glade: 'I had to break it down to get past, though it gave me the spasms to go near it. The web was more like elastic than anything and strong enough to hold a pigeon I should think. I had to throw 3 heavy boughs at it before it was demolished.'

Having overcome that obstacle, Henry continued to Kandy, the main city of Ceylon's central hill region, where he hoped to pick up some mail (including a package of new clothes) and find a room in the RIM quarters there. In a spirit of optimism he showered in a roadside waterfall before arriving and was able to dress for dinner in his new apparel. As he sat down to eat, Captain Hunt and the RIM paymaster appeared and invited him to join them for dinner. During 'yarns' about butterflies and other topics, Henry learned that the Shah of Persia had capitulated to the nationalists' demands for a constitution but that several RIM vessels were still 'hanging around' Bushire. Despite the *Fox* still being on twenty-four-hour alert, Henry had time to enjoy Kandy's lake, parks and palaces, and to visit the sacred Dalada Maligawa, the Temple of the Tooth, where Buddha's eponymous relic was enclosed in a magnificent golden casket. In the temple Henry also saw wall paintings portraying the Buddhist equivalent of Hell, in comparison with which he decided Dante's *Inferno* described 'a pleasure garden'.

On his way back to Colombo Henry visited Nawara Eliya, Ceylon's highest hill station:

I cannot describe my feelings yesterday as the agony of superhuman exertion always passes when over. … Nobody has – to the knowledge of the Secretary here – ever taken a bike up the Rambodda Pass, though many have risked their necks by going down it. The best way to go downhill is to make fast a heavy log astern. This acts as a continual brake and your brakes only come in for emergency. … I must knock off, as I want to climb Mt. Peduratalagota (usually called Mt. Pedro). It is 8,295 ft. and the highest peak in Ceylon. As I am over 6,000 ft. up here, the remaining 2,000 should not be arduous and I shall not have a heavily laden bike with me this time.

After a 30-mile downhill 'spin' into Colombo, Henry dispatched some picture-postcards and rejoined the *Fox* which had, in his absence, undergone a major clean-up as the RIM admiral was currently in port. Unprepared for the flurry of inspections and drills, Henry gave a lacklustre performance and felt fortunate to escape a 'wigging' from Captain Hunt. During 'Colombo week', with its horse races, games, tournaments, dances, dinners and 'At Homes', Henry slipped away with his new butterfly specimens to the museum, where he learned he had caught a perfect example of a rare species. Back in port he watched enviously as his contemporaries left for England and courses at the Naval College in Greenwich, but he was happy enough to hear that he was due an unexpected extra forty-eight hours' leave.

The next morning he left before dawn and rode uphill for 38 miles until he reached Habarane: 'Before long I regretted not having a lamp as there was no moon and where the trees overhung the darkness was pitchy ... By the time I could read a milestone, I had done 12 good miles – a pleasant surprise.'[27] He continued to Polonaruwa, which had been constructed by eleventh-century Ceylonese rulers fleeing assaults on Anuradhapura by Tamils from the Indian mainland. The city had enjoyed something of a golden age before being seized by the Tamils and, when the latter had abandoned it, swallowed up by the jungle. Henry found a bed for the night and first thing the following morning called at the home of Archaeological Commissioner H.C.P. Bell:

> He was still in pyjamas but was most kind ... Mr Bell has dug out all the ancient places I have gone to. He has years of restoration and jungle clearing before him at this out-of-the-way place. Buried in the densest jungle are the ruins of a great city and the Capital of some ancient and powerful dynasty. All these vast tanks, some with an area of 50 square miles, were built artificially by these people. In fact Mr. Bell says there is not a natural lake in Ceylon. Vast images of Buddha in all attitudes are there, hewn in solid rock, besides temples of remarkable design and structure.

When he returned to Colombo Henry felt tired, but was glad to have done justice to this beautiful island, reduced his weight and improved his fitness.[28]

7

UNCERTAIN TIMES AND
A NEW BEGINNING

In late July 1909 Henry turned 26. He had now been at sea for ten years and in the Royal Indian Marine for almost four. He still thoroughly enjoyed life on the *Fox* under Captain Hunt but felt frustrated at not being selected to go on a promotion-enhancing training course in Greenwich.

In August Henry received an unexpected letter from Sir Clements Markham, who told him that plans for Captain Scott's second Antarctic expedition would soon be publicly announced, and that should Henry decide to apply for a place he would have Sir Clements' full support.[1] Henry responded immediately thanking Sir Clements for his suggestion and confirming his interest. He also wrote to Captain Scott expressing his keenness; he felt duty-bound, however, to explain that his current terms of engagement precluded him from making an application other than through the RIM's official channels – which frustratingly he could not do until he had secured a place on the expedition. With little likelihood of being in London in the foreseeable future, Henry could only hope that these letters and providential happenstance would bring his boyhood dream to fruition. For the moment at least, all he could do was be patient.

The political situation in the East and Europe remained volatile. Henry wondered if war, which was certainly in the air, might not be altogether a bad thing as 'the effect of some terrible struggles has been for a long spell of prosperity afterwards'.[2] In Colombo Captain Hunt and his crew awaited instructions. Theories abounded: '... trouble in the Aden hinterlands – another Somali show – Bushire again – arms traffic at Muscat – trouble in India, etc.' Henry had a long 'yarn' with the captain who was 'like a boy in his keenness ... hoping for Somaliland'.[3] Eventually, the *Fox* was dispatched to the Yemen (from where the British consulate had summoned assistance to deal with a local uprising), but as she struggled westward through a series of monsoon storms, Captain Hunt received a telegram standing him down and recalling him to RIM headquarters in Bombay. With no immediate duties to fulfil, the *Fox* was entered for the annual RIM regatta – in which she won thirteen out of seventeen races – and took part in the RIM 'fleet cruise' to the beautiful, coral-edged Laccadive Islands.[4]

As May and Emily were soon due to leave Bute for their prolonged stay in Switzerland, Henry sent a final donation to their holiday fund and wrote enthusiastically about the prospect of 'alp ranging' with May on his next home leave. He also told them about his new friend, Captain Hunt's nephew Lieutenant Hunt, who had turned out to be an 'excellent chap' despite his political views:[5]

> He calls himself a 'Socialist' & is great on the 'Fabian Society', Bernard Shaw, the earlier poems of Swinburn & other things. All these things are unlooked for in a Naval Officer but Hunt sticks to his guns & only drinks 'The King' at mess out of pure condescension. ... As a companion a better chap could hardly exist, though we used to have long & heated arguments [in Bushire]. ... He at last gave me up & never starts on me. ... nobody – including the Captain – takes his views seriously.

When the new *dhow*-chasing 'season' opened in October Captain Hunt gave Henry his own cutter and strip of coast to patrol. Although some *dhows* were as large as galleons (with sterns resembling 'the craft of Drake's day'), a burst of speed from Henry's cutter, a volley of warning shots and a prominently displayed ensign generally secured bloodless surrender by the smugglers. Henry enjoyed being in command of his own small ship, working in the open air and living the 'simple life'. The only drawback to this 'delightful picnic' was the lack of a regular mail service, which meant Henry needed to start sending Christmas messages to Switzerland in late October. He recalled the previous year's festivities fondly but admitted he was suffering doubts about certain aspects of the Church's role: 'I never look on Christmas as a "Church" festival – in fact the word "Church" is one I dislike, its meaning is always perverted into organisations of minor sects who claim to be <u>the</u> Church. I think "Christ's people" is a much grander term.'[6]

As temperatures in the Gulf soared Henry slept on deck with his crew, 'like sardines, head and feet alternating', an arrangement which provided a level of comradeship he suspected he would not have experienced as a Royal Navy officer. Unfortunately, he also burned his bare feet so badly on the ship's deck that he could not wear shoes for weeks.

In early November Henry was delighted to hear that his tenure on the *Fox* would continue until at least the end of the year, but when he received Emily and May's missives from the Hotel Beau-Site in Clarens on the shores of Lake Geneva, his thoughts turned to cooler climes:

> Are you broiled, baked, frizzled & glared upon from sunrise to sunset like a relative of yours is or is that most delightful of all scenes – a driving Scottish mist – obscuring everything else? I can remember when this persistent orb <u>was</u> welcome – Down South when he had not been seen for weeks.[7]

By way of afterthought he added: 'Talking about Down South – I would enjoy a nitch in the forthcoming expedition under Capt. Scott – however I am afraid chances are not in my favour this time. If I were on leave I would worry them alright.' While Henry's last sentence was technically correct, it was Emily and May he had decided not to 'worry' about the Antarctic. When he received a letter from Captain Wilson-Barker, he shared with Emily the news that a high proportion of 'Worcesters' were now joining the RIM in preference to the merchant or Royal navies, but not that Captain Wilson-Barker was championing Henry's cause with Captain Scott. As far as Emily and May were concerned, Henry had everything he wanted from life: 'good plain food & an open air life with plenty of swimming & plenty of work & a dash of excitement – or at least anticipation occasionally – & no luxuries.'[8]

As Henry's time in the Gulf continued his face became leathery and, even when clean, the colour of mulligatawny soup; his red hair became matted and his chin sprouted 'a bristly beard of a lighter though more intense hue'. Perhaps fortunately given his current appearance, his posting at this time involved few encounters with the opposite sex, but he was still open to settling down: 'there can be no imaginably earthly joy greater than the possession of a good girl for your very own' – although he was conscious that the wives of young officers who could be posted far away at short notice had a rather 'thick time' of it. In terms of politics, Captain Hunt's socialist nephew was bringing Henry round to thinking that taxation of inherited wealth was a good thing; regarding religion, Henry admitted to Emily that he felt less close to some of the Evangelical 'brotherhood' than he had in the past.

While Henry was in the Gulf two letters arrived on the subject of Captain Scott's expedition. Sir Clements Markham confirmed that he had promoted Henry's cause with Captain Scott as far as possible but could do no more.

Captain Wilson-Barker told him that some 5,000 would-be Antarctic explorers had now applied to join the expedition. Henry felt stymied by RIM protocol, but when he realised that 'Old Worcester' Lieutenant Teddy Evans (whom he had met with Captain Wilson-Barker some eight years previously) had been appointed as Scott's second in command and was involved in the recruitment process, he quickly dashed off another letter.[9] In mid-December Henry received a 'poisonous telegram' from RIM headquarters summoning him to Karachi.[10] During his leave-taking from the *Fox* (an event enlivened by Lieutenant Hunt's champagne-based 'Stirrup Cup') Captain Hunt spoke warmly of Henry's contribution to the work of the ship and gratifyingly suggested that Henry's multifaceted 'little niche' would not be quickly filled.[11]

In Karachi Henry learned he would be joining the troopship *Northbrook* as senior watch-keeper. Although he now had a palatial cabin and opportunities to spend time on shore with 'feminine society', he regarded his new position, at best, a sideways move, and found his new captain to be a 'dear old Granny' compared to Captain Hunt. Despite social 'bashes' galore Henry felt very '*Fox*-sick'. He spent Christmas, his favourite season of the year, in 'an absolute void' with little or no Christmas mail and without finding a nearby Christmas service to his liking.[12] The few letters which reached him did little to lift his spirits: an old friend had died and George Foucar (Louis' younger brother) had eloped, thus causing a major rift in the Foucar family. As he fretted and sweltered Henry envied Emily and May their Christmas at Hotel Beau-Site, where he imagined them strolling in the snow or admiring views of Lake Geneva and the Alps.

On the *Northbrook* his captain had, against Henry's will, appointed him 'President of the Wines', in which capacity he was expected to organise Christmas crackers and swimming parties. When the *Northbrook* sailed past Ceylon Henry longed to revisit the 'pear-shaped island' or, following receipt of a postcard of Swiss skiers from May, to be risking his neck at skiing or other 'glorious sports'. Over the next few months the monotony of transporting troops, prisoners and dignitaries was broken only by news from far shores: Captain Pattman had, after almost thirty years, finally relinquished command of the *Loch Torridon* and turned his hand to steam; 'Old Worcester' Eric was in Queensland but, due to his lack of success at exams, was still a fourth mate; and Americans Peary and Cook had been (according to newspaper cuttings sent by May) in dispute regarding their claims to have reached the North Pole.[13]

In late January, however, Henry had the opportunity to try out some new diving equipment and walk along the seabed in a pressurised suit – and to visit Calcutta for the first time:

The 'Dollar Princess' is on at the theatre here.[14] It is tremendously popular. Calcutta is an enormous change after the other prosaic places such as Bombay, Madras & Rangoon. It is almost like coming home. The wide streets, big parks … shops, colossal buildings, theatres, music halls – motors by the thousand & traffic that would do credit to even London. The signs of blatant wealth are everywhere. No talk of slack trade or unemployment here. … How a change of rule could be desired amid this prosperity seems hard to understand.[15]

By now Henry was having regular 'differences of opinion' with his new captain and the current oversupply of ambitious young RIM lieutenants was making him wonder if he would make commander before his mid-thirties – unless war intervened and eliminated any distinctions between 'Imperial, Indian or Colonial officers'.[16] By late February his frustrations regarding postal services were amplified by the fact that any letters he posted to Emily and May in Switzerland now might not reach them before they left Hotel Beau-Site; as he had no further addresses for them in Europe, all he could was write to them in Bute 'in accordance with instructions'.[17] Everything seemed unsettled: unseasonably cold weather in the Gulf, huge storms in Europe and indications that the Germans (whom Henry generally regarded as 'not bad chaps') were 'busting themselves to wipe [the British] out', a move Henry felt would result in their receiving 'a terrible hammering'.[18]

During his midnight watch on 1 March 1910 Henry poured out his heart out in a letter to May, wherever she might be.[19] After beginning cheerfully enough, thanking her for a picture-postcard of a Swiss snow scene and asking whether she had yet heard the music from *The Dollar Princess*, he admitted to feeling confused on several fronts. Politically, while his views on the taxation of the rich chimed with Liberal policy, those on foreign affairs reflected the Unionist standpoint; he felt as if he had been born out of time and might have been happier as a Puritan Cromwellian Roundhead. In terms of religion he also felt torn, as during a recent visit to Bombay an Evangelical clergyman, 'Brother Tompson', had stated that Evangelical Christians should not carry swords or fight – even for a righteous cause such as defence of the British Empire. As an officer in an armed service Henry could not accept this: 'Are the soldiers of Christ to withdraw themselves from the "Services" of their countries? At that rate – theoretically – armies and navies would be Christless, depraved & hopeless.' In terms of Henry's own salvation he knew he had become worldly but still clung to Christ's promise of redemption for those who were not 'perfect & free from sin'. As regards women, Henry hoped to find a soul mate with whom he shared the kind of 'indefinable sympathy' and 'sound intellectual understanding' he did with May. He admitted, however, that he suspected he had never really been truly in love or found himself particularly compelled by 'the animal side or physical love' – a trait he wondered if he had inherited from their father who had only married in his fifties. As his midnight watch drew to a close, Henry signed off his letter with an apology to May for having wandered 'from the beaten tracks of letter writing' and a determinedly cheery 'good night old bird'.

Henry's long confessional seemed to serve its purpose, as two weeks later he was writing home describing an encounter at a dance with Captain Hunt's niece and several of her friends:

> I cannot analyse which I liked the best … one of the sub [lieutenant]s shared Miss H[unt] with me … all shared my liking for Miss Brown. They were all 3 pretty – quite young – only recently out I think – very sensible, well-educated girls – full of fun & absolutely 'pukka memsahibs' to their fingertips. How could we mere men help ourselves … I was quite sorry to say goodbye but feel that it is the best thing possibly for yours truly. I saw Miss Short a good deal. She is very tall & not half a bad sort of girl … much sought after for her dancing which she does splendidly.[20]

That evening Miss Short's mother, an erstwhile resident of Rangoon, approached Henry and asked him to send her best wishes to Emily and May – a request to which he gladly acceded. Not long afterwards, however, Mrs Short's cousin accosted Henry and asked him about rumours involving May and Alfred Aldridge (including their alleged engagement and Alfred's reported demise). Henry cut her short, furious that such scurrilous and ill-informed gossip should be circulating, and vowed never to 'have any truck with that lot' in future unless Emily told him that Mrs Short's family had been particularly kind to her in the past.

Emily and May, blissfully unaware of this unfortunate encounter and Henry's general unhappiness, were by now enjoying the architectural and artistic treasures of Milan and Florence.[21] They had given him an address to which Henry wrote saying that he was pleased they liked Italy but warned May against being seduced by the 'paraphernalia, ancient customs, buildings or pictures' of the Catholic Church, an institution he still distrusted despite now regarding individual Roman Catholics as his brothers in Christ.[22]

Henry's brief tour of duty on the *Northbrook* was due to come to its unlamented end, but he had heard nothing from Captain Scott in London or from Captain Hunt, who had been investigating the possibility of Henry being reassigned to the *Fox*. All he could hope for was that his name might eventually drift to the top of the 'Greenwich' list.

Now, at least, Henry could read Ernest Shackleton's *Heart of the Antarctic*, the explorer's account of the *Nimrod* expedition, a copy of which had been obtained for the *Northbrook's* library at Henry's instigation.[23] Wilkes Land, Henry's boyhood Antarctic goal, was mentioned in the book's opening pages and subsequent chapters provided information on Antarctic rations (pemmican, chocolate and cheese), clothing (Burberry gabardines, fur mittens and finnesko), transportation (ship, sledges and ponies rather than sledge-dogs) and weather conditions (rough seas, howling winds and treacherous ice).[24] He read of the tortuous, dangerous journey south and the combination of poor weather and surfaces, ailments and gnawing, life-threatening hunger which eventually forced Shackleton, Wild, Marshall and Adams to plant their flag at a new 'Furthest South' rather than trying to conquer the South Pole and risk dying in the attempt.

Henry's own hopes of seeing Antarctica were dealt a blow when he received a letter from Teddy Evans in London saying that almost 8,000 men had now applied to join Scott's expedition. His mood was not improved by an encounter with his nemesis, the 'horror of horrors':

I woke at 1 a.m. and opened my eyes wide – you can guess what it was, but you can't guess what I felt like. Not 3 inches from my nose and making straight for my cheek was the incarnation of my conception of the blackest and most horrible fiend the powers of darkness can produce. I did not utter a sound but if ever a man got out of a bunk with alacrity I was out of mine. Fast as the huge tarantula was he had only covered about 6 inches before we faced each other for a war to the death. ... I grabbed a shoe, but I hadn't the pluck to dab him with that ... I wasn't going to risk a miss though, and running out got hold of a hard broom. When I came back he was *gone*. I have searched in vain, but there are so many cracks and crannies especially under the washstand ... that bunk – or any other in that cabin – will never see my sleeping form again. It seems a long yarn about nothing, but I would rather dive on to the back of a 16-ft. shark than face that awful thing. I could see its hairs in the dark.[25]

When Henry learned that his next posting would be on the troopship *Minto* rather than his beloved *Fox* he gloomily reported to headquarters for duty. On arrival he was, somewhat to his surprise, told to go immediately to the director's office; when on entering he saw several severe faces he wondered if he had inadvertently done something wrong or was due for a 'wigging'. Two telegrams were handed to him: one stated that Lieutenant Bowers' services were required on Captain Scott's expedition to the Antarctic (subject to his release by the RIM); the other that, should Lieutenant Bowers wish to accept this offer, he must report for duty in London by 15 May at the latest.

Henry tried to explain to his RIM superiors – who were as much in the dark as his family regarding his clandestine correspondence with Markham, Scott, Wilson-Barker and Teddy Evans – that he had not actually applied for the post. When he realised that everyone in the room regarded his new appointment as a compliment to the RIM as well as his own personal achievement, he knew that all he now had to do was break the news to his family and get himself to London. He checked on the availability of passages over the coming weeks and fired off a series of succinct cables in the hope that one would reach Emily and May before he did: 'Arrive 27th [April]. Appointed Antarctic.'[26]

That done, he composed a long letter to Emily (addressed to Caerlaverock) setting out the long chain of circumstances which had led to his appointment.[27] He acknowledged that she had always 'stuck out against Polar Exploration' for him, but hoped she might feel some maternal pride about his being selected without formal application or interview from among 8,000 would-be explorers. His appointment was, he told her, yet another example of the 'unseen arrangement' which guided his career: 'One can only say it is destiny – it cannot be helped, it had to be. This may seem foolish but it is not. God knows how & why I was appointed & I am in His hands entirely.' Things were, he told her, already moving fast:

> Cables are flying about like smoke & your son has become a curio. I expect now to leave on Thursday by M. Maritimes to Marseilles & I shall in any case be in London by 1st May.[28] Capt. Hunt is highly pleased & I was dined by the Foxes at the Yacht Club last night ... I receive congrats daily of course for the sake of the Service. ... It is great honour mother & though it temporarily alters our plans I shall have a week or so with you & much time when I come back.

Henry's next letter was to Captain Wilson-Barker who, it transpired, had personally taken a copy of Henry's credentials to Captain Scott's office:

> I don't know how to thank you for getting me appointed to this Expedition. Really I am so surprised and pleased that I can hardly realize it now. It is all settled and the Government of India has approved ... I shall be leaving by the next French mail to Marseilles and should be in London by the 1st May.

I shall look forward to seeing you then and thanking you for what I consider to be the climax in a long succession of kindnesses you have done me. Needless to say I was never keener on anything in my life.[29]

Henry's final weeks in India passed in a flurry of packing, parties and presentations, until on the morning of his departure his fellow officers roused him at 4.30 a.m. and waved him off. During his homeward voyage Henry reclined in his new deckchair (a leaving present from his colleagues) and in a belated attempt to soften the blow of his brief cable, wrote more letters to Emily:[30]

The Director has now given me 3 months privilege leave so that if I fail the medical exam I shall at least have 6 weeks at home ... I cannot think how you will have received the news about my going ... consideration of dangers will have first entered your mind, secondly that it will be back to the old sailing ship days for letters again. I have not forgotten that you once said you hoped you would be dead before I started on anything so foolhardy. ... I know I lay myself open to a grave charge of selfishness. It is quite impossible to call it that though. What made me go to sea at first? ... In the case of this expedition hundreds – in fact 8000 applicants ... are rejected in favour of a paltry half dozen. To imagine that such a thing is mere chance is out of the question. It simply had to be – nothing could be clearer. ... It will, I am afraid, be very necessary to stay in town [London] – at least I shall know what can be done after I have seen Capt. Scott. ... Isn't it great – this expedition – you see I shall only be away for a couple of years & then a good spell at home after it. ... they say everybody has his chance & if ever I have had mine it is now. When I come back I shall be able to do much – in fact everything is possible after a show of this sort. I am sure you will look on the rational side of the question – life is just as precarious up the Gulf ... I am going to do a man's work, only a man could do it who is a strong one at that. No weaklings will be included in the Expedition that professes to have carefully selected that collection of British Sailors which will best further its ends. It is a National show & I am sure you will not fail to feel glad that your son should have such an honour.

... I do regret that cablegram, but that is no good now. I hope it did not curtail your stay in Italy ... I must come home well-lined and strong so I am working towards that end. I do quite a lot of exercising before breakfast which always gives me the best of appetites. I am as fit as anything of course & shall arrive home as strong as a mule this time (D.V.).[31]

* * *

One of Henry's brusque cables reached Emily and May in Rome on 15 April.[32] They both felt 'very wretched' as they crammed in some last-minute sight-seeing before taking the train to Florence and on to Clarens and the Hotel Beau-Site. There, fellow residents – in many cases also now friends – gave them a warm and sympathetic welcome before waving them off on the northbound train which would eventually take them to the Channel. After a choppy cross-ing, which left Emily 'more dead than alive', they arrived in London where they went to the Chiswick home of their long-standing friends, the Hills. They arrived two days ahead of Henry's stated arrival date of 27 April, but there was no news of him. As days passed without word they began to wonder if he might have landed in Plymouth and was taking a train to London.

On 1 May 1910, almost precisely two years since Henry had arrived in London for his long home leave, he, Emily and May were reunited in the capital. Henry reported for duty at the expedition's Victoria Street offices and to West India Docks where the *Terra Nova* was moored. Built in Dundee in 1884 as a sealer and whaler, she had been requisitioned by the Admiralty in 1903 to accompany the relief ship *Morning* to the Antarctic to help free Captain Scott's *Discovery*, which had become trapped in the pack ice.[33] Scott had wanted to use the *Discovery* for his second expedition but when her new owners declined to release her he had purchased the *Terra Nova* for £12,500. Since then her bows had been reinforced to withstand ice and she had been completely overhauled – although some noticed a whiff of whale oil still lingering in her timbers.[34]

When on duty at West India Docks Henry stowed and sorted cases, avoided as many official farewells as possible and stopped only to eat or to sign auto-graphs for particularly insistent or important well-wishers or visitors.[35] During his limited off-duty hours he spent time with Emily and May, visiting Kew Gardens, shopping for a new hat for May (a gift from Henry) and an Antarctic-weight Burberry overcoat ('identically the same as Shackleton's', according to May), visiting friends, dining at the recently opened Strand Palace Hotel and – to Henry's delight – going to a performance of *The Dollar Princess*.

On 6 May 1910 King Edward VII died at Sandringham. In the lull between his death and the state funeral Emily returned to Scotland, while Henry visited Edie in Chapel-en-le-Frith, Derbyshire (where she was currently working), and May stayed in London. On his return to West India Docks Henry met Sir Clements Markham, a regular visitor to the *Terra Nova*, and thanked him for supporting his application for the expedition.[36] On 20 May Henry joined naval colleagues in attendance at the king's funeral; May watched the proces-sion from Horse Guards Parade from where she had a good view of the new

King George V, nine crowned heads of Europe and the late king's dog Caesar, which trotted along in the wake of the royal gun carriage.[37]

By the end of May the *Terra Nova* was loaded to her gunwales and Henry, with May's help, had almost finished his own packing. They enjoyed a farewell outing to the Strand Palace and the theatre; May thought Henry seemed 'much older in his ways' and looked over-worked and worried, but when they discussed the expedition he assured her that, while he was not convinced he would return to the RIM, he was 'absolutely confident' of returning safely from the expedition. On 31 May Henry attended a farewell luncheon for the expedition party given by the Royal Geographical Society, at which Scott made a jocular reference to the fact that Henry, early in his new career, had fallen into the hold but emerged unscathed.[38]

On 1 June 1910, exactly a month after Henry's return from India, May, Emily and Edie joined Henry at West India Docks, where he showed them around his ship and introduced them to Captain and Mrs Scott. In the late afternoon, as the *Terra Nova* cast off, Emily, May, Edie and family friends waved Henry and his companions away.

That night, the *Terra Nova* moored at Greenhithe alongside the *Worcester* so that cadets could see over the ship and meet 'Old Worcesters' Teddy Evans and Henry Bowers. The next morning Henry and Teddy Evans breakfasted with Captain Wilson-Barker and bade farewell to Sir Clements Markham, who was travelling back to London with Scott, who still had matters to attend to there. Henry sailed with the *Terra Nova* to Portsmouth before taking the train back to London to spend a few more days with Emily and May (which Scott had allowed him given his recent return from long-term service in India). They visited the recently opened Japan-British Exhibition, met up with friends and, on their final weekend together, went to church and enjoyed a farewell tea of strawberries.[39]

On Monday 6 June 1910 Emily and May waved Henry off again, this time at Waterloo station, where, according to Henry, 'the dear old Mother was very upset but held up'; a truckload of coffins on the platform alongside the train did not lift anyone's spirits.[40] The next day, Emily and May returned to Scotland to prepare for a visit from Alfred Aldridge. By then, Henry was back on the *Terra Nova* ready, willing and able to serve Captain Robert Scott and his British Antarctic expedition in whatever way he could.

8

HEADING SOUTH

Before leaving Portsmouth Henry, now nicknamed Birdie in deference to his nose, wrote to Emily in Bute. While they knew that some of the men's relations would be following the ship to Cardiff, neither had wanted to prolong the farewells associated with Birdie's chosen life:

> If we never experienced the unhappiness of parting we would never realize the joy of living & thus it must go on until we reach the place where we never more shall part & where God shall wipe away all tears from our eyes.[1]
> ... I am perfectly confident without a shadow of doubt that I shall come back to you as I have gone, no worse and I hope a better man.[2]

Birdie was now embarking on the longest single journey of his life. After calling at New Zealand the *Terra Nova* would sail down the great Southern Ocean to Antarctica, where Birdie would help unload the ship, construct the expedition hut and sort and store provisions. He would then return with the *Terra Nova* to New Zealand, probably by early 1911; the ship would return to Antarctica at least once more and eventually sail back to Britain in 1912 or 1913.

From Portsmouth the *Terra Nova* continued to Weymouth where Scott rejoined his ship. In Cardiff piles of donated coal lay on the dockside ready for loading, and following days of hard work in poor weather, Birdie joined his new colleagues for a grand civic farewell dinner at the Royal Hotel. Birdie enjoyed fillets of beef 'Terra Nova', soufflé 'Captain Scott' and 'South Pole' ice pudding, while Roberts' Band played tunes from his favourite musical, *The Dollar Princess*, and the suitably stirring *The Hero of the South* and *Farewell to Gladiators*.[3] At lunchtime on Wednesday 15 June 1910 the *Terra Nova*, with Teddy Evans in command, left Cardiff to the sounds of crowds cheering and bands playing. Scott was returning to London for final negotiations with the Central News Agency, following which he would travel by steamship to South Africa with his wife Kathleen, Oriana Wilson (wife of the chief of scientific staff, Dr Edward Wilson) and Hilda Evans (Teddy's wife, whom he had met in New Zealand with the *Discovery* expedition). Scott's plan was to arrive ahead of the *Terra Nova* so he could start raising the funds still required to cover the costs of the expedition.

As soon as the *Terra Nova* was at sea, Birdie felt 'as right as rain, righter if anything' and happy to be handling sails again.[4] He had posted a bundle of letters from Cardiff and knew he could send and receive mail until the *Terra Nova* left New Zealand towards the end of the year. Following that, Birdie warned Emily, there would be a 'period of silence' until early the following year.

Now they were under way, Birdie had the opportunity to make the acquaintance of his new companions, many of whom were not naval men.[5] The scientists – a new species for him – were mainly Cambridge University graduates personally chosen by Dr Edward Wilson (a Cambridge man himself) and seemed to be 'the pick of 1st class talent in all scientific branches'. One such, Apsley Cherry-Garrard (known as Cherry), a friend of Dr Wilson, was a 'young millionaire' who seemed 'a thorough gentleman & very keen' and had travelled extensively 'in the lap of luxury'. The expedition's only military man was Captain Lawrence Oates of the Inniskilling Dragoons (nicknamed Titus after his seventeenth-century namesake); he had, like Birdie, recently returned from service in India. Birdie decided he was an 'awfully good chap' who, despite having a private income 'beyond the dreams of avarice', and his own yacht, the *Saunterer*, dressed more like a 'half-deck apprentice than a Captain'.[6] Birdie felt Titus would be a great asset to the expedition as his years as a cavalry officer and huntsman gave him a great affinity with horses and dogs, which would be the mainstay of the expedition's transportation. As most of the expedition animals were being purchased in northern Asia (from where they would be shipped direct to New Zealand), Oates had few current duties so had signed on as a midshipman. He immediately took to shipboard life and told Birdie he would rather be sailing to New Zealand than heading back to Asia to where Cecil Meares (the expedition's dog-handler) had gone to purchase sledge-dogs.[7] Teddy Evans and first mate Victor Campbell were naturally keen to hold on to a strong, willing crewmember like Oates and were relieved when Mrs Scott's brother, Wilfred Bruce – a late addition to the expedition party and another 'Old Worcester' – offered to go to Asia at his own expense to assist Meares with purchasing and transporting the animals.[8]

Of Birdie's fellow lieutenants, the one who impressed him the most was the ship's navigator, Lieutenant Harry Pennell (known as Penelope), who seemed even-tempered, highly intelligent, an excellent mathematician and accurate navigational observer, and who, although only eighteen months older than Birdie, was almost equal in rank to Teddy Evans. Since leaving Cardiff, Teddy Evans had gained Birdie's respect by holding regular onboard Sunday services but was, Birdie felt, turning out to be rather a 'man of moods ... a good friend – but a bad enemy ... & the most charming of chaps ordinarily'. Evans' effortless charm had so impressed the expedition's London manager, George Wyatt (an 'A1 chap with many irons in the fire'), that the latter had, Birdie believed, offered Evans £1,000 a year to join him in business when the expedition returned.[9] On their shared watches Birdie and Teddy found much to talk about, whether 'Old Worcester' gossip, Teddy's tales of the *Discovery* rescue mission or Birdie's RIM exploits. Birdie immediately liked his cabin-mate, Henry Rennick – who would be staying down in Antarctica as expedition storekeeper – and Dr Edward Atkinson, a naval research scientist who Birdie thought of as 'one of the best' and 'the most Christian character of any of us'.

The person Birdie most admired overall, however, was chief scientist Dr Edward Wilson, who happened to be a fellow redhead. He was, in Birdie's eyes, 'the soundest man we have'; a veteran of the *Discovery* expedition (of which he had tales to tell), he was also a wonderful artist and 'a real Christian' who was always ready to help others. Birdie found 'our Bill' or 'Uncle Bill', as he was known, to be a 'pre-eminent chap – the perfect gentleman ... the finest character in my own sex that I have ever had the privilege to meet'. Wilson, for his part, seemed to enjoy Birdie's sense of humour and spent a lot of time with his younger fellow Christian, with whom he shared a fascination for the natural world.[10]

In Madeira, the *Terra Nova's* first port of call, Birdie enjoyed the beautiful gardens and steep cobbled streets, and was glad to be able to dispatch and pick up letters and buy souvenirs to send home. He played in a football match against the Western Telegraph 'chaps' and enjoyed a 'sumptuous lunch' at the home of Mr Reid, owner of the island's luxury hotel.[11] For Birdie the latter occasion ended on a rather sour note after Mr Reid took his guests to see his 'collection', which turned out to be an exhibition of erotica which Birdie found (and declared to those present) to be thoroughly offensive. The *Terra Nova* left Madeira on 26 June and made good progress until she became becalmed in the Doldrums; her engines had to be fired up and the delay meant bypassing Tristan da Cunha and Gough Island, both of which Birdie had been keen to visit.[12]

Birdie's first official zoological expedition took place on South Trinidad island, an uninhabited wildlife haven 700 miles east of Brazil, where, according to sailors' lore, Captain Kidd had buried his pirate gold. After landing in the ship's 'pram' they spread all over the island.[13] Wilson and Cherry-Garrard led a bird-hunting party, Dennis Lillie sought out rare plant and geological specimens, Edward Nelson and George 'Sunny Jim' Simpson scoured the seashore and Atkinson searched for parasites lurking on other animals. While the naturalists were busy, Oates exercised the few dogs already on board, Tryggve Gran (the expedition's Norwegian ski expert) lent a general hand, and Birdie, Teddy Evans and 'Silas' Wright (a Canadian geologist)[14] were dispatched to hunt for 'small beasts' and insects the other scientists were too busy to deal with.

Birdie did not particularly enjoy his encounter with the island's infamous yellow and pink land-crabs, whose 'dead staring eyes follow your every step … with a sickly deliberation' and which seemed to him, next to spiders, 'the most loathsome creatures on God's earth'. He was somewhat perturbed to find spiders on his party's collecting list but he, Teddy and Silas (a fellow arachnophobe) managed, with the aid of a long-handled butterfly net, to trap fifteen new species of spider and a selection of other insects.[15] After a successful day they regrouped at their landing spot, laden with specimens − only to find themselves separated from the *Terra Nova* by an expanse of crashing breakers on which their pram bobbed like a cork. Birdie and two others swam out to retrieve the pram and helped others aboard. After a choppy passage to the *Terra Nova* and a night's sleep, Birdie and six others rowed the pram back to rescue their specimens and two 'maroons', Atkinson and a sick sailor, who had come ashore the previous day for some exercise but had been unable to face the return journey. The embarkation was not easy:

> You could go in to the very edge of the breaking surf, lifted like a cork on top of the waves … in a lull we got our sick man down … the next minute the boat flew out on the back-wash with the seaman absolutely dry, & I was of course enveloped in foam & blackness two seconds later by a following wave. … very scratched & winded, I clung on with my nails & scrambled up higher. … Atkinson & I then started getting the gear down … the next minute the pram passed over my head & landed high & dry, like a bridge, over the rocks between which I was wedged. … The next wave − a huge one − picked her up, & out she bumped over the rocks & out to sea …

As the heavily laden *Terra Nova* ploughed laboriously through the waves towards Simon's Bay, near Cape Town, Birdie enjoyed seeing the 'usual crowd' of seabirds from his *Loch Torridon* days. After they crossed the equator the intense heat – much to Birdie's great relief – abated; some people were wearing Shetland sweaters but he was, being something of a 'generator of heat', still comfortable in cotton shirts and his RIM 'whites'. On the subject of temperatures, he casually mentioned to Emily that there was an outside possibility he might be spending longer in Antarctica than he had initially expected:

> By the bye, Evans & Wilson are very keen on my being in the Western party, while Campbell wants me with him in the Eastern Party. I have not asked to go ashore, but am keen on anything & am ready to do anything. In fact there is so much going on that I feel I should like to be in all three places at once – East, West and Ship.

Life on board under Teddy Evans' command was a relatively relaxed affair.[16] In the evenings Birdie played tunes from *The Dollar Princess* or *The Merry Widow* on the pianola (which Oates hated) or joined in Teddy's 'entertainments' – a highlight of which was an all-male rendition of a music-hall number featuring 'the Sisters Hardbake' with their 'goo-goo eyes'.[17] On 23 July Birdie, although not much of a dancer, joined Teddy Evans and Rennick in executing a war-dance on the main hatch in honour of Edward Wilson's 38th birthday.[18]

On 15 August, just over two weeks after Birdie's 27th birthday, the *Terra Nova* docked in Simon's Town, where running repairs would be carried out free of charge. In Cape Town, which lay just over an hour's train ride away, Birdie picked up a month's worth of mail from Britain and dispatched his lengthy letter-cum-journal, letters and newspaper cuttings to Emily, May and Edie.[19] He knew the overloaded *Terra Nova* had been running behind schedule but was shocked to read newspaper 'panic stories' based on imagined reasons for her late arrival. Birdie knew Emily ('the wife & mother of a sailor') was well used to ships running late, but thought that 'blighters … who do that sort of thing to make money ought to be fried in their own fat', as should the 'silly jacks in offices who get a penny a line for writing rot … [and] put down any yarn we spin them'.

Since arriving in South Africa, Scott had been trying to raise funds from the government in Pretoria and private backers in Cape Town. He was glad to have his crew with him for a final push and although Birdie hated 'banquets & other horrors', he knew success in South Africa might mean they could go straight to New Zealand rather than stop to do more fundraising in Australia. This would save valuable time and avoid competing for funds with Australia's Douglas Mawson, a member of Shackleton's *Nimrod* expedition who was currently planning his own Antarctic expedition.

Birdie was learning something about Antarctic rivalries, as on the journey south Edward Wilson (not one to speak ill of people) had hinted that Shackleton had not 'played the game' by Scott after the *Discovery* expedition, and had 'sometimes worked for his own hand at the expense of others'.[20] Despite this, Birdie still regarded Shackleton as a 'splendid chap', although he was not particularly impressed by rumours that Shackleton and Mawson were both hoping to locate valuable mineral deposits which might later be exploited.[21]

In Simon's Town Birdie spent most of his time rearranging cargo in the ship's holds and on deck in preparation for the arrival of additional stores and fuel. He also spent time with Harry Pennell who was teaching him how to operate a theodolite:[22]

> I thought I could work, but I can't keep pace with Pennell ... [he] is a most indefatigable instructor. ... when I think of all he has in his brain I begin to wonder if I know anything at all. His accuracy is extraordinary. He never makes a statement or puts down anything that is not correct. Rather than say anything at random he will profess ignorance. Yet he is no prig and does not mind doing hard work with his hands either ...

Pennell knew Teddy Evans was keen that Birdie should join the landing party, but hoped that Teddy would keep that thought to himself rather than suggest it to Scott; Birdie was flattered to be in demand but still more than happy to sail back to New Zealand with Pennell:

> With my practical knowledge and Pennell's marvellous brain, & my shove-along [informal] disposition tempered by his feeling of responsibility, I think we shall do much with a minimum of risk. We will not hurry back from the South as when the sea freezing over drives us north we will investigate the islands between N. Z. and the Antarctic Circle. It will be a stormy time in the blackest & stormiest of oceans with perhaps only a 6 hour day. Still we should be as snug as a bug in a rug in a ship like the *Terra Nova* ...

In South Africa, Scott sought out Birdie and thanked him for 'doing splendidly' on the voyage south. To Birdie, Scott appeared to be 'a top-hole leader' who took a personal interest in his men, wanted straight answers to questions, expected everyone to know his own job, stuck to his decisions and knew a great deal about science as well as nautical matters. In Cape Town, Scott and Wilson spent time with potential funders and with people they knew from their *Discovery* days, while Teddy Evans threw himself wholeheartedly into the local social round.[23]

Birdie, Cherry-Garrard ('a sensible youth'), Atkinson and Oates (with whom Birdie had already discussed the idea of exploring the Amazon after Antarctica)[24] formed a 'peace-loving party'. They headed out of town to Wynberg, an attractive British garrison town where Oates had been invalided following Boer War heroics that had left him with a limp due to one leg now being an inch shorter than the other.[25] They stayed at Cogill's Hotel, a popular spot with the British military, from where Birdie wrote to Emily. The South African winter was, he told her, warmer than summer weather in the north of Scotland – an area he discovered Edward Wilson knew from his recent work for the Grouse Commission. Cherry, who had also spent time in Scotland, was a very generous young man who loved to 'treat' everyone when they were ashore – something which left Birdie feeling torn between not wishing to 'sponge' (even on an alleged millionaire) and appearing ungracious or over-independent (a trait he felt he had inherited from his parents).

On one of Birdie's few free days he and Cherry took two 'bewitching maidens' for an outing. The Misses Williams, whom they had met at a dance and who had already visited the ship, were 'as nice as their looks'. Cherry had organised a car and driver and they enjoyed a pleasant drive to Houw Hoek, a beautiful but remote area on the high plateau some 50 miles south-west of Cape Town. All went well until 10 miles into the return journey when, in the midst of uninhabited rolling moorland, the car 'did the romantic touch' and broke down. After tinkering with the engine yielded no results, the foursome abandoned the car and driver and set out to walk to Elgin, a small village some 5 miles away. Cherry rushed ahead across the moors to telegraph to Cape Town for another car, while Birdie and the girls continued along the road at a more leisurely pace. The girls, in Birdie's view, 'stuck it out most pluckily', despite being dressed in formal clothing and nearly losing their hats in the stiff breeze, but when they finally arrived in Elgin there was no sign of Cherry. At the village hotel they learned that he had already sent a wire, hired a cart and driven back along the road to fetch them. Birdie snatched a quick, much-needed meal, left the girls in the lounge and hired his own cart:

> I went in search of Cherry who had meanwhile got back & so we missed again & I arrived at the motor again about 8.30 pm & found driver only as before. We provided for his bodily wants for the night & I found them all in the hotel – not having seen Cherry for 4 hours through our little game of hide & seek. ... So all was well ... we were O.K. & had a nice little sing-song in the parlour.

Suddenly, a welcome 'toot' announced the arrival of the relief motor car from Cape Town; the day was saved and they enjoyed a 'jolly drive' back, arriving at 2 a.m. Although Birdie suspected he would not meet the girls again, he looked back on the day as 'a very happy little interlude which ought to be considered a sailor's right' – but he admitted that given a longer acquaintance he might have lost his heart to Miss Betty Williams. He told Emily that he enjoyed 'feminine society' while in port but rarely missed it when with his 'good salt lady', the sea; he admitted to occasionally 'flirting' but assured her he was not a girl-chaser and always treated women with respect. He knew in any event that, lacking private means, he could not afford to get 'spliced' for several years.

In Cape Town, however, other men's wives drew Birdie's attention: Kathleen Scott, a well-known sculptress, seemed to be very ambitious for both her husband and her brother (Wilfred Bruce) and to show rather too much of an interest in the expedition's plans; Teddy Evans' wife Hilda, although rather tall for Birdie and not his 'style' of beauty, was a 'brick', 'one in a hundred' and a good advertisement for a happy marriage; Oriana Wilson, while sometimes seeming 'coldly genuine to a fault, impatient of nonsense & without a particle of frivolity', was a 'woman of strong will & fertile brain', 'thoroughly good' and the right wife for Wilson.

From Cape Town the wives would sail direct to Melbourne, this time with Edward Wilson, whom Scott, tired of the 'incessant begging', had persuaded to start the next round of fundraising which was required due to the South African government having contributed £500 rather than the anticipated £5,000. Scott would now be sailing with his men for the first time, albeit as a passenger rather than at the helm.

On 2 September Birdie completed his final loading duties in torrential rain and posted a letter and updated sailing schedule to Emily. Although Scott reckoned on arriving in Melbourne by 3 October, Birdie felt that mid-October was more likely, in which case they would arrive in New Zealand in late October and leave for Antarctica at the end of November.[26] As he prepared to embark, Birdie felt, as ever, torn between his love for 'Kipling's immense & contemptuous surges' and that for his family:

> Why did you give me this nature that loves & longs more than anything to be at home, and yet when once away glories in the fact that he is. ... my life is cast in the midst of the unceasing racket of a ship's routine, without peace, without privacy & yet revelling in it ... everything in me longs for the Great White land to the South.[27]

9

TO THE POINT OF DEPARTURE

The *Terra Nova*'s passage to Melbourne was marked by rough seas, howling gales and periods of dead calm.

Birdie found Scott to be very different when away from Kathleen Scott and her 'constant suggestions & projects', but suspected Scott was on board largely to 'spy out the land' and learn 'anything & everything about everything & everybody'.[1] Although Birdie noticed something of 'a gulf fixed' between Scott and his men, the atmosphere gradually became as relaxed and lively as it had been on the voyage from London. One day Birdie received an unexpected summons to Scott's cabin – and was delighted to learn that Scott had decided to include Birdie in the expedition landing party. When Birdie realised that this would be at the expense of his cabin-mate Rennick, however, he wondered if he should decline the opportunity, but Scott's decision was final and Rennick, although clearly 'terribly fed up', behaved like 'a brick' and displayed no ill will towards Birdie in public or private.

Birdie immediately began planning how he would arrange all the stores and equipment in the expedition hut. Within the landing party he would rank after Scott, Wilson and Teddy Evans in terms of authority. He would also, Scott told him, take part in the first season's journey south to deposit food and other supplies in preparation for the second season's assault on the Beardmore Glacier and South Pole.[2] As Birdie tried to explain Scott's plans to Emily and May, he suggested they both reread Scott's and Shackleton's accounts of their *Discovery* and *Nimrod* expeditions (the latter of which he felt was more suited to the 'casual reader'). Birdie now felt as 'happy as a king & as fit as a fiddle' and ready for any weather thanks to his Burberry overcoat and outerwear, Wolsey underwear and several Shetland sweaters. Now, he told May, all he lacked was a sledge-flag:

From antiquity in Polar Exploration an unwritten law has been that officers in charge of sledges shall have a flag mounted on their sledge. These in our case must consist of a pennant about 2½ feet long by 1 ft broad made of silk with Saint George's cross at the hoist and the owner's private crest, colours or device on the other part marked X [on accompanying diagram]. Thus I shall have to think of a device though the other chaps who had theirs made at home had them done to proper heraldic form.[3]

Birdie hoped his family did not blame him for seizing the opportunity of joining the landing party; it might seem riskier than returning to New Zealand on the *Terra Nova*, but it could well pave the way to future promotion or other opportunities. A cutting from *The Buteman* about his Antarctic adventure made Birdie realise, however, that any subsequent fame could come at a price: 'I don't enjoy being identified with a locality ... As I am fortunate in being half & half I can claim either nationality – though why differentiate between English & Scotch. ... To have publicity at home would destroy the charm of home life.' On the subject of newspapers, he explained to Emily that Scott's agreement with the Central News Agency precluded Birdie – and his family – from communicating with any reporters without Scott's prior written consent. No one could publish a book, deliver a lecture or show magic-lantern slides for a period of two years after the return of the expedition without special permission – something to which Birdie had little objection as otherwise 'every man on the ship would be writing rot about the expedition & the press would publish more incorrect rubbish'.

As the ship sailed slowly southwards Birdie contributed to increasingly noisy evenings with his rendition of the drinking song *The Barley Mow* or his self-penned *Terra Nova* version of *The Rollicking Rowdy Crew*. He looked forward to visiting Melbourne again and seeing old friends, particularly the Brearleys who had welcomed him to their home a decade earlier. Although Birdie's 'mild attachments' rarely lasted more than three or four weeks, he had, he confessed to Emily, thought of 'Miss Nancy' Brearley for considerably longer. When the *Terra Nova* finally docked in Melbourne on 12 October, Edward and Oriana Wilson, Kathleen Scott and Hilda Evans were already there to meet them.[4] On landing, Birdie learned that King Manuel II of Portugal (whom he and May had seen at King Edward's funeral a few months previously) had been deposed following a revolution, which made Birdie realise how quickly things changed – and that if members of their expedition reached the South Pole, man would, in Birdie's short lifetime, have reached both ends of the earth, taken to the air, travelled beneath the ocean and communicated across the ether.[5]

When the *Terra Nova* docked in Melbourne, Scott asked two crewmembers to leave the expedition, leaving Birdie in little doubt that his leader set high standards.[6] Birdie checked into his hotel, enjoyed a long bath and went with Cherry to see the theatrical 'spectacular' *The Whip*.[7] He had accepted an invitation to stay the night at the home of Cherry's host the Reverend Fitchett,[8] a well-known Evangelical preacher and founder of a Methodist ladies' college, and had agreed to give a short address on the expedition to a hundred or so young ladies from the college the following day. Birdie also met several old acquaintances, attended the shipboard visit by the Governor of Victoria, Scottish-born Sir Thomas Carmichael, and joined *Terra Nova* officers on a tour of the Australian navy's flagship, the warship *Powerful*. Birdie regarded the latter as something of a white elephant but enjoyed meeting its padre (son of a RIM officer) and a lieutenant who had recently served on the *Fox*. Birdie and Oates shifted tons of coal from the *Terra Nova*'s hold to her bunkers and went to collect 30 tons of compressed pony-fodder. Oates, not one to stand on ceremony, wore his coaling boots into town and on to dinner that evening with Wilson and Teddy Evans. Birdie was also invited to join the Scotts and Lord Neville, the governor's private secretary, for a dinner, during which the latter announced a grant of £2,500 towards the expedition.[9] Later that evening, at a ball at Melbourne's town hall, Birdie was emboldened – despite the discrepancy in their heights – to partner Hilda Evans in a two-step. Between dances he bumped into Gladys Brearley who informed him that 'Miss Nancy' was also at the ball; Birdie enjoyed two dances with the now-married erstwhile object of his affections and a good 'yarn' with Charles Timmins, her husband, whom he decided was an 'excellent chap'. That night, Birdie retired to bed late and rose weary for his last full day's work in Melbourne.

While much of Scott's time in Melbourne had been spent fundraising, he was very distracted by a recent telegram advising him that Roald Amundsen, the Norwegian explorer, was also heading for Antarctica.[10] Birdie tried to convey the significance of this development to Emily and May:

Our previous arrangements for the depot journeys may be changed now this Norwegian fellow Amunsden [*sic*] is going to McMurdo Sound. Capt Scott may land with us instead of going on to King Edward's Land & if he comes [Teddy] Evans will probably take my place with the dogs for the first journeys this season. ... Dog, horse or man haulage – I am equally keen on each & all. Amunsden has done a wily trick. He raised funds for a scheme of drifting across the N. Pole from the Behring St[rait] in the famous *Fram*, strangely enough though – he took sledges & ... about 150 dogs in the ship to go twice through the tropics (round the Horn) when he could have sent them via Canada. We find his game has been a deep laid plot to forestall us – the R.G.S. [Royal Geographical Society] having found out that his intentions are really – & always have been – to attempt the S. Pole. He has now cabled to the King of Norway & you will have heard all the details. Now there is not one of us who does not welcome fair competition & if he selects a new base he will be doing a sporting & reasonable thing. If however he comes to McMurdo Sound – which for 18 months has been known to the world as our projected base – it will be another matter.[11]

On 17 October the *Terra Nova* left Melbourne with Edward Wilson back on board, as Scott would be travelling ahead to New Zealand with 'the wives' to start a final fundraising push. On 27 October, following a frustratingly slow voyage across the Tasman Sea and up the New Zealand coast, the *Terra Nova* arrived at Lyttelton harbour, the main port for Christchurch. Scott and Shackleton had both previously used Lyttelton as their departure point, due to its well-equipped dry dock, magnetic observatory and timeball against which ships' chronometers could be reset before sailing. The natural harbour, surrounded by hills which rose straight from the sea, reminded Birdie of the Firth of Clyde or a highland loch. He and several others were billeted at the Marine Hotel,[12] 5 miles away across the hills at Sumner, which was also home to Joseph Kinsey, the *Discovery*'s New Zealand agent. Each morning Birdie strode across the hills to reach Lyttelton for 8 a.m. and returned in the evening to eat dinner with his hosts, Mr and Mrs Hatfield, whom he found to be, like all New Zealanders he met, extremely kind and hospitable.

Certain New Zealanders had, Birdie found, more than kindness to recommend them: 'The charms of the Fair Sex have not been exaggerated. The girls here as a whole are good looking & the average would pass as pretty. They are all very good to me too but the little we see of leisure at present precludes the possibility of my falling this time.'[13] Birdie's limited free time was largely taken up by outings organised by Joseph Kinsey or by Hilda Evans, whose family lived in Christchurch. He attended three dances in one evening and spent a day at the Christchurch races with a party organised by Teddy and Hilda Evans, and including Hilda's famously glamorous younger sister Rita ('fascinating girl but not my type'). Birdie learned that Hilda Evans' family, the Russells, were very wealthy and that Mrs Russell had offered £25,000 towards Teddy Evans' own Antarctic expedition. The fact that Teddy had been planning his own expedition before Scott's plans were announced was an open secret, but while Birdie regarded Teddy as 'the best of skippers & friends', he felt Scott channelled other people's energy more effectively. He noticed, however, that

Hilda Evans was well liked by everyone but that Kathleen Scott's appearance on board was sometimes greeted by a painful silence; Birdie tried to give each woman her due and to understand what lay behind an increasingly evident hostility between them:

> I like Mrs Scott & admire her many excellent qualities ... she has been kindness always ... [and] marked all my expedition clothes for me. ... Mrs Evans is a person apart ... not my style in most ways but for a womanly woman of remarkable beauty & charm she stands out of the crowd as almost everything a wife should be. Unfortunately her excellent qualities have laid her open to very much jealousy ... the hand of Mrs S. can be seen in Scott's coming with us from the Cape (owing to Evans' unbounded popularity) & Wilson – the one man to pour oil – removed. Finally, as if Evans might make a dash for the Pole this season ... S. has announced his intention of going on the depôt journeys with us ... it was the last straw that broke the camel's back ... [and] Mrs E's pluck after her most trying of times must nearly have given way.

After Teddy Evans made it known to Birdie and others that he was on the point of resigning, they asked Edward Wilson to intervene. During the eve-of-departure ball, Mrs Wilson came over to Birdie's group and quietly confirmed that all was well as 'Uncle Bill' had talked to Scott and Evans at length and prevented 'the feminine point of view' from jeopardising the expedition.

By now the expedition hut had been assembled on Lyttelton quay, dismantled and re-stowed, the *Terra Nova* was in good repair and all were present and correct. Recent arrivals included scientists Raymond Priestley, Griffith (known as Griff) Taylor and Frank Debenham, engineer Bernard Day and explorer and dog-handler Cecil Meares (who had brought with him Dimitri Gerof and Anton Omelchenko to help with dogs and ponies respectively). Photographer Herbert Ponting, who had stayed behind in London to launch *In Lotus Land* (his newly published photo-journal on Japan), had now caught up with the *Terra Nova*, as had Birdie's chum George Wyatt, the expedition's London manager, who had travelled to New Zealand via America to collect some dogs used on a recent Arctic expedition.[14]

Although the *Terra Nova* now carried 60 tons more cargo than when she had left Cardiff, Birdie knew where everything was, from fuel and provisions to ponies (nineteen), dogs (thirty-four) and motor-sledges (three).[15] They reluctantly left behind tons of ballast Pennell wanted for his return journey, 'Sunny Jim' Simpson's observatory, several cases of beer and barrels of rum,[16] and personal effects not required on the expedition. Birdie managed, nevertheless, to find a corner for some crystallised fruits, sweets and crackers, which he had purchased by way of a gift for the expedition party from Emily, and extra fodder for the ponies, which Oates swore was vital if they were to be in any fit state to haul laden sledges on the depot journey:

> Oates wanted to take more than his 30 tons of fodder – in fact he wanted to make it 50. The question was thrashed out & the Owner [Scott] gave his permission on the understanding that I could take it without overloading the ship. ... Oates was anxious to procure an expensive linseed meal & Scott was keen on the compressed variety Shackleton had used. Finally my opinion was asked, (knowing nothing of horse-fodder) I got in a wink from Oates & said I was sure nothing could equal the linseed meal, and to O.'s great delight the motion was carried there & then.[17]

Before leaving Lyttelton Birdie sent May early good wishes for Christmas (as he would by then be 'down in the Pack') and wrote to Emily:

> As I am just packing the last of the things I am leaving here with Mrs Hatfield it has struck me that a little note to you – in case of eventualities – would not be unnecessarily sentimental or out of place. My aims and objects in going into dangers & difficulties are well known to you – they are not for self-advancement or anything sordid as you know. The chief thing that impels me is the indefinable call that is unexplainable as it is insistent. ... Anyhow I go from here today with a joyful heart that nothing on earth could take away – trusting in my Heavenly Father – our Father – who will lead me & keep me till we meet again. If it is His will for me to slip over the narrow border which is so close to us daily, you will know that in this narrow spell of time it will be soon, very soon, when we shall meet on the joyful tomorrow when He shall wipe away all tears from our eyes. Should you be taken before me my feelings will be as yours would be for me, but we know in whom we believe ... I go South with no other Earthly affections greater & dearer than to yourself.[18]

On 25 November crowds waved the *Terra Nova* away from Lyttelton harbour; Captain and Mrs Scott left the ship by tug and returned to Joseph Kinsey's home for a few days' peace before taking the train to Port Chalmers, the expedition's last port of call before McMurdo Sound. The *Terra Nova* rounded the Banks Peninsula and sailed across Canterbury Bight, past Timaru and Oamaru to Port Chalmers, where Birdie helped load final coal supplies and cargo and, with Wyatt's help, complete his stores' records. He wrote to Emily, May and

Edie with news from Christchurch, Lyttelton and Sumner – and further details of the sledge-flag he hoped they would be able to send to New Zealand by late 1911 so that Pennell could bring it south for him. He had cobbled together a makeshift pennant from some spare silk but wanted a 'proper' flag with an embroidered Bowers family crest (a half-bent single leg pierced by an arrow) and the family motto *Esse quam videri* ('to be what I seem').[19] He assured May that Cherry, who also lacked a wife or fiancée, already had one which his sister had made.

Birdie had greatly enjoyed New Zealand, with its kindly people and familiar scenery, but he was beginning to long for his 'element', the sea. He told Edie he was 'as happy as a king', despite having recently parted from 'Miss Dorothy' of Christchurch, whom he had met at a dance. She was younger than him, 'ridiculously small', 'extraordinarily pretty with a delightful self-awareness & will of her own' and just his type. At his invitation she had visited the ship with her mother and younger siblings, but had told Birdie that she and her family would be leaving Christchurch for the countryside before the *Terra Nova* left Lyttelton. Birdie was sorry the relationship had not developed further but decided that Miss Dorothy's early departure had perhaps spared him 'an unhappy or not unmixed parting'.

All in all, Birdie was now ready to leave New Zealand 'with great éclat & no regrets'.[20]

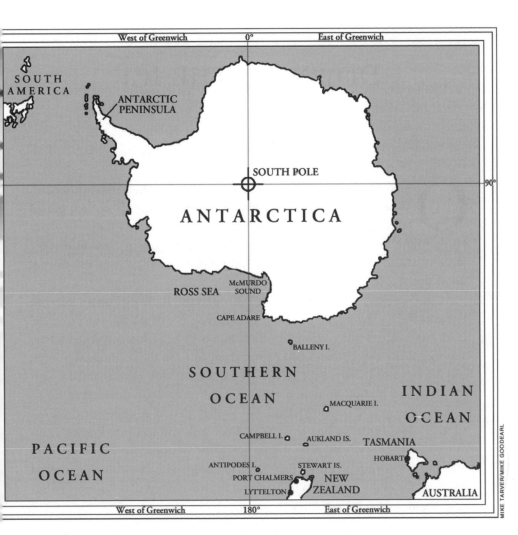

Map 2 Antarctica, showing surrounding countries. © *Michael Tarver, Mike Goodearl*

10

DOWN TO THE ICE

On 29 November 1910, nearly six months after she had left London's West India Docks on an early summer's day, the *Terra Nova* pulled out of Port Chalmers harbour in bright sunshine. As Kathleen Scott, Hilda Evans, Oriana Wilson and Joseph Kinsey left the ship, crowds of well-wishers waved and cheered Captain Scott and his men away to the frozen, uninhabited south.[1]

As the over-laden *Terra Nova* passed through the Roaring Forties into the Furious Fifties she began pitching violently in a stiff north-westerly gale. Birdie and others not confined to their bunks by seasickness worked virtually round the clock; Oates and Anton tried to calm the frightened ponies, and Meares and Dimitri kept an eye on the dogs, which were chained up on the deck and getting drenched by waves and spray. Scott decided to forgo a planned stop at Campbell Island, but as they passed by they encountered another gale.[2] Birdie rushed aloft, helped lash sails and scrambled down again to try to stop bags of coal from rolling across the swamped deck and smashing into dogs or precious cans of fuel. After floating and half-swimming around the deck for hours, he retired to his cabin for his allotted two-hour break but could hardly sleep for worrying:

> … the water that came aboard was simply fearful, & the wrenching on the old ship was enough to worry any sailor called upon to fill his decks with garbage fore & aft. Still 'Risk nothing & do nothing', if funds could not supply another ship, we simply had to overload the one we had, or suffer worse things down south. … the shaking up got the fine coal into the bilges, & this mixing with the oil from the engines formed balls of coal & grease … the water started to come in too fast for the half-clogged pumps to cope with.

During his next turn at the helm Birdie tried running the engine at 'full-steam-ahead' in the hope that the motion might clear the blockages in the pump. As huge waves pummelled the ship the holds began flooding. When the gale rose to Force 11 more sails were taken in and, to make space around the failing pumps, vital coal was unceremoniously dumped overboard. Desperate not to lose any of the expedition's precious fuel cans (now bobbing around the swamped deck), Birdie ripped planks from the gunwales to provide an outlet for the swirling water:

> ... one was constantly on the verge of floating clean over the side with the force of the backwash. ... [The ship] sagged horribly & the unfortunate ponies – though under cover – were so jerked about that [they] could not keep their feet in the stalls ... Oates & Atkinson worked among them like Trojans, but morning saw the death of one, & the loss of one dog overboard. The dogs ... were washed to & fro, chained by the neck, & often submerged for a considerable time.

By now the wardroom and cabins were awash, water had extinguished the fires in the furnaces and Birdie feared the waterlogged ship might soon sink. With the main hatch covered with heavy cargo, Birdie knew the only way of reaching the stricken pump was to cut a hole through an iron bulkhead in the engine room – a twelve-hour job. In the midst of apparent chaos, however, Scott seemed, to outward appearances at least, impressively calm:

> ... he might have been at Cowes, & to do him & Teddy Evans credit at our worst strait none of our landsmen who were working so hard knew how serious things were. Capt. Scott said to me quietly – 'I am afraid it's a bad business for us – What do you think?' I said we were by no means dead yet, though at that moment, Oates, at peril to his life, got aft to report another horse dead; & more down.

As one of the heavy motor-sledges began straining at its chains, Birdie started scrambling after petrol cans again:

> Captain Scott calmly told me that they 'did not matter'. This was our great project for getting to the Pole – the much advertised motors that 'did not matter'; our dogs looked finished, & the horses were finishing, & I went to bale with a strenuous prayer in my heart, & 'Yip-i-addy' on my lips, & so we pulled through that day.

As they baled, Birdie and the other mariners led the scientists in endless renditions of 'every silly song' they knew; during his two-hour breaks Birdie grabbed any food or drink on offer or retired to his cabin in his dressing gown ('a great comfort … a lovely warm thing'). Eventually, the storm blew itself out, the water stopped rising and it began to look as if the *Terra Nova* might stay afloat until the pumps could be repaired.

Around midnight on 3 December Birdie, Teddy Evans and shipwright Francis Davies crawled through a newly cut hole from the engine room; they managed to dive through the water and locate the blocked pipes and, after several hours of wet, dirty work, coax the pumps back into life. By the following afternoon the deck was clear of water. They had lost two ponies, one dog, about 10 tons of coal and about 65 gallons of fuel. Birdie decided things could have been worse and that Scott had behaved 'up to our best traditions at a time when his own outlook must have been the blackness of darkness'.[3]

On Tuesday 6 December, a week out of Port Chalmers, the *Terra Nova* crossed 60° South. The following day, at around 62° South, Birdie saw his first iceberg in the distance, flickering in and out of sight as shafts of sunlight pierced the clouds. Whale birds, fulmers and skuas, albatrosses and cape chickens wheeled round the ship, hour-glass dolphins leapt through the air and the Southern Ocean became so still that Antarctic veterans predicted that pack ice was not far away. On 8 December the wind, which was now pushing the *Terra Nova* along at a steady pace, suddenly dropped; as sails were furled and the engine fired up she suddenly began pitching and twisting. By 65° South she was surrounded by icebergs of all shapes and sizes: some towering more than 80ft above the sea, others extending for over a mile; some rough and jagged, others smooth but marbled with veins of vibrant blue. Ponting persuaded Teddy Evans to steer the ship as close to the icebergs as possible so he could record them on camera. On smaller ice floes penguins scuttled hither and thither issuing their distinctive 'wah, wah' cries or slithered on their bellies into the icy water in search of their next feast of krill. In the middle distance, spouts of spray emitting from shrinking patches of open water indicated the presence of the massive blue rorqual and other whales.[4]

On 9 December, at 65½° South, the *Terra Nova* reached the pack ice and entered 'a sea of such silence as to have appalled many in times past'. When they breached the invisible Antarctic Circle – which crossed Wilkes Land, Birdie's boyhood goal – they were still some 700 miles from McMurdo Sound. On some days the old whaler was hemmed in from all sides by ice floes – engines silent, sails useless; on others (less frequent) she managed up to 40 miles by weaving through slender leads of open water.[5] Scott was clearly frustrated by the lack of progress, but Birdie found the conditions 'great fun & so interesting [that] the hours go like the wind'; he particularly enjoyed being at the helm and using the *Terra Nova* as a maritime battering ram to 'punch, punch, punch at a crack' until, with engine at full speed ahead, he split the offending ice floe or butted it out of his way. As deafening crashes and thuds juddered through the *Terra Nova* and her mast whipped fore and aft, Scott would rush up from his cabin to the bridge to establish exactly what Birdie was doing.[6]

On ice-bound days Teddy Evans or Pennell anchored the ship to a large, stable ice floe so Gran could give skiing lessons to the landing party. The 8ft-long skis (designed so the user could pass safely over narrow crevasses) were not ideal for one of Birdie's dimensions, but he welcomed the exercise and joined in enthusiastically.[7] It had recently occurred to him that he was about to become 'a longshoreman' for the longest time since he had gone to sea; he was also getting used to seeing 'fields of whitest ice & great big bergs of marvellous colours' and feeling the 'glorious wind that chills you to the marrow'.[8]

On 18 December, after several days at a standstill, the *Terra Nova* finally crossed into the Ross Sea. On Christmas Eve she ground to a halt again and Birdie joined a hunting party on the ice to chase down some unusual Christmas fare:

> The Adelie Penguin has the curious feature of a light eyelid which gives him an absurdly 'surprised curiosity' appearance. When he sees you he waddles towards you waving his flippers and shouting a guttural Aha or Wahah, and gets most excited if you sing to him. To shoot these wonderful little beggars as they come towards you or stop to bow to each other – looking foolishly serious – is nothing short of murderous. Still, with a gun and a true aim all is over in a second and we must have them for food and specimens. ... I know of nothing I can think of nicer than well-cooked penguin ...

As midnight struck, Birdie realised he was among the first people in the world to celebrate Christmas Day 1910.[9] Everyone was in good spirits and Captain Scott, despite his worries, was 'geniality itself'.[10] The wardroom was festooned with sledge-flags and they all agreed that Thomas Clissold, the ship's cook, had risen to the occasion with his festive offerings of tomato soup (Heinz), a stewed penguin breast entrée, roast beef and asparagus, plum pudding and mince pies.[11] Wine, champagne, port and liqueurs (all rare treats) flowed and post-dinner carol singing lasted until well after midnight. Before turning in, Birdie and others went on deck to enjoy the ice-reflected light and to watch penguins scuttling around on ice floes. Below deck Tom Crean's pet rabbit and her new litter (some twenty in number) were already dozing comfortably among bales of fodder.

On 28 December, as leads began opening up between the floes, the engines were fired up again and at 1 a.m. on 30 December 1910, at latitude 71½°S, Birdie had the honour of steering the *Terra Nova* into open water.[12] As he gazed around at what looked like sunlit clouds, he realised he was looking at the glaciers and peaks of Victoria Land which, although 70 miles away, were 'as clear as bells'. He felt in the best of moods:

> ... all our troubles seem to have fizzled out with the glad New Year and the anticipation of actually landing. I cannot give any idea of the beauty of a clear Southern day. The atmosphere is so clear & sharp that the very air seems permeated with vitality. The inhospitable mountains look from the distance inviting & grand beyond conception, and the sea itself is as blue as in the Tropics, with glittering ice-bergs here and there. Yesterday with the wind shrieking through the rigging – which was hung with icicles – & the air filled with driving snow, it was a different scene.

Birdie reminded May that he would now receive no further letters from Britain until the *Terra Nova* returned from New Zealand to McMurdo Sound in early 1912, but that news of his first Antarctic season should reach his family in late spring 1911. Ponting's photographs of the journey and their arrival would also be sent back with the *Terra Nova* and would appear in British newspapers and periodicals, while his moving pictures would be shown in Gaumont cinemas. Birdie was sure it would be easy to identify him:

> I am either bare-headed or in my green hat – you will remember the old dear – I have worn no other hat or cap hitherto since leaving home (except in uniform when in port). It is quite a feature of the Expedition now, and has been as useful in the Tropics as here, and in the rains of the Doldrums as in the blizzards of the Pack. I wear it thus [sketch provided] with a chin-strap.

Birdie was well prepared for cold conditions as latterly he, Wilson, Atkinson and Nelson had been bathing in buckets of slush hauled up from the semi-frozen ocean.[13] As they approached the ice, Birdie had been considering how Scott would choose the men who would make the final assault on the Pole in late 1911.[14] Sixteen men would, he understood, set off from their base with ponies, dogs and sledges (wooden and motorised); as the long march progressed, small teams of men and animals would turn back until one team of four men remained. This last group would, Birdie suspected, include Scott, Wilson and Teddy Evans, plus a fourth man chosen depending on the form of transport used for the attempt on the Pole. It could be, for example, Meares if sledge-dogs were still being used, Oates if ponies, Day if motor-sledges or Gran if skis.[15] If pure manpower was needed for sledge-hauling, obvious candidates included the three strong seamen who had served on Scott's *Discovery* expedition: Edgar 'Taff' Evans, Tom Crean and William Lashly. Birdie felt he had a good chance of being in the initial sixteen and perhaps of even being asked to navigate the last supporting party back to base; in any event, he felt honoured to be the only member of the expedition whose status had been upgraded so far. He knew that the Southern journey would not be a 'glorified picnic' and that, with almost a year to go, 'a frost-bitten toe or *nose* might upset all these calculations' or that forces of nature might intervene. Whatever happened he would abide by Scott's decision and do whatever he could towards 'the great object in view'.

As the ship entered McMurdo Sound, Scott began looking for a good landing spot and stable base for the hut. He first considered Cape Crozier, close to the twin volcanoes of Terror and Erebus.[16] It was conveniently close to the colony of Emperor penguins that Edward Wilson had begun researching during the *Discovery* expedition, and which Birdie thought looked 'for all the world a Saturday afternoon football club'. There was, however, no sheltered, flat area of appropriate size. Birdie began taking photographs of the 'phenomenal' bergs and pack ice, which Antarctic hands told him was considerably more extensive than they had seen previously.

From Cape Crozier the *Terra Nova* followed the 60ft-high ice barrier towards Cape Royds, Shackleton's *Nimrod* expedition base, where there was a heavy swell and no suitable place for landing animals or the motor-sledges. As they rounded Cape Bird, *Discovery*-hands pointed out Mount Discovery – and several potential landing places, including Hut Point, where the *Discovery* hut still stood. After due consideration this was rejected in favour of a larger, flatter site some 15 miles further north which had, in the *Discovery* days, been known as The Skuary, but which Scott now renamed Cape Evans in honour of his second in command.

On 4 January 1911 unloading began. The ponies were thin and worn from the journey but clearly glad to be on solid ground; the dogs immediately began rushing around, barking at any penguins who ventured too close and arousing the interest of orcas, the killer whales which lurked near the ice edge. Two of the three motor-sledges were immediately hoisted off so that other deck cargo could be reached. Birdie joined the hut-construction party led by Teddy Evans, which would be living on land in tents to save the 1½-mile trek across the beach and sea-ice edge to the ship every night. Campbell was now in charge of unloading and transporting the rest of the deck cargo to the hut site. Ponting began taking photographs: his shots of the *Terra Nova* through the entrance to an ice cave promised to be spectacular, but his early attempts to photograph orcas at close quarters almost ended in disaster when his subjects started butting the ice floe he was standing on in an effort to deposit him and his equipment into the icy ocean.[17] Oates declared two of his equine charges to be unfit and three in need of further breaking-in, but the other ponies were soon pulling laden sledges to and fro across the ice while the motor-sledges dragged heavier loads. As hundreds of crates were unloaded onto the black volcanic 'sand' beside the site of the hut, Teddy Evans, Atkinson and two seamen helped Birdie unload and stack them systematically; between loads, Birdie worked on building the hut or rushed down to the ship to check what was being unloaded next.

By 12 January, thanks largely to shipwright 'Chippy Chap' Davies and seamen Robert Forde, Patrick Keohane and George Abbott, the hut was well on its way to completion. They had also started constructing a stores annexe ('my annexe', according to Birdie) from wooden storage cases and spare wood; this would supplement the ice 'Grotto' (for fresh meat) and give Birdie working space to prepare precisely weighed packages of rations for the different groups of explorers and scientists. Adjacent to the hut they constructed a stable block with an adjoining fodder-storage annexe and a lavatory block.[18] Over at the ship, long hours of sunshine, high temperatures and constant traffic continued to weaken the ice 'wharf'. This had already resulted in the loss of one of the heavy (and expensive) motor-sledges, which had, to Scott's visible distress, plunged through ice into over 100 fathoms of water, almost taking Pennell and Priestley with it. Following fruitless attempts to retrieve the machine, the *Terra Nova* moved to a more solid mooring further along the bay. The sunshine had also been responsible for several attacks of snow-blindness and almost universal sunburn and blistering (particularly of redhead Birdie's fair skin).

On Sunday 15 January Scott, apparently satisfied with progress, declared a day of relative rest. After morning service and lunch he led a small party to Hut Point and Cape Royds to check whether his and Shackleton's erstwhile headquarters were in a fit condition to be used by the expedition. He returned satisfied that they were but evidently annoyed at the state in which the *Discovery* hut had been left by Shackleton. In terms of the forthcoming depot journey, however, he was more worried about the ponies. Oates had made it very clear what he thought about their condition when he first inspected them on Quail Island in Lyttelton harbour: several were well past their prime or simply unsound and their conditions had certainly not been improved by the voyage

W. Mc LENNAN & Cº   GREENOCK.

Above left: 1. Emily Bowers (Bower's mother) shortly following her wedding in 1877, Singapore. *Image licensed by and © Scott Polar Research Institute (SPRI)*

Above right: 2. Captain Alexander Bowers (Bower's father), photographed in Greenock, date unknown. *Courtesy of and © the owners*

3. Bowers as a toddler, Greenock. *Image licensed by and © SPRI*

W. Mc LENNAN & Cº   GREENOCK

4. Portrait of the Bowers family (clockwise from left): Edie, May (standing), Emily, Henry (seated, wearing kilt and sporran). *Image licensed by and © SPRI*

5. Bowers as a schoolboy, London (possibly Sidcup). *Image licensed by and © SPRI*

6. Bowers (right, seated) receiving instruction on HMS *Worcester* (detail). *Original by unknown photographer, photograph by Anne Strathie, courtesy of and © Spink, www.spink.com*

7. *Loch Torridon* in full sail, off Melbourne Heads. *Postcard from collection of and © State Library of Victoria, Australia*

8. Bowers in the countryside near Auckland, January 1901 (when serving on *Loch Torridon*). *Photograph: V.O. Banneho, 3rd Mate. Image licensed by and © SPRI*

. Bowers in RIM dress uniform, *c.* 1905 detail). Original photographer unknown. The photograph was later used for a postcard titled 'Henry Bowers, Hero of the Antarctic'. *Photograph by Anne Strathie, courtesy of and © Spink, www.spink.com*

10. Letter of 8 October 1908 from Bowers to sister May from the Irrawaddy (showing the sideways writing he regularly used). © *private*

11. Group photograph at dockside SY *Terra Nova*, June 1910, including Bowers (fourth from right) and (left to right, the only women) May, Emily and Edie Bowers. *Photograph: London Stereoscopic Company. Image licensed by and © SPRI*

12. Bowers and Edward Wilson indulge in horseplay on board the *Terra Nova*; Silas Wright looks on. *Photograph: Frank Debenham. Image licensed by and © SPRI*

«THAT'S THE BUNTLINE YOU'RE PULLING ON! I SAID THE CLEWLINE!»

13. Bowers in RIM 'whites'; caricature by Dennis Lillie (in the *Terra Nova South Polar Times*, 1911). © *Cheltenham Art Gallery & Museum*

THE MIDDLE WATCH. 12-5 A·M.

14. Bowers in his 'cool weather' gear, including his favourite green felt hat; caricature by Dennis Lillie (in the *Terra Nova South Polar Times*, 1911). © *Cheltenham Art Gallery & Museum*

15. Bowers (presumed) aboard the *Terra Nova*, Lyttelton, 1910. *Photographer unknown; Kinsey collection © Canterbury Museum, Christchurch, New Zealand*

16. The 'Tenements' at the Cape Evans hut. Bowers stands at his improvised 'desk' second from the left; Cherry-Garrard is below him. Oates is in the middle bunk, and Meares (above) and Atkinson (below) are in the right-hand bunk. *Photograph: Herbert Ponting; © Kerry Stokes Collection, Perth, Australia*

17. Bowers and others trying to rescue some of the ponies, sledges and equipment from the sea-ice following the depot journey, April 1911. *Painting: Edward Wilson; from the Terra Nova's South Polar Times © private*

Dr. E. A. Wilson, del.

Sledge-hauling on Ski. March 1911

18. Sledge-hauling on ski, March 1911. Watercolour by Edward Wilson. This shows five men pulling a sledge rather than the more usual four. *Image from Wilson 1914 print series © private*

19. Bowers and Wilson taking readings on the ramp at 'B' station ('Bertram') during winter 1911. *Photograph (by flashlight): Herbert Ponting; © private*

20. Watercolour by Edward Wilson showing Bowers on the ramp in winter 1911. *From Scott's Last Expedition,* Vol. I, *facing p. 306* © *private*

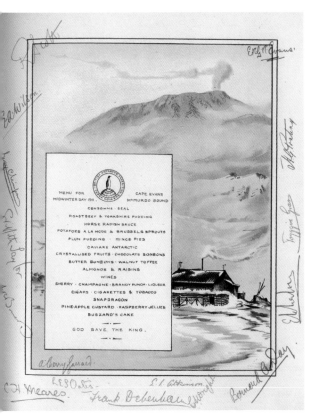

21. Menu prepared by Edward Wilson for Midwinter Day dinner, 22 June 1911, showing the hut and Mount Erebus, and signed by expedition officers and scientists ('H.R. Bowers' on left). © *Cheltenham Art Gallery & Museum*

22. Midwinter Day tree, 22 June 1911. Tree made by Bowers, decorated with feathers, gifts and crackers. *Photograph: Herbert Ponting; image licensed by and © SPRI*

23. Wilson, Bowers and Cherry-Garrard at the Cape Evans hut after the Cape Crozier journey, August 1911. *Photograph: Herbert Ponting; from* Scott's Last Expedition, *Vol. II, facing p. 72* © *private*

24. Bowers with a laden sledge. *Photograph: Herbert Ponting;* © *Kerry Stokes Collection, Perth, Australia*

25. Bowers with a camera, possibly at Cape Evans, October 1911 (when Ponting gave photography lessons). *Photograph: Tryggve Gran (developed by Debenham)* © *Canterbury Museum, Christchurch, New Zealand*

26. On the march: Bowers ('HRB' and 'B'), Cherry-Garrard ('ACG'), Oates ('TO'), Scott ('RFS'), Keohane ('PK') and unnamed ponies. *Drawing by Edward Wilson; from* Scott's Last Expedition, *Vol. I, facing p. 540* © *private*

27. Bowers' sledge-party and others on the Beardmore Glacier, December 1911. Front, pulling (left to right): Cherry-Garrard, Bowers, Keohane, Crean; pushing: Edward Wilson and another (hidden). *Photograph: Robert F. Scott © Kerry Stokes Collection, Perth, Australia*

28. Members of the South Pole party on the plateau, near Three Degree depot. Left to right: Oates, Evans, Scott, Wilson. *Photograph: Henry R. Bowers © Kerry Stokes Collection, Perth, Australia*

29. Members of the South Pole party at Roald Amundsen's tent,
18 January 1912. Left to right: Scott, Oates, Wilson, Evans.
Photograph: Henry R. Bowers © Kerry Stokes Collection, Perth, Australia

30. At the South Pole, 18 January 1912. *Left to right*: Oates, Bowers
(pulling the string to the camera with his bare-fingered right hand),
Scott, Wilson, Evans. *Photograph: Henry R. Bowers © Kerry Stokes
Collection, Perth, Australia*

31. HMS *Worcester* memorial to Bowers, originally mounted on the mast of the ship, now at SPRI, Cambridge. *Photograph by Anne Strathie; by permission and courtesy of SPRI*

32. Royal Indian Marine memorial to Bowers, originally at St Ninian's church, Port Bannatyne, Bute, now at Bute Museum, Rothesay (an identical copy of the memorial is in Bombay Cathedral). *Photograph © and courtesy of Bute Museum*

33 & 34. Bowers' medals (obverse and reverse), left to right: Royal Geographical Society Memorial Medal (Captain R.F. Scott's expedition 1910–13); Polar Medal (George V, clasp Antarctic 1910–13); Italian Royal Geographical Society (Scott expedition 1913). © *private*

5 A John Player's cigarette card depicting Bowers
a confirmed non-smoker). © *and courtesy of Dr Max Jones*

36. This sledge-flag with the Bowers crest was sent to the Antarctic by Bowers' family in autumn 1911. It remained unused as it did not reach Cape Evans until after the departure of the southern party. This flag was given by May Bowers to Waitaki High School for Boys, Oamaru, New Zealand, where it still hangs. *Photograph © and courtesy of Paul Baker*

37. The 'Birdie Bowers' skiff (built by John Glover for the Royal West of Scotland Amateur Boat Club) at the Viking Festival 2011; crew, from bow: Yvonne Christie, Lorna McCartney, Charlie Baxter (age 7), John Glover, Campbell McCall, Ian Clark. *Photograph © and courtesy of Jim Ford*

south. Now, with two ponies lost during the voyage and others not ready for travelling, Scott and Oates began recasting Scott's carefully worked-out transportation plans for the forthcoming journeys.

The Cape Evans hut was declared ready for occupation on 17 January. At 50ft by 25ft it was considerably larger than the *Discovery* hut (in which seamen slept in hammocks rather than bunks) and had two distinct sections – one for officers and scientists, the other for seamen – each with a dining table. The officers' section included all the laboratories and Ponting's darkroom, while the men's section contained the galley and cook's table.[19] Birdie had an upper bunk in a section which was nicknamed the Tenements, due to its lack of home comforts, and which he shared with Cherry (his lower-bunk mate), Oates (neighbouring bunk with storage below), Atkinson and Meares. The Tenements had no writing table but Birdie soon improvised a desk by standing on a stool beside Cherry's bunk with his papers propped up on his own bunk; everyone's kit and belongings were stowed under lower bunks or festooned from the ceiling or nearby hooks.

Adjacent to the Tenements, Scott, Wilson and Teddy Evans shared an area with three bunks, a plotting table, bookshelves and storage for Wilson's medical supplies. The hut's homely atmosphere was completed after Rennick reassembled the pianola and Clissold began producing his expanding repertoire of dishes, which now included variations on penguin meat, seal rissoles and stewed skua.

Outside the hut blizzards gradually covered the beach and sea-ice with deep snow and, as chunks of ice broke off the *Terra Nova*'s ice-wharf, Pennell kept shifting the mooring. With everyone now settled in, it was time for the scientific and depot parties to prepare for departure. The Western party (Griff Taylor, Debenham, Silas Wright and Taff Evans) were going to investigate the Ferrar Glacier and the geology of the neighbouring valleys; Victor Campbell and his Eastern party (Levick, Priestley, Abbott, Browning and Dickason) would be transported along the barrier by the *Terra Nova* to King Edward VII Land,[20] where they would continue exploratory work begun by Scott and Shackleton.

Scott and the depot-laying party would head almost due south from Cape Evans to leave caches of provisions (for men and animals) for consumption during the journey to the South Pole the following season. This, the largest group by far, included twenty-six dogs, eight ponies and thirteen men: Scott, Wilson, Teddy Evans, Birdie, Oates, Cherry-Garrard, Gran, Atkinson, Meares, Crean, Forde, Keohane and Dimitri. They would head for Glacier Tongue and on to Hut Point to prepare the *Discovery* hut as a secondary base to be used when Cape Evans was cut off from Hut Point following the break-up of the sea-ice. From there they would continue on to the Great Ice Barrier and leave several depots along the first part of their proposed route south.

While others loaded the *Terra Nova* with sledges, stores and equipment to take over to Glacier Tongue for the depot-laying party, Birdie spent hours in his annexe calculating, weighing and packaging rations for all three parties. Just before leaving he prepared his own kit and frantically scribbled last-minute journal entries and letters for Pennell to take back on the *Terra Nova*. He was short of sleep but knew this was his last chance to send a letter to Emily for many months:

> I am finishing up at 3 am with my last letter … & you will hear nothing more for a year. However, you will know that I am having & have struck the most glorious of jobs in a climate that suits me in every way, with a great object [and] a responsible position. … I dare say you will think I have been working too hard. Well I have not nearly reached the limit of my capacity … I never seem tired only sleepy at times & the hours fly. … you would not believe the work there is in preparing everything for a big sledge journey. … Capt. Scott is simply extraordinarily nice to me & I cannot help feeling that I am going to hit it off with him permanently. Our special sledging kit has required much preparation & sewing … I have changed mine as little as possible so as to evolve my own ideas from personal experience. … The actual windproof kit … consist[s] of a helmet, blouse & breeks; only Wolsey underwear is worn underneath & our allowance of spare gear including all other clothing, books, tobacco etc is 12 lbs. … As to whether we are coming back next year or not I cannot say & more ponies or dogs or rather mules & dogs are being ordered as well as provisions – it all depends of course as whether the pole is reached next Summer. … you will hear if you get into communication with Mrs Scott & Mrs Wilson … I will write much of the winter & tell you everything, in the meantime make my apologies to those I ought to have written to.
>
> With dearest love & best wishes & God's blessing & all good things on my own Mother, from your loving Son, Henry.[21]

Birdie, suddenly remembering he had previously told Emily he would be leading a dog team on the depot journey, added: 'P.S. I am in command of pony division for forthcoming journey.'

North
Bay
C. Evans
Hut
Wind Vane Hill
South
Bay
Inaccessible I.
Lt. Razorback
Turk's Head
Tent I.d
Gt. Razorback
Shackleton's
Fodder Depot
Glacier Tongue
Sultan's Head
Rock
Cone Hill II.
Hutton Cliffs
Turtle Back I.
Cone Hill I.
Third Crater
Second Crater
Castle Rock
First Crater
Arrival Heights
Crater Hill
The Hut
Pram Pt.
Hut Point
Observation
Hill
C. Armitage
Fodder Depôt
Safety Camp
Edge of Barrier

White
Island

Map 3 McMurdo Sound, showing the scene of the pony 'disaster' on the depot
journey, April 1911. *Map by Stanfords, 1913 © private*

11

THE DEPOT JOURNEY

On 24 January Birdie and his pony, Uncle Bill (named in honour of Edward Wilson), were last to leave the Cape Evans hut.[1]

After only an hour's sleep Birdie rose, dressed, ate breakfast, made his final check of the stores, left instructions for Clissold and harnessed Uncle Bill to the sledge. By the time he had done everything the others had already set off. He grabbed Uncle Bill's nosebag and stumbled along, 'perspiring in every pore & constantly tripping over'. When he banged his knee on a sharp stone he began to worry that an early injury would prevent him from continuing on the journey, but that evening Cherry – who had suffered his own traumas that day – took him aside and bandaged his knee tightly so Birdie could have a good night's rest in a historic spot:

My dearest Mother

I am not going to miss a chance though it is a line dashed off sitting in a sleeping-bag in a tent close to where the 'Discovery' was frozen in for 2 years. It is the end of my first sledge journey & has been a glorious day as well as a successful one. ... It took over 4 hours to reach [Glacier] tongue where the ship arrived shortly after & gear, sledges, etc. were put ashore. There was a rather bad series of crevasses about a mile distant on the route so we man-hauled the sledges safely over leading the beasts later. ... we often caught our feet in small cracks & all had falls. ... Cherry's pony broke through & was all but drowned ... My pony is an A1 beast, the biggest & fastest of the lot. The dogs are faster but less sure. ... The green tent & nice warm bags are a contrast to the white ice flows [sic] yet I shall sleep like I would at home in the acme of comfort. Capt. Scott is highly pleased with our march and everything has gone A1.[2]

On 25 January they unloaded the stores and equipment that the *Terra Nova* had brought round from Cape Evans. Birdie bade farewell to the Eastern party (who would be returning to Cape Evans later) and the *Terra Nova* crew, of which Birdie would particularly miss Harry Pennell, 'one of the very best & soundest officers & friends'. At the *Discovery* hut the depot-laying party found provisions which had been abandoned by Shackleton, but were, despite being covered with two years' worth of snow, still edible.[3] The next evening the dogs (pulling loads of 500lb per team) seemed tired and hungry, and Wilson, who was keen to try his hand at sledge-driving, volunteered to join Meares in trying to get the best out of them. The ponies generally seemed to be coping with pulling sledges weighing up to 900lb each; Scott was keen to pick up the speed but when Gran tried skiing alongside his pony Weary Willie, the normally lethargic animal bolted with his sledge leaving the athletic Norwegian in his wake.

They constructed their first depot, Safety Camp, at 77° 55' South. Birdie, Cherry and others managed to excavate two half-hidden tents left by Shackleton's *Nimrod* party which contained a primus stove (battered but in working order), tins of sheep's tongue, cheese, biscuits, tea and Rowntree's cocoa – all pronounced edible. As snow fell and covered the ice, Uncle Bill and the other heavier ponies began to struggle in windswept drifts, but the dogs came into their own. Unfortunately, only one pair of pony snowshoes had been brought from Cape Evans, but Meares and Wilson agreed to go back with a dog team to fetch more. They returned early the next day having found that the sea-ice between Glacier Point and Cape Evans had broken up and floated out to sea, leaving anyone travelling with animals cut off from the hut at Cape Evans. Gran offered to ski back to Hut Point with everyone's last-minute correspondence in the hope someone from Cape Evans would think to check there before the *Terra Nova* finally left for New Zealand.

Birdie, who felt he had not recently 'played the game' in terms of correspondence, bundled up his 21 January to 31 January journal (scribbled somewhat haphazardly on the pages of a small pocket-diary purchased in New Zealand) and added a few letters.[4] He described his pony ('a good puller & steady & solid'), his new food, pemmican ('A1 but very rich ... could not look at it for breakfast') and his companions (in largely favourable terms), before wishing his family well during the 'long silence' that would succeed their receipt of these missives. Gran sped off to Hut Point with the mail but by the time he returned drifting snow had almost covered the camp; despite his struggles he volunteered to make another trip the following day to collect the sole pair of pony snowshoes, which had been accidentally left behind at their previous camp.

By now Atkinson's foot – which he had chafed but then ignored – had turned infectious and he reluctantly agreed to return to Hut Point, accompanied by an understandably even more reluctant Tom Crean.

On 2 February, with Birdie at the head of the column, the depot-laying party set off across the Barrier. The going was initially firm but by the afternoon the equine Uncle Bill began floundering in deep, soft drifts. Until Gran got back with the snowshoes, Birdie could only try to coax his lathering pony through the white, swirling silence, which was broken only by low-pitched human voices and the involuntary sounds of straining animals. After they stopped early and made camp Scott suggested they start marching overnight. There would be sufficient light, the part-frozen surfaces should bear their weight better and the ponies would benefit from resting during the relatively warmer day. It was agreed to implement the plan immediately so they ate, slept briefly and rose at 10 p.m., ready to set off just after midnight. Nine miles into the march, Birdie and Uncle Bill suddenly plunged into a deep drift, but Gran returned in the nick of time – snowshoes were strapped on Uncle Bill's hooves and the column marched on until morning.

Early on 4 February, about 40 miles from Cape Evans, they made their sixth camp and second depot, which they named Corner Camp for the abrupt change of direction required on leaving it. That afternoon a blizzard swept in from Cape Crozier and pinned them in their tents for three sunless, frustrating days, during which they could only arrange supplies, check on the animals and sleep. When the blizzard eventually blew itself out late on 7 February, the ponies looked, despite Oates' ministrations, listless and noticeably thinner; the dogs, by contrast, seemed refreshed by their enforced rest and eager to sprint across the fresh snow.

During each of their next three overnight marches they covered between 10 and 12 miles. Despite a halfway break to let the weaker ponies recoup their strength, Teddy Evans' pony, Blossom, was visibly wilting and Scott decided that Evans, together with Forde and Keohane (whose ponies, Blucher and James Pigg, were also struggling), should return to Hut Point. Scott was confident that, without the weaker ponies, they would soon reach 80° South, the planned location of their largest depot. Temperatures were dropping but Birdie continued to wear his favourite green felt hat (in preference to a balaclava or wind-helmet) and would potter around outside for hours, checking and adjusting sledges and carrying out the small tasks he considered vital for the expedition's success.[5]

On 14 February sticky snow limited their progress to 7 miles. By now Gran's ailing pony, Weary Willie, was regularly being harassed and bitten by the dogs and Birdie's Uncle Bill was frequently grinding to a complete standstill in deep snowdrifts. Conditions did not improve and when they camped on 16 February at 79° 28½' South (some 30 miles short of Scott's goal of 80° South) several ponies were flagging. The ponies were not the only ones suffering: Birdie's exposed ears had (much to his indignation) turned white from frostbite; Scott and Cherry's cheeks and Oates' nose had also been 'nipped'; and Meares was suffering from a troublesome toe. Scott had to decide between continuing on to his originally planned destination with Weary Willie (thus risking the pony dying on the journey) or leaving him at their camp (where he might die of exposure before they returned).

After considerable deliberation they started building their largest depot where they had stopped, naming it One Ton depot for the quantity of food it would hold. The pile of provisions, animal feed and fuel oil made a 6ft-high pile, to which they added two 12ft sledges, two pairs of skis and other spare equipment, and marked it with the usual black flag and with several empty biscuit tins, which would act as reflectors. One Ton depot should not be difficult to find.

On 17 February they embarked on the return journey in two parties. The two dog-sledge teams – driven by Scott and Meares, Wilson and Cherry – would bypass Corner Camp and go straight to Safety Camp, where they hoped to find Teddy Evans, Forde, Keohane and their three ailing ponies. Wilson and Cherry would then continue with Evans' group to Hut Point, while Scott and Meares ferried further supplies from Safety Camp to Corner Camp. In the meantime, Birdie, Oates and Gran would lead five ponies (their own plus Scott's and Cherry's) to Corner Camp, where they would meet up with Scott and Meares before returning to Safety Camp and Hut Point. Birdie, Oates and Gran set off following their outward tracks; as they marched Birdie found his eyes playing tricks:

> ... the snowy mist hid all distant objects & made all close ones look gigantic. Although we were walking on a flat undulating plain, one could not get away from the impression that the ground was hilly ... Suddenly a herd of apparent cattle would appear in the distance, then you would think: 'No, it's a team of dogs broken loose & rushing towards you.' In another moment one would be walking over the black dots of some old horse droppings which had been the cause of the hallucinations.

When they camped they built protective snow-walls for the five ponies, although the beneficiaries did not seem particularly grateful:

Weary [Willie] was the most annoying, he would deliberately back into his wall & knock the whole structure down. In the case of my own pony, I had to put the wall out of his reach as his aim in life was to eat it, generally beginning at the bottom. He would diligently dislodge a block, & bring down the whole fabric. One cannot be angry with the silly beggars – Titus says a horse has practically no reasoning power, the thing to do is simply to throw up another wall & keep on at it.

Whenever the snow-clouds lifted, Birdie could see their route-marking cairns from miles away, either directly or through mirages which shimmered above the cairns like distant pools of open water. Progress was slow: Weary Willie, although now pulling a considerably lighter load, was reluctant to march and low stratus clouds 'as thick as a hedge' regularly plunged them into 'fuzzy nothingness' that made steering difficult for Birdie, particularly given the effect of the magnetic pole on his compass. He and Oates took turns at leading but neither could keep a straight course; after several hours of zigzagging all over the Barrier they finally found some established tracks, but were puzzled to see a cairn they did not remember building on the outward journey. With the wind in their favour and another blizzard threatening they decided not to investigate and to press on. They struggled to pitch their tent in a snowy gale but rose the following morning to perfect marching weather:

Erebus & Terror were showing up as clear as a bell & I got a large number of angles for Evans' survey. We started out as usual, & had the most pleasant, as well as the longest, of our return marches on the last day of summer ... We did 18 miles right off the reel, the sun was brilliant from midnight onwards. ... All the old cairns were visible a tremendous distance, 6 or 7 miles at least for big ones. Mount Terror lay straight ahead & looked so clear that it seemed impossible to imagine it 70 miles away.

When Birdie spotted a second cairn he did not recall from the outward journey he wondered if it might conceal the body of Blucher, Forde's pony, the timing of whose demise had already been the subject of a wager between Oates and Gran. A note from Teddy Evans attached to the top of the cairn confirmed that this was Blossom's final resting place, which suggested to Birdie that the earlier mysterious cairn must have been Blucher's grave.

At 9.30 p.m. on 24 February, almost a week after leaving One Ton depot, Birdie, Oates, Gran and five tired, hungry ponies arrived at Safety Camp in a snow-laden mist. After they had been greeted by Wilson, Meares and a pack of barking, enthusiastic dogs, they tethered and fed the ponies and ate a good meal of pemmican, biscuit and seal's liver. Wilson and Meares told them about the dog teams' short but near-disastrous return journey from One Ton depot. A snow-bridge at the edge of a crevasse-field had unexpectedly collapsed and plunged half of Scott's dog team into a huge chasm. The lead dog, Osman, had already crossed over and the sledge was still on firm ground at the other side of the abyss, but the dogs in the middle dangled precariously by their harnesses, howling and wriggling. Thanks to Osman's strength and the still-substantial weight of the sledge, the four men had, with some difficulty, managed to retrieve the struggling dogs. All had survived their ordeal but some, who had been dangling for over an hour, were badly injured and might not recover.

On arriving at Safety Camp the sledge-drivers (who had bypassed the new cairns) learned from Teddy Evans that Blucher and Blossom had both collapsed and died on the return journey from One Ton depot. As there was still no sign of Atkinson and Crean, the dog teams and Evans continued to Hut Point, where they found a note suggesting that Atkinson and Crean were probably on their way to Safety Camp with messages from those on the *Terra Nova*. When Scott and the other sledge-drivers arrived back at Safety Camp, Atkinson and Crean handed Scott a note from Victor Campbell, whom they believed had been deposited by the *Terra Nova* in King Edward VII Land, well to their east.

Campbell recounted how, on their way east, they had encountered the 'famous *Fram*' in the Bay of Whales. With no other ships for thousands of miles the two teams of explorers could hardly ignore each other and the *Fram*'s crew (and later Amundsen when he returned from his own depot journeys) had been very hospitable and shown them round the ship and their hut. The *Terra Nova* party had reciprocated the invitation but Campbell decided against spending the coming months near Amundsen's base and asked Pennell to take him to Cape Adare. Campbell had left his note at Cape Evans with instructions for it to be delivered to Scott as soon as possible; Campbell and his Eastern party now headed north on the *Terra Nova* for Cape Adare.

Scott digested the news: Amundsen's base was 60 miles closer to the Pole than Cape Evans, and the smaller Norwegian team of expert skiers and dog-handlers would be able to leave earlier in the season than Scott's party could do with the ponies.

Scott then left Meares and Wilson at Safety Camp to wait for Birdie's party and sped back to Corner Camp with the rest of the depot-laying party and two laden sledges of provisions.[6] By 28 February everyone had gathered at Safety Camp but with heavy snow falling, temperatures below safe limits for the ponies, nights drawing in and the sea-ice between Safety Camp and Hut Point deteriorating, they needed to get back to Hut Point immediately. Wilson and Meares left at 4 p.m. with the dog teams. Birdie and his pony Uncle Bill were soon ready to leave but Oates was still helping Scott with the other horses, including Weary Willie who could hardly rise to his feet. Scott told Birdie to go ahead. After a mile or so Birdie arrived at the Barrier edge and stopped to wait for the others; when he looked back he was surprised to see only a small group of men and ponies, which turned out to be Cherry and Crean leading Punch, Nobby and Guts. When they arrived they explained that Scott, Oates and Gran were still tending to Weary Willie. By now snow was whirling and, with the light deteriorating, Birdie could barely see anything, let alone which direction Wilson and Meares had taken.

Birdie decided he should follow Scott's original plans and head straight across the sea-ice towards Hut Point, camping on the way if necessary. As darkness fell cracks in the ice became harder to make out, seawater began squelching up through unseen fissures and ice floes shifted under the weight of the ponies and sledges. Birdie decided to retreat onto older, more solid ice that was still attached to the shore and on which he felt they could camp safely. They built pony-walls, fed the ponies and ate a modest meal of pemmican. As Birdie waited for the water to boil for a nightcap of cocoa, he fumbled around in the dark, found a small bag of powder and carefully blended the contents and some sugar into the water; he stirred the steaming pannikins and handed one each to Crean and Cherry. Crean had almost finished his before he began gasping and spluttering – too late, Birdie realised he had mixed curry powder into the water. At 2 a.m., having forgone his own nightcap, Birdie went outside to check on the weather. Everything looked calm and visibility was improving, although dark sky over McMurdo Sound made him think open water might not be far away. He went back to the tent and climbed into his sleeping bag. About two hours later a noise outside the tent jolted him awake. Suspecting it might be Uncle Bill helping himself to extra fodder he went outside to investigate:

> I cannot describe either the scene or my feelings ... We were in the middle of a floating pack of broken-up ice. ... as far as the eye could see there was nothing solid; it was all broken up, & heaving up & down with the swell. Long black tongues of water were everywhere. The floe on which we were had split ... Guts [the pony] himself had gone, & a dark streak of water alone showed the place where the ice had opened under him. ... I shouted to Cherry & Crean, & rushed out in my socks to save the two sledges; the two floes were touching farther on & I dragged them to this place & got

them on to our floe. At that moment our own floe split in two, but we were all together in one piece. I then got my finnesko on, remarking that we had been in a few tight places but this was about the limit. I have been told since that I was quixotic not to leave everything & make for safety. You will understand, however, that I never for one moment considered the abandonment of anything.

They packed up their equipment and harnessed the remaining three ponies. Their floe was drifting westwards towards the open ocean so Birdie knew they must try to reach a floe that was near an accessible point on the Barrier. They cajoled Punch into jumping onto the next floe, which encouraged Nobby and Uncle Bill to follow suit. Once the three men had dragged the sledges across, they stood as still as possible until the floe drifted against another one in the right direction and repeated the process:

Sometimes it would take 10 minutes or more, but there was so much motion in the ice that sooner or later bump you would go against another piece, & then it was up & over. Sometimes they split, sometimes they bounced back so quickly that only one horse could get over, & then we had to wait again. We had to make frequent detours & were moving west all the time with the pack, still we were getting south, too. ... [Crean] behaved as if he had done this sort of thing often before. Cherry, the practical, after an hour or two dug out some chocolate & biscuit ... I felt at that time that food was the last thing on earth I wanted, & put it in my pocket; in less than half an hour, though, I had eaten the lot. The ponies behaved as well as my companions, & jumped the floes in great style. ... After some hours we saw fast ice ahead & thanked God for it.

As a pack of killer orcas raised their heads in the water, Birdie decided to make for a big sloping floe which looked as if it might be touching the Barrier. As they reached the top of the incline they found themselves looking down on a 30–40ft channel of heaving brash ice in which more orcas were prowling. As Birdie somewhat anxiously considered his next move, their ice floe calved in two forcing them to retreat onto another more stable floe. They gathered the sledges and ponies round them and discussed their predicament. Birdie knew they must fetch help:

To go myself was out of the question. The problem was whether to send one, or both, my companions. As my object was to save the animals & gear, it appeared to me that one man remaining would be helpless in the event of the floe splitting up, as he would be busy saving himself. I therefore decided to send … Crean, as Cherry, who wears glasses, could not see so well. … I sent a note to Captain Scott, & stuffing Crean's pockets with food, we saw him depart.

Birdie tried to follow Crean's progress through the theodolite telescope, but the rise and fall of their floe and the appearance of several Emperor penguins (looking from a distance remarkably like Crean) made it difficult. To make things worse, the orcas, with their 'large black & yellow heads with sickening pig eyes', were paying rather too much attention to Birdie, Cherry and the ponies.

By the time Crean returned with Scott and Oates, the floe carrying Birdie and Cherry was within reach of the Barrier but they had decided to remain with the ponies and sledges as the latter were loaded with the rations they needed for their stay at Hut Point. Birdie was somewhat taken aback at Scott's reaction:

He said: 'I don't care a damn about the ponies & the sledges. It's you that I want, & I am going to see you safe here up on the Barrier before I do anything else.' … I realized the feeling he must have had all day. He had been blaming himself for our deaths, & here we were very much alive. He said: 'My dear chaps, you can't think how glad I am to see you safe.'

Birdie and Cherry persuaded Scott to let them start hauling provisions and equipment onto the Barrier. They were making good progress when, at around 4 a.m., Scott suddenly ordered them off the floe. A few moments later Birdie was on the Barrier, watching helplessly as the three ponies drifted out to sea. The five men pitched camp – a safe distance from the ice edge – and started cooking the first meal Birdie, Cherry and Crean had eaten in over twenty-four hours. Birdie, despite feeling thoroughly miserable himself, tried to cheer Scott up with the thought that there were more ponies back at Cape Evans, as well as plenty of dogs and two motor-sledges. Scott confessed that the accident in the crevasse-field with the dogs had shaken his faith in them as a safe means of transport on the crevasse-strewn Beardmore Glacier and that he was worried the motor-sledges had been damaged while being unloaded from the ship. Now, with Weary Willie dead at Safety Camp, Blossom and Blucher buried under cairns, Guts drowned, and Uncle Bill, Punch and Nobby currently drifting out to sea, Scott was beginning to wonder if they would make it to the Pole next season.

After a sombre meal, Birdie walked over to the Barrier edge. When he spotted the ponies heading out to sea on their ice floe he ran along the edge until he was parallel with them – they looked over at him and he wondered if they thought he was bringing their next feed. He returned to the camp and snatched a few hours' sleep before returning to the Barrier edge armed with a pair of binoculars. When he realised the ponies' ice floe was jammed against the Barrier further along the rim, he ran back for Oates and Cherry who, with Scott's reluctant consent, joined him in jumping across floes towards the ponies. They coaxed Punch into starting the run-up to a jump onto the next floe but the stiff, cold animal suddenly skidded to a halt and toppled into the icy water. As the pony struggled in the water the orcas drew in and Oates reluctantly dispatched Punch with a pickaxe. Scott shouted at them to return to the Barrier immediately but they continued to try to coax Nobby and Uncle Bill across to safety. As soon as they were within reach of the Barrier they identified a suitable landing place and persuaded Nobby to jump to safety; as a dozen orcas suddenly appeared beside them, Uncle Bill, frightened by the sudden movement in the water, missed his footing and began slipping off the floe. They managed to haul him back to safety but 'the undefeated old sportsman' could not rise. As chunks of Barrier ice crashed into the sea around him, Birdie tried to revive his pony, but when he realised Uncle Bill was beyond help he grabbed a pickaxe and, following Oates' shouted instructions, ended the animal's misery. They disconsolately packed up what they could from the ice floe and led Nobby round to Hut Point.

The *Discovery* hut was now clear of snow and fit for habitation, but 3 miles of Glacier Tongue (which Birdie had regarded as 'practically terra firma') had broken off and floated out to sea.[7] When describing the incident to his family, Birdie concluded that there had been an almost uncanny element of chance in what had happened:

My own opinion is that it just had to be ... Six hours earlier we could have walked to the hut on sound sea-ice. A few hours later we should have seen open water on arrival at the Barrier edge. The blizzard that knocked out our beasts, the death of Weary [Willie], the misunderstanding of the dogs, everything, fitted in to place us on the sea-ice during the only 2 hours of the whole year that we could possibly have been in such a position. Let those who believe in coincidence carry on believing. Nobody will ever convince me that there was not something more. Perhaps in the light of next year we shall see what was meant by such an apparent blow to our hopes.

Birdie also wrote an official report to Scott outlining 'the succession of unfortunate circumstances' which had resulted in the loss of the ponies. He made it clear that he had expected Scott to be with the pony party as they crossed the ice and that when Cherry had arrived and explained that the condition of Weary Willie made that impossible, he had passed on Scott's instruction that Birdie was to 'press on to Hut Point without delay having due regard to the condition of the sea ice'. Birdie took some time to write his twelve-page report and toyed with alternative conclusions to it before handing it to Scott. To Birdie's surprise and relief, Scott, at least in public, took this and other reversals of the depot journey 'like a brick'.[8]

By now the sea-ice between Hut Point and Cape Evans had completely broken up, but the lower slopes of Mount Erebus were currently too dangerous for any men, let alone animals, to clamber round to reach Cape Evans. They were now effectively trapped at Hut Point, but Birdie led a party back to the Barrier edge to clear the remains of what they now called Disaster Camp and joined a party led by Teddy Evans to move more provisions to Corner Camp. Knowing that the death of so many ponies would probably make manhauling vital on the Southern journey, Birdie began to hone his technique:

> I found a steady plod up a steep hill without spells [breaks] is better and less exhausting than a rush & a number of rests. This theory I put into practice with great success. I don't know whether everybody saw eye to eye with me over the idea of getting to the top without a spell. ... Atkinson said: 'I don't mind you as a rule, but there are times when I positively hate you.'[9]

By 15 March the geological party – Griff Taylor, Wright, Debenham and Taff Evans – joined the depot party at Hut Point. For the next few weeks Birdie became a 'pseudo-scientist' and hunted out rocks which he presented to Debenham or Wright with a triumphant flourish and volley of recently acquired geological terminology.[10] He had a spell as Hut Point cook, in which capacity he played an April Fool's Day trick on Cherry and Wright by filling the bottom of their pannikins with wheat-chaff rather than seal meat – a joke which somewhat rebounded when he felt duty-bound to replace the missing meat from his own allowance.

Eventually they began to run out of things to do and had read all the *Discovery* expedition reading material, from ten-year-old issues of *Girls' Own Paper* and *Contemporary Review* to a thawed-out copy of *My Lady Rotha*, a romantic novel of which the ending was missing. On 13 April, with the sea-ice between Hut Point and Cape Evans showing little sign of freezing over, Scott decided he must now try to lead a party, including Birdie and several scientists, over the lower slopes of Mount Erebus to Cape Evans.

When they arrived at Cape Evans after a challenging clamber through a raging blizzard, they found everyone in good spirits but learned that another pony, Hackenschmidt, had died. As it was Good Friday, Scott led a short service, following which Birdie gave himself a brisk wash and shave and retired early to his cosy bunk for a good night's sleep.

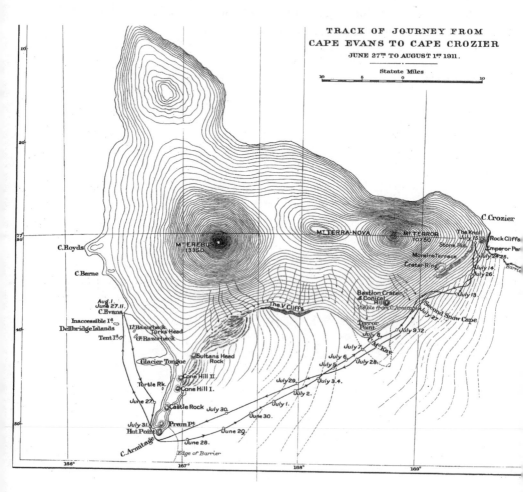

Map 4 Ross Island, showing the track of the Cape Crozier journey, June–August 1911. *Map by Stanfords, 1913 © private*

12

DEEPEST WINTER

On 23 April Birdie watched the sun disappear below the horizon for the last time until August. Over the coming months the only natural light would come from the sun's glow from beneath the horizon, moonlight on snow and ice or ephemeral displays of aurora and parhelia.

Birdie, currently the sole occupant of the Tenements, was more than happy to join Scott and others in taking more provisions over to Hut Point. It had been agreed that Meares and a small group would stay with the animals until the sea-ice froze over, but that Wilson, Cherry and some others would return to the hut. Outdoor activities were gradually being curtailed by the lack of light but Birdie kept busy, helping 'Sunny Jim' Simpson with his air-temperature balloon flights (a process which involved hydrogen, numbered scientific instruments and miles-long threads) and making the closer acquaintance of Victor, his new pony who had been named in honour of the absent first mate Campbell.[1] Birdie's attempts to ride Victor bareback ended prematurely when the 'lively beggar' bolted back to Cape Evans with Birdie on his back and charged through a low stable door only seconds after Birdie, fearing a nasty blow to the head, had managed to slither off his back.

This and other episodes reinforced Birdie's reputation as one of the expedition's 'characters', recognisable from a distance by his rotund silhouette,[2] prominent nose and distinctive green felt hat. He took teasing (including about his snoring and snow-bathing habits) in good part, cheerfully did what was asked of him and was always willing to help others with their tasks. Birdie was always happy to take temperature and wind readings outside and formed a close partnership with Wilson, who was equally dismissive of the effects of biting cold on exposed fingers. The pair became such a fixture at 'B' station (known as Bertram), which lay high on an exposed natural ramp of volcanic rubble near

Mount Erebus, that Ponting took a flashlight photograph of the two of them on the ramp and Wilson sketched his friend and later produced a fine watercolour.

As long as there was enough sunlight emitting from below the horizon, lunchtime football matches continued to help maintain fitness and work off excess energy. In terms of talent, Gran had played for Norway, Atkinson was reckoned the expedition's finest British player, and Frederick Hooper, Taff Evans and Crean were the cream of the defensive players – Birdie, playing at full back with Wilson, rushed around with more enthusiasm than finesse.[3]

As the scientists worked in their labs, Birdie and others constructed small outbuildings and screens, melted ice for water, hunted for fish or seals (for Clissold to transform into *galantine* of seal and other delicacies), exercised the animals that were not at Hut Point or went for walks:

> We had a very pleasant range of walks around the station. For rock-climbing there was the Ramp or Inaccessible Island which despite its name is quite accessible when frozen solidly in. Further afield there is Turk's Head … Cape Barne & C. Royds … & a splendid collection of grounded icebergs off the Cape … One of these had a complete arch of ice in it … 25 feet at least. It collapsed one day with a great roar & as we knew the Owner [Scott] & Silas were out inspecting it Bill & I walked over as quickly as we could to see if all were well. Fortunately it was alright though Silas had been under it inspecting the ice only a short time before.[4]

To make the most of the dark months, Scott organised, as he had on the *Discovery* expedition, a series of lectures which were compulsory for officers and scientists, but optional for seamen. The 'term' opened with Wilson's lecture on Antarctic flying birds, Simpson's on 'Coronas, Halos, Rainbows and Auroras' and Griff Taylor's introduction to modern physiography. Birdie took copious notes and began research for his own talks on the history of polar clothing and polar rations. On non-lecture evenings he caught up with correspondence and started a new journal which, written out carefully in ink in a handsome new leather-bound notebook, would form a permanent record of his adventures that he could send to Emily.

He began writing on 1 May 1911, the anniversary of his return to England from India. He admitted that during this first 'long silence' there had been occasional 'might-have-beens' (particularly during the depot journey), but that despite being in 'one of the uttermost parts of the earth', he felt he was still in God's care. He told her about the hut ('simply splendid') and sleeping arrangements ('tip-top'), before waxing lyrical about his 'marching kit'.

This multi-layered affair included Wolsey undergarments ('simply comfort itself [and] specially strengthened in vulnerable places'), multiple pairs of socks, windproof outerwear ('asleep or awake they never come off') and finnesko ('the lightest & most delightful footwear'). While he still found his favourite Army & Navy Stores' green felt hat indispensable, he acknowledged that a woollen balaclava or windproof helmet protected the ears better against frostbite. As winter set in he found his mitts (worn strung around his neck with lamp-wick) ideal for protecting the fingers and was glad his cosy Wolsey pyjama jacket had handy waterproof storage pockets for anything damp. All in all, everything in the clothing line was very satisfactory.

On Monday 8 May Scott gave his own first lecture in which he outlined plans for the Southern journey.[5] The attainment of the South Pole was, he explained, the most important object of the expedition, both in terms of reaching an as-yet unconquered goal and because success in this would result in the expedition's scientific work receiving the attention it deserved from public and learned societies alike. He had not yet finalised plans but had identified the main challenges that they would all need to consider over the coming months. Members of the Southern journey party would be chosen nearer the time based on fitness and suitability for the work involved; he knew some people would inevitably be disappointed but hoped that everyone would accept his final decision in good spirit. Scott assured them that (contrary to rumours) he had made no promises to date and would not do so until he felt the time was right. He would also welcome suggestions regarding the journey from anyone even though these might be contrary to the outline plans he would lay out before them that evening.

The journey to and from the Pole was, he told them, some 1,530 miles; based on Shackleton's times (duly adjusted for blizzards and the distance between Shackleton's 'Furthest South' and the Pole), Scott estimated it should take them 144 days – 84 days there and 60 days back to Hut Point. The main challenge would be the harsh conditions on the plateau. While dogs, ponies or motor-sledges could conceivably continue up the Beardmore Glacier, Scott had not relied on this and had assumed that the latter part of the journey would be carried out by men and sledges alone. Once they reached the Beardmore, three or four teams of men would haul laden sledges up to the plateau. As they sledge-hauled towards the Pole teams of men would turn back at pre-arranged points until one team was left to travel the final leg. Noting that Shackleton had been forced to turn back due to lack of food, Scott confirmed that he had, with Birdie's assistance, already begun calculating weights and quantities of food required for men and animals, taking into account the amounts already left at depots.

There were, Scott concluded, many factors in their favour: the availability of ponies, dogs and motor-sledges to assist with the journey across the Barrier; additional manpower to accompany the twelve-man team to the Glacier, which meant a good chance of the final South Pole party having ample rations for their journey; and the availability of skis to assist on the long, flat stretches of the Barrier journeys. There were, however, also risk factors: the complexity of the overall operation; the random chance of the weather being worse than that experienced by Shackleton; and the loss of ponies that they had experienced on the depot journey. The latter had also shown them that they needed enough snowshoes and goggles for the ponies as well as eye-protection for themselves. Scott had every confidence in Oates' management of the ponies and confirmed that, as long as the weather was not too cold for the ponies, he planned to set out on 3 November 1911. This meant that, based on his calculations for the journey, the final South Pole party would arrive back at Hut Point on or around 29 March 1912. He appreciated that the *Terra Nova* would have left for New Zealand by then, but assured everyone who would be returning with the ship that he had made arrangements for their salaries to be paid.[6]

Scott's lecture gave Birdie much food for thought, but Ponting's magic-lantern show the following evening transported him back to Burma and gave him and Simpson (who had also worked there) the opportunity to contribute their own experiences in that fascinating country. On 13 May Meares, the dogs, the final members of the Hut Point party and the two surviving ponies from the depot journey returned to Cape Evans. Birdie found the now-packed hut to be a convivial place where everyone mixed and mingled. Although horse-play was forbidden (in case of injuries), verbal sparring matches regularly broke out between the inhabitants of the Tenements – led by Birdie and Oates – and the scientists. Within the Tenements Birdie and Oates would argue the merits of ships versus horses, the navy versus the army, and sailor Nelson versus soldier Napoleon (of whom Oates had provocatively hung a portrait beside his bunk). As almost total darkness fell and gales howled, outdoor activities (other than vital meteorological duties) petered out and lectures became the high spots of the week. Wilson's talk on Adélie and Emperor penguins proved particularly popular and he spoke enthusiastically about his plans for a winter expedition to Cape Crozier to study the Emperors' breeding cycle and obtain eggs and embryos on which to test his theories on the origins of the flightless birds. One evening Oates (who addressed his audience as 'Gentlemen – and Scientists') explained the diet he had devised to prepare the ponies for the Southern journey, and on another Wright talked about the types of glaciers and crevasses those on the Southern journey might encounter.

On 22 May Birdie joined Scott, Wilson, Atkinson, Taff Evans and Clissold on a trip to Shackleton's hut at Cape Royds, where they were pleased to find abandoned fuel and provisions in good condition and to salvage a few useful scraps of leather and five hymnbooks for the Cape Evans Sunday service choir. Following three further scientific lectures, Birdie gave his talk on the history of polar rations. While he made no claims to be a dietician, he delivered an ency-clopaedic and entertaining overview of the range of foodstuffs used by earlier Antarctic explorers. His conclusion that cocoa (a relaxant) was preferable to tea (a stimulant) during marches provoked a long and lively discussion between 'tea-ites', led by Scott and Taff Evans, and 'cocoa-ites'. He then handed over to Wilson who led a more scientifically based discussion on the merits of fats and other components of the modern sledging diet. By contrast, Ponting's next lantern show transported everyone to springtime Japan, with views of snow-capped Mount Fuji, temples and blossom-laden trees.

Birdie, ever eager for exercise, was delighted when Wilson invited him and Cherry – acknowledged to be among the best sledge-pullers in the party – to join him on a 70-mile journey to Cape Crozier and the Emperor penguin colony. Birdie suspected the weather conditions might warrant something more than his green felt hat and began customising a balaclava with flaps which could be raised or lowered depending on prevailing wind and snow conditions.

On 6 June, Scott's 43rd birthday, Clissold produced a huge iced cake deco-rated with photographs of Scott, miniature flags, crystallised fruit and chocolate decorations. In the evening the wardroom was festooned with sledge-flags and everyone tucked into seal soup (Clissold's speciality), roast New Zealand mutton with redcurrant jelly and asparagus, jelly, fruit salad and chocolate, washed down with a somewhat mysterious cider cup, sherry and liqueurs. The next day Scott, apparently a little the worse for wear, lectured on 'The Ice Barrier and Inland Ice'. Birdie missed Teddy Evans' lecture on surveying (a subject with which he was very familiar) in favour of a trip to Cape Royds with Cherry. He was, how-ever, fascinated by Nelson's talk on Antarctic biology and as soon as he realised that pycnogonids or sea-spiders thrived in polar waters, he asked whether they were more closely related to crustaceans (against which he bore no grudge) or arachnids (his lifelong enemies) – a question which resulted in considerable amusement given his uncharacteristic use of correct biological names.[7]

With his departure for Cape Crozier imminent, Birdie completed work on his custom-designed balaclava and joined Wilson for snow-baths outside the hut. They would not be leaving, however, before the great feast of Midwinter, the Antarctic explorers' equivalent of Christmas.[8] On 22 June the hut was hung with sledge-flags and Union Jacks, Wilson prepared a special menu card and

Birdie quietly passed Clissold some 'special' rations, which did not appear on the general inventory. At 7 p.m. sharp everyone sat down to seal consommé, roast beef with all the trimmings, Clissold's homemade plum pudding and mince pies, and 'caviare antarctic' (anchovies mixed with cod's roe), washed down with champagne, wine, sherry, brandy, punch and liqueurs, and topped off with almonds and raisins, bonbons, toffees, crystallised fruits (Emily Bowers' 'Christmas' gift to the company) and cigars. Scott reminded them that their expedition was, like the winter, at the halfway point and thanked everyone for their contribution to date, including, in particular, Birdie and Oates' efforts with the stores and animals respectively. Toasts to the king and the success of the expedition were followed by lengthy expressions of mutual admiration and general goodwill, and Cherry's presentation to Scott of the first *South Polar Times* of the *Terra Nova* expedition.[9] Birdie featured on several pages: in Dennis Lillie's cartoons, Griff Taylor's pseudo-ornithological description of him as 'B. Avicula' ('little bird') and in Atkinson's open letter 'Celebrities who live in glass houses':

Sir, You were appointed to this Expedition in 1910, and joined it as 4th Mate, with charge of the stores. You performed your duties in London with great zeal, and in your anxiety to see where a split pea had been, fell down the main-hold. But being well endowed by a somewhat unkind Nature, you survived in a sitting position. ... On the voyage to New Zealand you again served with great zeal and ability. ... The Truculent Farmer [Oates] gave some trouble, but was unable to stump you in any question of seamanship. ...

Sir! Your ideas of heat and cold are peculiar, we are bound to confess. We are sure that in India you do not feel heat, and wear accordingly very thick and inappropriate clothes. Likewise in approaching the Antarctic you equally do not feel cold, and appear in a thin shirt and the Green Hat.

Your leanings towards Science are well marked. ... You are now following in the footsteps of a great Master [Wilson], and Evoluting is your subject. Your motto is 'Avoid Scurvy', and in this you play into the hands of the Chief, 'Reindeer Bill' [Wilson]. When your two heads are together he is generally in a sitting position.

You believe, Sir, above everything, in being a sailor. We agree with you; you can navigate ice-floes, especially with a crew composed of 'Cherry blaggards' and quadrupeds.

We wish you, Sir, all good luck and success.

After dinner everyone enjoyed Ponting's lantern show of recent photographs and a game of Snapdragon.[10] After they had toasted absent friends (particularly

Campbell's party and Pennell and the *Terra Nova* crew), Clissold brought in some final desserts. The unaccustomed consumption of alcohol affected people in different ways: Oates danced Russian-style with Anton; Keohane began debating the 'Irish question'; Clissold, his job well done, sat smiling broadly and issuing the occasional 'whoop' of pleasure. In the midst of the melee Birdie (who had imbibed less than most) slipped out of the room with a few cohorts, returning a few minutes later with his 'Christmas tree' decorated with feathers, candles, coloured paper, crackers and hung with gifts largely donated by Wilson's sister-in-law. Oates was delighted with his whistle and pop-gun and Griff Taylor with his trumpet (as were others with necklaces or earrings), although Silas Wright was clearly less impressed with an envelope marked 'In memory of my native land' (Canada), which contained a copy of the American 'Stars & Stripes' anthem.

A few days later Birdie wrote to Emily:

Just a line before we leave for Cape Crozier … Our life in the hut here has indeed been a happy one since our return from Hut Point. As usual I have found more than enough to fill my 16 waking hours & in spite of the lack of daylight am always on the go – chiefly out of doors. The weather so far has been most uncertain & inclement, blizzard has succeeded blizzard … However it is not so bad that as a rule one can't get out sometime in the 24 hours, though frequent frostbites are often the result. Captain Scott is a topper, I cannot say too much for him as a leader & as an extraordinarily clever & far-seeing man. Our Cape Crozier party consists of Dr Wilson, Cherry-Garrard & myself. Two more congenial companions I could not have found. Uncle Bill is as ever my beau ideal of an English gentleman & I feel it an honour to have been asked to accompany him. … We are going to undertake what I believe is a unique thing in polar travel – a mid-winter journey – I am very keen on it – though what is in store for us in the darkness I cannot say. The scientific value of the journey will be very great – more than worth it. It is 70 miles (geog) – about 82 miles statute – from here & we are taking provisions for 6 weeks. I do not anticipate any unusual danger but am leaving this in case anything should happen. DV all will be well. … I hope you & the girls are as happy as I am.[11]

On Tuesday 27 June Birdie, Wilson and Cherry set off for Cape Crozier.[12] By the time they reached the Barrier the temperature had fallen to -50°F and their sledges became so difficult to pull over sand-like surfaces that they had to relay them with the aid of a hurricane lamp.[13] Initially, they made barely 2 miles a day for eight or nine hours of back-breaking work, during which Cherry's fingers and some of his and Wilson's toes became frostbitten. Daily routines were a struggle: when Birdie lit their candle in the morning the matches were damp and the metal matchbox ice-burned his fingers; when he recorded his daily meteorological readings his pencil slipped on ice-coated paper:

> I was beginning to think I could stand most things but when one has to deal with 100 degrees [F] below freezing point I did not want to ask for any more. We were now pretty well iced up. All three of us slept & lived in the same clothes, windproofs & all, & they were frozen so stiff that they stuck out all round like armour. To get into one's bag was an effort that required … skill, care & time; once you were thawed out by the heat of the body everything became sopping until you were soft all over & comfortably wet & warm. The discomforts of such a journey are so many & varied that life becomes a struggle for nothing but the most primitive aids to existence.

There were, however, compensations:

> We had auroras the like of which I had never imagined as … Erebus must hide the best from Winter Quarters. At times the sky was ablaze with brilliant curtains of light being shaken along as if by a breeze & whirling into vortices etc or opening like a vast mushroom overhead with all colours to be seen – though yellow predominates as a rule.

Overnight their outerwear froze solid and dressing each morning in pitch darkness took about four hours, despite each man helping his companions. In terms of food they were each testing (for the Southern journey) varying combinations of pemmican, biscuit and pure fat, none of which appeared to agree with their stomachs, at least initially. About a week out from Cape Evans the temperature rose:

> We were hung up 4 days with Blizzard … [it] seemed offensively warm after what we had had. We got wetter than ever in this heat & our bags were now so saturated that Bill's began to split & we had to knock off rolling them up for fear of breaking them. … We lay them on the sledge like 3 corpses.

At Cape Crozier they found the only suitable site for their igloo was on top of an exposed ridge, but they persevered and after three days of digging had sufficient rocks and chunks of ice for the walls and to weigh down the canvas roof against the wind. They could hear penguin cries but the rookery lay beyond a series of deep crevasses and 70ft-high pressure-ridges, and with the moon on the wane, they had barely five hours of reasonable visibility per day in which to reach it and return with specimens to the safety of the igloo.

After a first attempt to reach the rookery took them into a cul-de-sac, Wilson found a route through a gap in an 800ft-high ice gorge (which reminded Birdie of Dante's dark valleys of hell) – and Birdie and Wilson became the first people to see the 'lordly Emperor' nursing its eggs. As total darkness enveloped the area, they grabbed, killed and skinned three penguins, gathered five eggs and turned tail. On the way back Birdie, whose finnesko were almost frozen solid, slipped into a deep tide-crack; he managed to save his eggs, but Cherry, whose glasses were completely iced up, tripped in the dark, fell onto his and smashed them. By the next morning a gale threatened to whip the canvas roof off the igloo and, with temperatures tumbling and only a week's oil remaining (needed to melt ice for water), Wilson decided they must return to Cape Evans.

The next day, which was Wilson's 39th birthday, Birdie awoke to find that their tent (being used as a store while they lived in the igloo) had blown away. They battled outside, collected what they could find and spent the rest of the day in their sleeping bags wondering how they would make the return journey to Cape Evans without a tent for shelter.[14] They celebrated Wilson's birthday with a few sweets Birdie had thoughtfully brought from Cape Evans and hoped that the canvas roof of the igloo would hold:

> … it started to go at the door … [then] crack & the whole business flew to ribbons & I dived for my bag … I was resolved to keep warm & beneath my debris covering I paddled my feet & sang all the songs & hymns I knew to pass the time. I could occasionally thump Bill & as he still moved I knew he was also alright; what a birthday for him. We had been 48 hours without a meal …

Following an unsuccessful attempt in almost total darkness to find their tent, they moved their sleeping bags to the leeward side of their damaged igloo walls and heated up some debris-covered pemmican. Restored, they went outside to try again to find the tent; when Birdie returned triumphant after finding it half a mile away, Wilson decided that, now they had shelter for their return journey, they must set off for Cape Evans immediately.[15] While sorry to abandon further research into the origins of the Emperor penguin, he declined Birdie's suggestion of a further trip to the rookery before they left. On the return journey gales howled around them as they stumbled in the dark over pressure-ridges and through mazes of crevasses:

My helmet was so frozen up that my head was encased in a solid block of ice & I could not look down without inclining my whole body. ... Bill stumbled one foot into a crevasse & I landed in it with both mine – the [snow] bridge gave way & down I went. ... I hung with the bottomless pit below & the ice crusted sides alongside ... Bill said 'What do you want?' I asked for an alpine rope with a bowline for my foot & taking up first the bowline & then my harness they got me out.

With 'noon twilight' lengthening and sledges lightening, they increased their daily marches to about 7 miles. By now Wilson and Cherry were suffering from lack of sleep (Birdie generally snored through anything) and fuel was running low so they were glad to reach the smoother surfaces of the Barrier. But as night temperatures suddenly plummeted to -60°F and their sleeping bags froze solid, their contorted limbs would cramp. As their bodies shuddered and their teeth chattered to the point of shattering, Cherry reluctantly accepted Birdie's offer of a loan of his spare eiderdown sleeping-bag lining. The shivering friends discussed whether, on a longer journey, death might appear preferable to prolonged suffering or to knowing that one's condition was putting the lives of others at risk. Although Cherry preferred not to consider the matter in any great detail, Birdie concluded that he would, should the need arise, dispatch himself with a pickaxe, seek out a conveniently deep crevasse or find something suitable in the medicine chest.[16]

On 29 July, Birdie's 28th birthday, the three friends walked off the Barrier. Their sledges were virtually empty of rations but still heavy from the weight of ice trapped in the folds of their tent and sleeping bags.[17] After a night in the *Discovery* hut (which now seemed the height of luxury), they plodded back to Cape Evans and, on Tuesday 1 August, walked back into the hut. Their companions barely recognised the three thin, scruffy, ice-covered men, but helped them peel off their filthy marching gear and don warm clothes before plying them with hot drinks and as much food as they could consume. After a hot bath and shave, Birdie slipped into the warm pyjamas Emily had sent him and retired to his 'delightful bunk' which now felt like 'heaven itself'. His feet were less badly frostbitten than those of his companions but as they thawed out he felt as if he was walking on hot bricks. As soon as he heard that Scott was planning a short expedition to the Western Mountains and Ferrar Glacier in a few weeks' time, he made as light of his discomfort as possible – and was rewarded with an invitation to join the group.

Now he was back in the hut Birdie had time to finish the first volume of his journal for Emily:

If I have no time to more than touch on our Cape Crozier journey before the fast-flying winter ends you will know that it was from lack of opportunity. I have been helping Captain Scott work out an elaborate scheme for the polar journey as well as do all the 101 things that keep one at it from 8am to 11pm. ... I have simply enjoyed myself immensely. I love the life & the desolate country, the endless ice & snow & immense mountains & glaciers. ... The darkness is by no means unpleasant. The same old moon smiles down on us as you see so far away & the glorious auroras alone would be worth coming down to see. I have never missed civilization so far & except for seeing your dear face again would be in no hurry to return. I am proud to be under such a leader & to be associated with such an excellent lot of men. ... One realises [God's] Presence here in the uttermost part of the Earth more than anywhere.

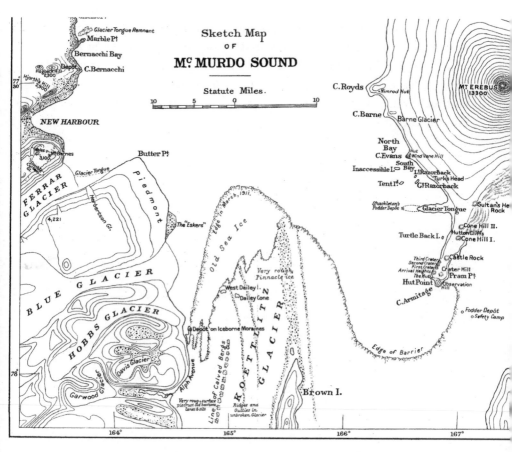

Map 5 McMurdo Sound, showing Cape Evans and the Ferrar Glacier. *Map by Stanfords, 1913 © private*

13

GETTING READY

By the time Birdie, Wilson and Cherry returned to Cape Evans, preparations were already well under way for the Southern journey.

Taff Evans had created special overshoes so people could ski in their finnesko, Meares had made dog harnesses, Oates had cleaned the ponies of parasites and the scientists had been busy in their laboratories. Atkinson, however, had not been able to help out much recently due to his fingers being severely frostbitten after becoming lost in a blizzard. He had set out one snowy evening to take the nightly readings at one of the stations; when he did not return for dinner search parties were mounted and Meares and Debenham eventually found him, completely disorientated and in a state of near-collapse. Since leaving the hut some seven hours previously for a journey of a few hundred yards, Atkinson had covered some 4 or 5 miles, zigzagging or walking in circles, had fallen into and clambered out of the tide-crack and finally started digging a snow-hole to rest in until the blizzard passed. It had been a close shave.

Birdie began researching for his lecture on the history of polar clothing and spending long hours working with Scott, calculating, recalculating, checking and rechecking details of provisions, sledge-weights and distances for the Southern journey. In August the weather at Cape Evans was largely fine; in September it was more variable but Birdie had plenty to do in his annexe. In the evenings he enjoyed reading the new issue of the *Terra Nova's South Polar Times*, which featured two items on the Cape Crozier journey: his own poem 'This is the house that Cherry built' and a retelling of the story in mock-hieroglyphs, illustrated by Wilson. Birdie's poem celebrating the return of the sun on 26 August (which could be sung to the tune of *Thou Whose Almighty Word*) had also been selected for this issue.

On 3 September, still fresh from the rigorous test conditions of Cape Crozier, Birdie gave his lecture on polar clothing. He concluded that, barring a lack of reindeer skin outerwear (not easily obtainable at this stage), Messrs Wolsey, Burberry and others had done them proud and that their marching gear, Shetland sweaters and undergarments should serve them well in most conditions.

Ten days later Scott gave his second presentation on his plans for the Southern journey; these were roughly as outlined on 8 May, with no concessions made to the presence on the ice of Amundsen's team. Teddy Evans, Day, Lashly and Clissold would leave in late October with two heavily laden motor-sledges, which they would drive as far as possible across the Barrier, ideally to the 'gateway' Shackleton had found that led to the Beardmore Glacier. The rest of the party would leave on or around 1 November, by which time temperatures should have risen sufficiently for the ponies to be comfortable. At the foot of the Beardmore any ponies that had survived the journey would be killed to feed men and dogs, and Meares and the dog teams would turn back, as would the motor-sledges if they had not already done so. From there three teams of four men would pull sledges up the Beardmore and across the plateau; one, then another team would turn back leaving four men – whose identities Scott would decide during the journey – to manhaul to the South Pole. As previously indicated, these four would probably not return to Hut Point until the end of March (by which time the *Terra Nova* would have undoubtedly left for New Zealand), so would need to stay for another season. They and others staying on would continue with scientific and surveying work and, should the South Pole team have been forced to turn back before reaching the Pole, might make another attempt to reach their goal. In any event, the *Terra Nova* would return in early 1913 to take those still at Cape Evans back to New Zealand and to England.

On 15 September Scott, Birdie, Simpson and Taff Evans left for the Western Mountains, the Ferrar Glacier and the adjacent coast; in his customary farewell 'line' to Emily, Birdie told her he was looking forward to something of a 'jolly picnic' and to climbing his first glacier.[1] The outward journey, however, brought back unhappy memories of the depot journey:

> … it seemed so strange to be marching over a plain that I could so well remember as an immense firth of turbulent water as broad as the mouth of the Firth of Clyde. I shall never enjoy sea ice much after my experience but felt no apprehension this time with about 4 to 8 feet thickness [of ice] between me & the black depths below while asleep.

After three days' march and a scramble across broken-up ice they reached the foot of the Ferrar Glacier. They climbed it for about 12 miles in semi-darkness (the surrounding mountains blocked out much of the afternoon sunlight), then camped for two days near Cathedral Rocks. They collected rock specimens, checked glacier markers left by the Western party the previous summer (Birdie's theodolite readings showed a movement of some 30ft). Birdie and Scott took photographs using the techniques Ponting had shown them to prepare them for being 'official' photographers for the Southern journey. After some more climbing and 'geologising' they descended to the coast where they found a series of capes, beautiful hidden valleys and several uncharted mountains – and stood in sunshine watching blizzards sweep in from the Barrier towards Cape Evans. After the blizzards swung in their direction they spent a day trapped in their tent and two days battling their way back to Cape Evans against 80mph winds. They had been away for ten days, covered some 150 miles and conducted useful scientific work; Birdie had also improved his photographic techniques and impressed Scott with his ability to operate a theodolite in low temperatures without gloves.

At the Cape Evans hut the main news was that Day's hard work with the sometimes-temperamental motor-sledges was paying dividends. On the pony front, Oates was still finding the equally temperamental Christopher difficult to control and Atkinson was worried that Jehu was not responding to extra feeding. On 6 October Wilson, Oates, Cherry and Crean went, with ponies, to take more provisions to Hut Point and to check the new telephone line that had recently been installed between there and Cape Evans. At 5 p.m. a bell rang in the Cape Evans hut and over the following days conversations took place about local weather conditions and other matters of mutual interest. Meares was particularly keen that the telephone line should be kept in good working order so that those returning from the Southern journey or other expeditions, and who might only be able to reach Hut Point, could telephone those at Cape Evans to advise their safe arrival or summon assistance.

Ponting, who would be leaving with the *Terra Nova* in a few months' time, was busily photographing and filming wildlife, icebergs, geographical features and any of his companions who would pose (or 'pont' as it was now known) for him. During one of Ponting's more ambitious sessions, Clissold fell almost 20ft from the top of a particularly picturesque iceberg and damaged his back, to the extent that his participation in the Southern journey as a member of the motor-sledge team was now in doubt. Birdie, when not consolidating his partnership with his horse, Victor (which he did with some success), taking readings or working in his annexe, helped Oates and Anton train the recalcitrant Christopher to pull a laden sledge. He finally managed to complete his account of the Cape Crozier journey, bring Emily's journal up to date and write a couple of letters to Harry Pennell, to be given to him when he arrived on the *Terra Nova* in a few months' time. There was much to tell:

> The news of the station will be showered upon you by everybody ... I don't think [Scott] is particularly keen on coming home this time ... Bill I believe has decided to stay under certain conditions in any case, provided he gets good news of Mrs Wilson's health, etc. Teddy I think is keen on leaving once the polar show is over. I am staying anyhow, so is Sunny Jim, Silas, Deb, Day, Nelson, Atkinson & probably Titus, Cherry & Trigger [Gran]. Meares, Ponko [Ponting], & Griff [Taylor] are returning in the ship. ... Evans, P.O., is a perfect godsend to us he can do anything in the sewing & repairing line & is general handy man. ... Cherry has developed into a great sledger so has Silas. ... Bill & Atch [Atkinson] never change & are just the good chaps we have always known. Teddy has changed a good deal, he is just as enthusiastic & energetic as ever but inconceivably quiet for his mercurial nature. One hardly ever hears him & we have never ... had a single sing-song since you left us. Trigger was a little flattened out by the cold in the autumn but has bucked up considerably since. Titus is much more cheerful than he was at the start of the depôt journey. We all hope that he & Cherry will stay with us next winter. Day is a good soul & a marvel at all mechanical jobs as well as being one of the most obliging fellows imaginable. The Owner [Scott] I think is the one & only. He & Bill are an ideal pair.[2]

Birdie outlined the vagaries of the depot journey before giving details of the Southern journey and expressing his confidence in his leader:

> Manhaulage is the main thing & I think it is the most reliable. All transport is being used to place 12 men at the foot of the Beardmore with necessary grub. ... We are ignoring Amundsen & I think we are relying on the soundest of schemes. Captain Scott will carry it through if anybody does. ... he does nothing without careful forethought & does everything for himself. Altogether I think most of us are agreed that he is one of the best.

Birdie closed with the hope that Pennell might be allowed to join the Cape Evans party for the following season and assured him that they would meet again after Birdie returned (he suspected) with the last Southern journey support party.

On 22 October, the last Sunday everyone at Cape Evans would be together before the motor-sledge party left, the scientists (who had less preparations to make) played football while Ponting filmed and members of the Southern party ferried last-minute sledge-loads of provisions to Glacier Tongue and Hut Point. All went smoothly, although Birdie, Wilson and Taff Evans had some unexpected exercise when Victor, Nobby and Snatcher all bolted in different directions (Victor had caught his nostril on Snatcher's harness) before being caught and coaxed back to Cape Evans. On 24 October, after a couple of false starts, Teddy Evans, Day, Lashly and Hooper (in place of Clissold) left with the motor-sledges. As others relayed final cases of provisions to Hut Point and other depots, Birdie weighed and bundled provisions into four-man ration packages. When there was no telephone call from Hut Point to confirm the safe arrival of the motor-sledges, Scott asked Gran and Simpson to ski after them to investigate. The next morning Simpson rang from Hut Point to say that the motor-sledges were stuck at Glacier Point where their caterpillar-tracks were slipping on bare ice. Birdie abandoned his rations work to help get the motor-sledges to Hut Point; the next morning they waved the motor-sledge party off again and marched back to Cape Evans.

On his return, Birdie ignored 'a slight touch of snow glare' (caught thanks to dashing off to Glacier Point without picking up his goggles) to complete a pre-departure letter to Edie:

We are on the eve of leaving for the Southern journey … Our winter here has passed very happily & I must say that I like this part of the world tremendously … The utter desolation has some attraction about it that no place peopled by man could have & the great mountains & cliffs that are always exposed to the icy winds command one's admiration. The wind here is terrible … [but] you get pretty hard after a bit & personally I would still sooner have frostbite than sunburn. Nothing I have had to put up with here compares with the burns I got on my bare feet when cruising in the Persian Gulf. … I have never seen such a spot, for every fine day you get you have to pay for it with interest in the successive blizzard … you get a heavy still day comparatively warm & full of snow when suddenly – piff & the storm bursts … you can't see 2 yards & very soon eyes & everything are bunged up with [snow]. This is thawed by the heat of your skin & immediately frozen on the outside so that your face is soon an ice mask. Altogether it is a most unpleasant experience to be caught to leeward of home in a blizzard & the safest course would be to bury yourself in snow if it were not for the danger of being frozen. … the advantage of being fairly plump down here is tremendous ... you keep warm when others are perished ... & on a long journey you draw on your supply after the lean ones have their clothes hanging on them like sacks. In a tent too I think it is an advantage not to be too tall. You can fit into a corner & sleep in comfort where a big man would be cramped. ... it is splendid to feel really fit & the satisfaction of a good meal & dry foot gear after a long day's march is not to be overrated & then the interior of the bag & delightful oblivion & let the tempest do what it may. ... hurrah for the South. May God give us what we are striving for – we will do all that man can do but one realizes more than ever down here how very much man is limited & how small a thing can upset his best laid plans. We are not going forward like a lot of schoolboys on a holiday picnic, but rather as a party of men who know what they have got to face ... the journey will be no child's game but a hard one – as hard as any have ever been – & the Pole will not be gained without a terrible struggle. ... If man can make for success we have the right stuff with us, but as I say when man has done all he can do he can only trust in God for the rest.[3]

Birdie also found time to write to Kathleen Scott; he assured her that, despite 'reversals' on the depot journey, all was well and expressed his continuing admiration for her husband.[4]

On Sunday 29 October Birdie became involved in a cinematograph filming session with Ponting, who was eager to capture members of the Southern journey party 'on the march' (for which Ponting would not be present).[5] Scott, Wilson, Taff Evans and Crean donned full sledging gear and plodded up and down dragging (lightly laden) sledges and demonstrated the difficulties of erecting tents against the wind. For the last session Birdie replaced Crean and joined Scott, Wilson and Taff in a tent where they cooked and ate a pemmican hoosh[6] and clambered into sleeping bags.

On 1 November Birdie finished his pre-departure letter to Emily and added it to the pile of his letters and journal pages which Pennell would take to New Zealand and post to Britain:

My dearest Mother

We are just away for the Southern journey ... all seems well for a start & the only thing to worry us will be the truculence of the ponies which are all very fit with the exception of Jehu who struggled up to Hut Point last night so as not to delay our march today. I shall write on the journey & send [letters] back with the dogs ... everything seems to be very promising & the weather has improved considerably w/in the last 10 days. I have had a tremendous lot of arranging about the stores & depots to fit in with the ship's movement etc. & also alternatively to allow for her not coming down at all. In every respect I think things are arranged & I leave with much pleasure except in the case of unwritten letters which I have put off & put off till the time has overcome. However I have travelled more from the base than anybody here as well as being one of the busiest people in the hut & so I have few regrets. On the contrary our sodjourn [*sic*] here leaves only the happiest recollections & my comfy bed last night was something to remember for long. … What a glorious return we shall have with all our letters & news waiting & the fellows on the ship to see again. Well if we only succeed it will be a happy return indeed & you may be sure I shall consider no sacrifice too great for the main object & whether I am in one of the early returning parties or not I am Captain Scott's man & shall stick by him right through. God knows what the result will be but we will do all that man can do & leave the rest in His keeping in which we are & shall remain.[7]

Map 6 Southern journey from Cape Evans to the foot of the Beardmore Glacier.
Map by Patricia Wright © Adrian Raeside

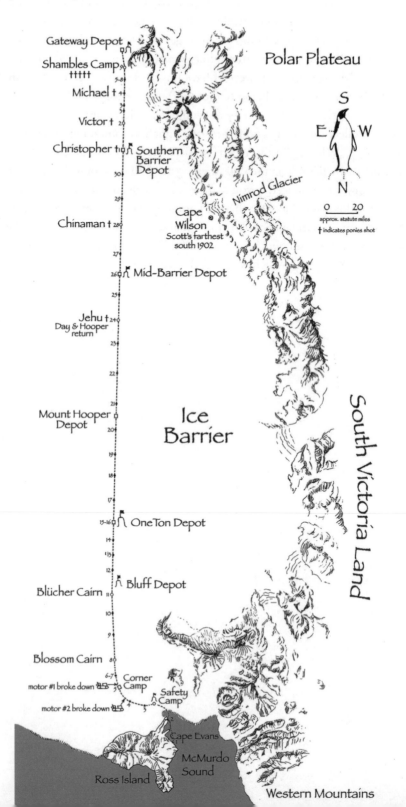

Gateway Depot
Shambles Camp
ttttt   5-8
Michael t
Victor t   26
Christopher t   Southern
                 Barrier
                 Depot
                 30
                 29
Chinaman t 28
                          Cape
                          Wilson
                     Scott's farthest
                     south 1902
                 27
                 26   Mid-Barrier Depot
                 25
Jehu t   24
Day & Hooper
       return   23
                 22
                 21
Mount Hooper
Depot   20
                 19
                 18
                 17
              15-16   One Ton Depot
                 14
                 13
                 12
Blücher Cairn 11   Bluff Depot
                 10
                 9
Blossom Cairn 8
              6-7   Corner
motor #1 broke down   Camp
                          Safety
                          Camp
motor #2 broke down

Polar Plateau

S
E   W
N

0   20
approx. statute miles
t indicates ponies shot

Nimrod Glacier

Ice
Barrier

South Victoria Land

Cape Evans
McMurdo
Sound
Ross Island

Western Mountains

14

ACROSS THE BARRIER TO THE BEARDMORE

A t approximately 11.30 a.m. on 1 November 1911 Birdie and Victor left Cape Evans in fine clear weather.[1]

As he waved goodbye to Simpson, Nelson, Griff, Debenham, Gran, Forde and Clissold, he could see the others ahead of him: Scott (leading Snippets), Crean (Bones), Taff Evans (Snatcher), Wilson (Nobby), Silas (Chinaman), Cherry (Michael) and Oates (Christopher). Atkinson and Keohane had left for Hut Point the day before so Jehu and James Pigg could rest overnight before setting off across the Barrier.[2] Victor was a little truculent at first but was soon pulling the sledge 'like a bird' and coped well with the icy surface at Glacier Tongue. By 4 p.m. everyone was safely at Hut Point and out of a gale-force blizzard.

The next morning Scott suggested they should change, with immediate effect, to marching at night, which should mean firmer surfaces for the ponies to march on and warmer temperatures for their rest. A late evening departure also gave Gran time to ski over from Cape Evans (where he had been contacted via the Hut Point telephone) with the Union Jack, which had been inadvertently left behind in the pre-departure rush. The staggered start began at 8 p.m. with the slowest ponies and concluded around midnight after Birdie had managed to coax a reluctant Victor from his warm stable and Oates had harnessed a lively, struggling Christopher to his sledge. Ponting filmed their departure before following the caravan by sledge to Safety Camp where he would leave them after a final cinematograph session. As Birdie passed Safety Camp (Victor was deemed not to require a lunch stop), he 'ponted' for the last time and bade his photographic mentor farewell – from now on it was down to him, Wilson and Scott to keep a visual record of their journey.

At their first daytime camp they built snow-walls for the ponies, fed the animals and themselves and retired for their own rest period. At 1 p.m. Birdie rose 'early' to help feed the animals and prepare for the new marching 'day', which for him and Victor would start at around 11 p.m. As he marched Birdie spotted first some abandoned petrol drums, then a 'mournful wreck' of a motor-sledge half-concealed beneath approximately two days' accumulated snow. On 5 November he and Victor arrived at Corner Camp to find that some of the party had suffered tumbles at the edge of the notorious crevasse-field where Scott's dog team had nearly come to grief on the depot journey.

After helping with camp-making Birdie checked the depot provisions and rearranged sledge-loads, taking into account the strength of the various ponies and dog teams. On their next march Birdie saw, through a thick fog, the second abandoned motor-sledge; he and Crean added as much fodder to their sledges as possible but reluctantly left provisions and fuel behind. At 4.15 a.m. on 6 November, having completed their requisite 10 miles, they camped in a blizzard, during which Birdie and others spent much of their supposed rest period digging out 'pretty miserable' ponies or rebuilding snow-walls that Snatcher and Jehu had kicked down.

The blizzard prevented them from marching the next day but they were able to set out again in the early hours of 8 November. As Birdie slipped and fell on treacherous surfaces, Victor calmly plodded along or nibbled at the snow, and by the end of the day they had again achieved 10 miles. They continued thus for several days, following cairns left by Teddy Evans, Day, Lashly and Hooper – who, judging by their tracks, were now manhauling two heavily laden sledges.

On 11 November Birdie noticed that the obstreperous Christopher had dislodged the sledgemeter on Birdie's sledge; on arriving in camp after a difficult march on tricky surfaces, he found Scott complaining that his team's sledges were now heavier than the others. After many calculations and some debate they agreed to leave things as they were. It occurred to Birdie that Scott was probably worried about the ponies and delays due to blizzards, but he consoled himself with the thought that Shackleton had experienced blizzards at this stage of the journey and then enjoyed a long spell of fine weather. On their next march they found, attached to a depot-journey cairn, a note dated 7 November from Teddy Evans, which suggested he was about four days' march ahead of them.

During their rest period the sun started to push its way through the heavy snow-clouds, but Jehu and Chinaman were clearly beginning to flag: 'Titus thinks … that they are the most unsuitable scrap-heap crowd of unfit creatures that could possibly be got together … It is most distressing as this continual bad weather depresses the animals & will shorten their usefulness.'³ Now, as fodder and rations were consumed, Birdie was regularly moving cases between sledges so Scott had no grounds for further complaints regarding fair distribution of weight.

Almost two weeks into their journey, on 13 November, the weather became 'about as poisonous as one could wish … with an awful surface'. Victor, who was now a 'lean lanky beast', struggled in deep drifts, but when long icicles regularly formed under his nose he would simply turn his head and wipe them off on Birdie's sleeve. Birdie was by now snow-blind in one eye and forced (to his intense annoyance) to wear snow-goggles. On 15 November they reached One Ton depot where they found their provisions buried under deep snow but otherwise in good order, despite winter temperatures equivalent to those at Cape Crozier. A note from Teddy Evans dated 10 November confirmed that the erstwhile motor-party would manhaul to 80° 30' South, where they would wait for Scott's party. Birdie joined a conference on the future of the ponies:

> [We] decided to reduce their weights in pony food. This means that there will not be enough food to march them up the glacier but as they are such a poor lot it is not worth while risking the success of the Expedition by over-loading them here with the idea of using them farther than the foot of the Beardmore. If we can get our man food there our chances are very good … Jehu & Chinaman cannot pull much even now … Michael & Jimmy Pigg are not fit for much either; the other six are more or less on a par.

The dogs also came into the food equation as Meares had fed them well during the early stages of the journey and Birdie knew ponies would need to be killed for dog food if the dog teams were to make it to the Beardmore Glacier and back to Cape Evans.

Scott now wanted to increase their average daily march from 10 to 13 miles, with a lunch stop for everyone. On 16 November Birdie redistributed loads on sledges according to the strength of the ponies (580lb for stronger ones, 480lb or 400lb for weaker ones); the dogs could pull a further 860lb of pony-fodder but an additional 400lb would need to be left behind. That evening they started out on the remaining 240 miles to the Glacier: despite marching into a cold southerly wind, even the 'crocks', Jehu (an 'unfortunate sack of bones') and Chinaman ('probably a good little pony 20 years ago'), managed to make 13 miles. During his rest period Birdie made a temporary fixing for his broken sledgemeter and, despite the lingering effects of snow-blindness, did some sky-gazing:

A splendid parhelia exhibition was caused by the ice crystals.[4] Round the sun was the 22° halo with 4 mock suns in rainbow arcs – outside this was another halo in complete rainbow colours: above the sun were the arcs of 2 other circles touching these halos & the arcs of the great all-round circle could be seen faintly on either side. Below was a dome-shaped glare of white which contained an exaggerated mock sun which was as dazzling as the sun himself.

By 18 November Birdie's snow-blindness had cleared completely, but having learned his lesson he now wore dark amber goggles which gave the world 'a warm sunset tint', and let him see his companions ahead in mirage and the outline of Mount Erebus some 150 miles away. Although they were making their daily distances, despite soft snow, Scott was still worried about sledge-weights, so Birdie reluctantly agreed to leave another bundle of forage behind. Scott wanted to leave more but Birdie objected:

> … it will be an awful pity if we have to shoot 6 strong ponies because we have no food for them. However one can only carry on & hope they will do the job now. I am sure that their performance in the next fortnight will decide the fate of the Expedition; … it is sad that for the poor ponies there is no return. They have been our pets for so long that I cannot bear to contemplate the fact that I shall have to shoot Victor in less than 3 weeks. They are all well treated & any beating or undue urging is out of the question, we have not a whip or stick in the party.

On 19 November Birdie took photographs of the camp showing the tents, pony-walls, men and animals; Scott had also been busy with his camera as he and Birdie wanted to send some completed films back to Ponting. The next day they crossed 80° South and caught up with the 'belated motor party' of Teddy Evans, Day, Lashly and Hooper. This foursome had all been manhauling for over two weeks and were, Birdie noticed, somewhat 'down in the mouth', particularly as they had been waiting for several days worrying whether something had happened to the others – although Day managed to joke that they hadn't seen Amundsen yet.[5] They had made good use of their time and built a sizeable Motor Party depot to which Birdie added enough four-man packages of rations and fuel to support each of the returning parties for a week. With their five tents, ten ponies, twenty-three dogs and thirteen sledges, Birdie reckoned they were the largest encampment ever seen on 'the old Barrier'. On 22 November, with good visibility and reasonable surfaces, they made almost 16 miles, confirming Birdie's view that it was all down to the weather:

... may we be granted the weather one would reasonably expect at this time of year, even in this most desolate and inclement region. The welfare of the animals is a continual worry to me though everybody seems to imagine that I am the ultra-optimist of the party. Certainly it worries Captain Scott as so much hangs in the balance on the performance of these animals. As far as we ourselves are concerned I have little fear[;] no matter how bad the conditions man can put up with them when an animal would succumb. I have the greatest confidence of success if we are only given a chance.

When they camped on 23 November they had crossed 81° South. Victor, who was proving to be a 'steady old goer' and as docile as a 'dear old sheep', happily headed the marching line as required. As Birdie marched, the bright night sun burned his face and lips and made him glad he was wearing his goggles – which Scott suggested made Birdie see the world 'through rose-coloured spectacles'. With enough pony-fodder for only twelve days they had to maintain their 13-mile average, and with dog food also running low, Jehu and Chinaman were due to be dispatched in a matter of days. As Day and Hooper were due to turn back in a few days, Birdie packaged up his completed roll of film and wrote notes for Ponting showing which camera settings he had used and which was which pony.[6] He tore out pages 1 to 23 from his journal notebook ready to send back and, in deference to Scott's agreement with the Central News Agency, wrote 'Strictly confidential. For personal friends & relations only' on the front page. He added a note to Emily:

My dearest Mother

Just a line to enclose herewith a portion of my journal with the first people returning. We are just over 3 weeks out from Hut Point – the motors have failed us but the ponies & dogs have come up trumps so far & we are doing splendidly. It is early to prognosticate but I have the greatest hopes of our successfully accomplishing the first part of our scheme – namely to arrive at the foot of the Beardmore Glacier with twelve strong men & 21 weeks provisions for a 4 man unit. This will enable one unit to go to the top of the Glacier & return & a second to go forward 2 weeks beyond the first & return, the last unit being left at that point with its return food depoted & 6 weeks food to go to the pole & return to that spot. This gives an ample scope & enough time & to spare for making the journey on full rations if it can be accomplished at all. As an offset against that the weather conditions on the Great Plateau even in summer are terrible beyond words, it will therefore be a matter of endurance. ... I cannot describe the fascination of this strange life … the surface of a vast field of ice the nature of which is still as full of mystery as ever. The shining mountains so far away & the wonderful lights & solar phenomena only seen in polar regions go together to make everything strange & unusual.[7]

He assured her he was confident, given sufficient food and rest, that those on the expedition would be successful and that he would return home safely; he knew there were risks and given that she now faced long periods without news from him, any news she received would be good news and she would never hear anything to make her ashamed of him. Just after 10 p.m. Birdie finished his correspondence, handed everything to Day and wished him and Hooper a safe journey back to Cape Evans. By now men and dogs were all feeling the benefit of some fresh meat: Birdie had been sad to lose 'poor old Jehu' but felt he had been well fed and treated to the last. On the subject of ponies, Birdie had noticed that Victor and his sledge seemed to move more easily after the sun had been shining on the frozen surface crystals for a few hours; he mentioned this fact to Scott and it was duly agreed that they would leave a little later the following night.

On 26 November the weather closed in and snow, fog and a 'dead white light' cut Birdie off from those marching only yards ahead of him. After a foreshortened march they built Middle Barrier depot with three large packages of rations, 84lb of biscuits, 2 gallons of fuel, matches, salt and a packet of toilet paper. As the ponies were now pulling sledge-loads of 450lb or less, Birdie was worried when Victor suddenly fell to his knees – but he seemed to recover and 'strode into camp like a bird'. That night, as ever, Birdie sat up late recording the meteorological readings and other navigational data for which he was responsible, until he received the order to return northwards and hand over to someone who would be continuing to the Pole. Birdie took great care of the tools of his trade: 'an excellent little sundial – an idea of Captain Scott's', his theodolite, a sling thermometer, a hypsometer[8] and an aneroid. But no instruments could help when they marched into a 'blank fuzzy snow wall' and compasses were particularly unreliable so near the magnetic pole.

On 28 November vivid parhelia were succeeded by another 'bliz', which filled Birdie's snow-goggles with driving drift. Victor struggled during the early part of the march but after his lunchtime feed 'turned up trumps … stepped & led the line in his old place & at a good swinging pace' and even, for the first time for many days, enjoyed a roll in the snow. For Birdie, marching on a full stomach seemed to enhance the scenery:

... a vast mountain chain towering high above the Barrier and looking tremendous in the bright twilight after 300 miles of monotonous snow plain ... To our left lay Cape Wilson & Shackleton inlet with the huge mountains to the south of them. Greatest of all was Mount Markham — estimated by Captain Scott's survey as 15,100 ft high & certainly the biggest mountain yet found down here. ... To come down from flights of scenic grandeur to the sordid, I must say that pony flesh is A1. As I was Cook I had ... cut up enough of Chinaman's undercut before it froze. This I dumped into the water cold with the pemmican ... when the water came to the boil the meat was cooked, as far as we were concerned it had to be as the allowance of oil always requires the primus to be switched off directly the article in the pot reaches the boiling point.

On 29 November 1911 they reached 82° 21' South, which was just beyond Scott's 'Furthest South' of 30 December 1902. Shackleton's 'Furthest South' of 88° 23' South lay some 360 miles away, less than 100 miles from the South Pole. Birdie's week as cook for his tent had just ended; it had, he thought, been rather a success thanks to the availability of fresh meat and his weekend 'special' of cocoa and arrowroot hoosh, which everyone had found delicious, if a touch heavy on the stomach. They would soon be changing over from 'Barrier' rations, which included luxuries such as raisins and chocolate, to simpler, more nutritious 'Summit' rations, which consisted largely of their staples — pemmican, biscuit and butter, plus cocoa, sugar and tea. On 1 December (a rare fine, sunny day) Birdie enjoyed magnificent views of Mount Markham (named for Sir Clements), Mount Longstaff and an immense, unnamed glacier ('an honourable namesake for anybody') on which, from a distance of some 20 miles, he could make out huge crevasses. He took out his camera and began creating a panorama photograph of the mountain range with the 'cavalcade' of eight ponies in the foreground.

With the timing of the demise of each pony now being critical, Scott asked Oates to join his tent so they could discuss equine matters in confidence. Cherry moved in with Birdie, Crean and Taff Evans. That evening they built Southern Barrier depot, filled it with 200lb of Summit rations, other provisions and fuel, and marked it with a sledge that was now surplus to requirements due to Christopher's demise: 'He died as he had lived — hard. At the moment of firing he tossed up his head & the bullet entered just below his brain. He charged away ... & was secured with difficulty nearly giving Keohane a bad bite. The next shot finished him.'

Birdie knew the ponies were generally doing their best but the sight of the dog teams racing into camp with their sledges, full of energy and oblivious to the conditions, made him wonder whether Amundsen, with his dog-sledges and skiers, might already be approaching the Pole. Before they set off on 2 December Scott sought Birdie out and took him aside:

> I guessed that he had decided to shoot another pony & was not wrong. It is all a matter of pony food now ... We are nearing the part where Shackleton met with an appallingly soft surface & it had to be decided against a heavy horse ... the lot fell on [Victor]. ... he is to go at the end of the march tonight. ... Victor did a splendid march, he kept ahead all day & as usual marched into camp first, pulling over 450 lbs easily. It seemed an awful pity to have to shoot a great strong animal & it seemed like the irony of fate to me as I had been downed for over-provisioning the ponies with needless excess of food & the drastic reduction has been made against my strenuous opposition up till the last & it is poor satisfaction to me to know that I was right now that my horse is dead. Good old Victor he has always had a biscuit out of my ration & he ate his last before the bullet sent him to his rest. The death is as swift and painless as it can be ... he is dead in the air, even before he falls. I have depôted one of his hoofs which I hope to take back with me. Here ends my second horse in 83° S, not quite so tragically as my first on the break up of the sea ice but none the less I feel sorry for a beast that has been my constant companion & care for so long. He has done his share in our undertaking anyhow – may I do my share as well when I get into harness myself. The snow has started to fall over his bleak resting place ...

The next morning, in a 'fizzing' south-easterly blizzard, Birdie sadly rearranged sledge-loads and planted the sledge he no longer required in the snow to mark Victor's grave. When they finally left at 2 p.m. he was on skis which, given bright sunshine and good surfaces made him feel as if he was on 'the perfect holiday'. Overnight the wind shifted round again and the driving snow became so thick that Birdie could barely see the neighbouring tent. He helped move the remaining ponies to the leeward side of their protective walls and turn the tents round so snow would not blow in whenever the flaps were opened. As Birdie lay in enforced idleness in his sleeping bag he remembered that Frank Wild (who had accompanied Shackleton to his 'Furthest South') had mentioned a long period of fine weather at this stage in the journey, and wondered whether Shackleton had enjoyed a particularly good season or if they were suffering from a particularly bad one. By now some of the seamen were debating who or what was the 'Jonah' in their midst (the cameras were cited as strong candidates),[9] but by late morning the blizzard had abated and Birdie enjoyed a fine afternoon's skiing:

... the mountains surpassed anything I have ever seen – beside the least of the giants Ben Nevis would be a mere mound & yet they are so immense as to dwarf each other. They are intersected at every turn with mighty glaciers & ice falls & eternally ice-filled valleys that defy description. So clear was every-thing that every rock seemed to stand out & the effect of the sun as he came round was to make the scene still more beautiful.

In the distance Birdie could now see a 'chaos' of ice where the Beardmore Glacier met the Barrier. Given that the Beardmore itself was still hidden behind Mount Hope, Birdie realised how lucky Shackleton had been to find the Southern Gateway which led to it – and what a 'stout hearted fellow' Shackleton had been to explore this region at all. After an afternoon's invig-orating skiing on ice-waves up to 20ft high, Birdie took some readings. He reckoned they were about 13 miles from Mount Hope and that the mountains to his east lay at about 86° South – considerably nearer to the South Pole than they currently were. This suggested to him that if Amundsen (the 'back-handed, sneaking ruffian') had found his way up a glacier like the Beardmore, he might, given a shorter summit journey, have already reached the Pole.[10]

That evening, Cherry's pony Michael was shot, which meant Birdie could now make up a sledge-team with Cherry and Scott, who had entrusted Snippets to Oates following Christopher's death. But the next morning – and for several days thereafter – they found themselves confined to camp, 'comfort-able but impatient', as an unseasonably warm, swirling blizzard half-buried the ponies and their tents:

When I volunteered for this expedition I did not expect or desire a bed of roses ... If I seem at times to growl ... it is because of my anxiety for the success of our object & not for myself. I have been down to bed rock in this country, brought there by the forces of Nature. I have more than once thought 'Shall I see this through?' ... A few miles from us is the greatest gla-cier known to man [and the] Gateway ... The day before yesterday it seemed within our reach – today it might with the Glacier & mountains all be at the North Pole for all we can see ... It is blowing a blizzard such as one might expect to be driven at us by all the fiends of darkness.[11] ... We try to treat it as a huge joke but ... we are wet through, our tents are wet, our bags which are our life to us & the objects of our greatest care, are wet, the poor ponies are soaked & shivering ... our food is wet, everything in & around and about us is the same – wet as ourselves & our cold, clammy clothes.

To conserve food and fuel during their days of idleness they cooked and ate two meals a day instead of three. To pass the time they 'spun yarns', read *By Order of the Company* and other novels Taff Evans had brought with him, and listened to Keohane's new poem, 'The snow is all melting and everything's afloat'.[12] Birdie reluctantly began opening packages of precious Summit rations, which were not due to be touched until they were two days in to their march up the Beardmore. Gradually, the weight of snow on their tents restricted their living space to the extent that even Birdie could not lie out straight in his sleeping bag; by 8 December the blizzard had surrounded them with waist-high snowdrifts. The pony-food had almost run out but they dug out the five 'poor wet sodden miserable creatures' and their sledges in case a march was possible. Birdie, in an effort to cheer Scott up, began 'prognosticating good signs out of everything' and suggesting the current delay meant only 'a little short commons[13] on our return – a trifling matter', although he added 'D.V. we shall march tomorrow' to his journal entry. He had plenty of time to write a letter to May to send back with Meares:

> The weather is what I should find delightful at home – really Christmas like in aspect. ... unfortunately we are unable to appreciate it. ... I don't feel a bit pleased at all the delays & rebuffs but it would be ridiculous not to expect them, neither would I like to see so great a journey pulled off without difficulty. We came down here to meet difficulties & if they are too great for man to overcome we cannot do more than man can do. At present our prospects of success are very bright. It is possible without a succession of such delays for Capt Scott to reach The Pole & get back at a reasonable speed on full ration. If we have more delays we must meet them by longer marches or shorter rations or both ...[14]

He assured May his accounts of events were 'in no way exaggerated', as his journals were private and he had no need to 'play to public sentiment'. He just wanted to do his best for 'Old England' and, although she might think he sounded depressed, he didn't think he really was and still felt privileged, as a person 'without an excessive number of good points', to be a member of Captain Scott's expedition. He was well aware they might not reach the Pole before the Norwegians, but reassured her he was in good spirits; after completing his letter with enquiries about the Maxwells and other Bute residents he signed off with 'hurrah for the Glacier' and a cheerful goodnight.

On 9 December the blizzard finally petered out and they began forging their way through huge snowdrifts towards the Beardmore Glacier. As temperatures rose conditions went from bad to 'diabolical', forcing them to cancel their lunch stop due to a lack of pony-fodder and anxiety about eating further into their precious Summit rations. Birdie and Scott had some differences of opinion regarding navigation, which left them zigzagging for about two hours before settling on Shackleton's route along a chasm – which Birdie had favoured in the first place. That evening, after Bones, Snippets, James Pigg and Nobby had been shot, Birdie helped prepare horse-flesh for immediate consumption and for depoting, along with provisions, more surplus sledges and pony gear.

Now, with the three motor-sledges and all the ponies gone, and the dog teams about to turn back, the next stage was all down to manpower.

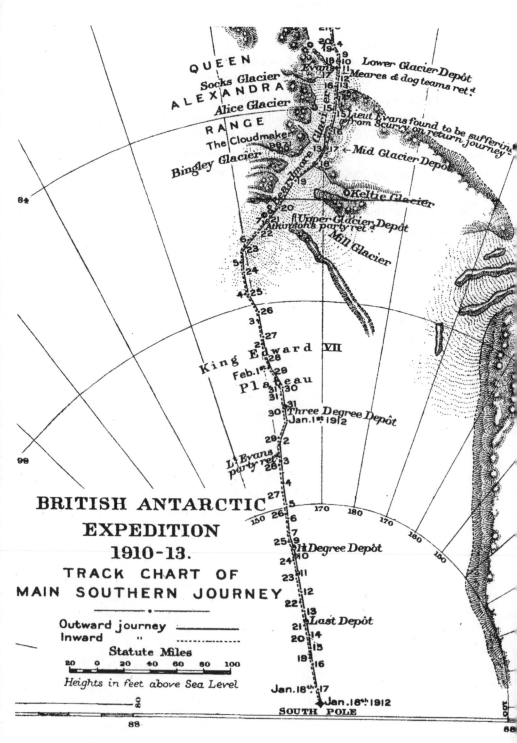

Map 7 Route to the South Pole (on plateau), January 1912. *Map anonymous © private*

15

TO THE POLE

On 10 December 1911 three teams of four men, each pulling a sledge weighing some 600lb, began climbing the Beardmore Glacier: Scott had Wilson, Oates and Taff Evans on his sledge; Teddy Evans had Atkinson, Silas Wright and Lashly; and Birdie was with Cherry, Tom Crean and Pat Keohane.

Birdie's team initially 'bust off with great success on ski', but as the slope steepened, drifts deepened and the sun beat down, Birdie found pulling 'a fearful grind'. The morning's seven hours' labour yielded only 2 miles and a brief afternoon interlude of downhill skiing came to a halt when they encountered a snow-laden williwaw[1] wind rushing down one of the Beardmore's tributary glaciers. Meares, who had postponed his return with the dogs to assist the twelve men to their next depot, was now anxious to leave before fresh snow completely obliterated their outward tracks on the Barrier. Birdie took the opportunity to dash off another letter to Emily:

> In this land of wonderful desolation & grandeur one has the strange feeling that appeals so much to the roving mind. ... I simply revel in the life for its own sake. The delicious feeling of having earned one's meals and rest – no worry now – only marching, observing, navigating, grooming, cooking, etc. – living out one's full allowance of time under conditions that fulfil one's ideas of manliness ... you may be sure of one thing that though I may not get to the Pole or make a splash in the public eye – I shall do much towards the object in hand & the honour of my mother who deserves to have something better than a rolling stone for a son. Alls well for a start. The finish is in the hands of a higher power.[2]

He tore out pages 24 to 46 of his journal and scribbled a few lines to May:

> We are through the Gateway – Oh what a pull we've had! However, here
> we are on the Great Beardmore Glacier at last. It stretches away before us
> like an immense strait ending too far for us to see on high. ... The rocks &
> hills around are simply splendid. The Glacier itself is so immense & huge in
> appearance that it is difficult to conceive it more than a Great Strait with a
> rising floor.

By the next morning Birdie, who had forgotten to put on his goggles the previous day, found his right eye had 'gone bung' and his left was 'pretty dicky'. His
sledge-mates and Oates were also complaining of snow-blindness, and Teddy
Evans and Lashly were feeling the cumulative effects of their long weeks of
enforced manhauling. Birdie organised Lower Glacier depot with Summit provisions, biscuits and cans of fuel oil, changed into a fresh new set of Wolsey
under-drawers and depoted his spare gear – which made room on his sledge
for some Christmas fare he had hidden on a dog-sledge at Cape Evans. After
a farewell lunch, Meares, Dimitri and the dogs sped northwards and the three
manhauling teams began tugging their 800–900lb sledges up the glacier.

The day's journey passed without major mishap, bar Taff Evans half-falling
into a crevasse (skis and all) and Birdie's snow-blindness limiting his navigational abilities. By the evening Birdie could not bear to look at white paper and
it was not until 14 December that he restarted his journal and told Emily about
the most 'back-breaking' work he had ever done. The snow had been deep
and if one member of a team slackened off, the sledge immediately sank, and
required up to fifteen violent jerks to start it up again.

On the morning of 12 December they took five hours to cover a mile;
in the afternoon, despite improved surfaces, they made only 3 miles due to
a snow-blinded Birdie following Teddy Evans' sledge into 'a frightful bog' of
snow, from which they only extricated themselves ninety minutes later. The
next day Birdie's sledge sank in the snow the moment they left camp and it
took four hours to cover less than half a mile: 'I have never pulled so hard or so
nearly crushed my inside into my backbone by the everlasting jerking with all
my strength on the canvas band round my unfortunate tummy.'

On 14 December they worked hard to make 8 miles (still below their
required daily average) but the following day Birdie, with 'sight duly restored
& a more rosy outlook', did a 'splendid bust off on ski' leaving Scott's sledge in
his wake and eventually overhauling Teddy Evans' sledge team (which had left
before them). They covered 8 miles that morning but when swirling snow and

bad light made crevasses impossible to see, Scott reluctantly gave the order to camp. Birdie noticed his leader was in 'quite a paddy with the weather & said [they] had not had a piece of good luck since [they] started'. In terms of food, however, Birdie and several others were finding the fat-rich Summit ration more than they needed – but despite feeling full they were all getting noticeably thinner. On 16 December the weather improved sufficiently for Birdie to resume what he now regarded as something of a sledging competition with Scott. When Birdie failed to keep up with Scott that morning he realised the runners on his sledge had become iced up (due to handling with damp mitts or hands), but when they cleared them at lunchtime the sledge ran so well that two of them had to act as brakemen at the back to prevent it from overrunning the skiers at the front.

Near Cloudmaker Mountain, drift-covered pressure-ridges forced them to abandon skis and resume a monotonous plod, broken only when someone's foot shot into a half-hidden crevasse. That night they camped near the turbulent junction of the Keltie and Beardmore Glaciers – an area where Shackleton had also struggled – and Birdie photographed the 10,000ft Cloudmaker Mountain in bright sunshine.

On 17 December, using crampons and ski-sticks, they inched their way up the glacier until suddenly they came upon a series of huge pressure-ridges:

> … we had the greatest fun in our lives. … It was just like the Scenic Railway,[3] you poised the sledge on a giddy height, aimed her carefully, all four men breaking [sic] with their feet & then a shove & down you would fly, often faster than any switchback. Sometimes … we would all jump on & let her rip. A broken sledge however would be a most serious matter & it needed much care. As an offset against these delightful rushes we had hours of dragging, uphill & across snow filled slopes & hollows that made lifting the feet a labour. We often had to face the sledges & manhaul them inch by inch. However all these were forgotten in one good rush down.

Their roller-coaster journey ended abruptly in hard blue ice, but when they camped for lunch they found to their pleasant surprise that they had covered a good 5 miles that morning.

In the afternoon, despite reasonable surfaces, Birdie's team fell behind Scott's sledge again, but after adjusting their pulling formation and harnesses they caught up. That night they camped halfway up the glacier at an altitude of 3,600ft, in the midst of a sea of pale-blue ice. The next morning Birdie rose early and, having admired the beautiful feathery frost-crystals on the socks he had left out to dry, set up Middle Glacier depot. That morning they struggled over 'hard rippled blue-ice ... like a sea frozen intact while the wind was playing on it'; their sledges regularly capsized but Birdie noted approvingly how Scott avoided the snowy glacier edge as he weaved his way through a chaos of ice. When they camped, visibility was so bad that Birdie abandoned his surveying duties in favour of making a new fixing for his sledgemeter to replace the one Christopher had broken a few weeks previously.

After a late night and short sleep, Birdie awoke to a glorious morning and went outside to photograph the 'tremendous array of splendid mountains', which looked like a source of interesting geological specimens. As they crossed a crevasse-field Birdie found blue ice made fissures easy to see, but his short legs were not ideal for stepping over wide cracks with a heavy sledge behind him. They made almost 15 miles for the day, and after taking observations with Teddy Evans, Birdie was soon sleeping like a log. On 20 December they spent the morning marching over 'the most delightful blue ice surface imaginable' for over 10 miles, but in the afternoon their progress was hampered by bumpy ice. When Birdie stopped to check their distance he saw to his dismay that the entire recording dial of his sledgemeter had been jolted off. Wilson kindly accompanied him back along their trail for about 1½ miles until blizzard conditions forced them to return to camp empty-handed. Scott had already unstrapped his own sledgemeter as a precaution so it fell to Teddy Evans to announce that they had made a record run of over 19 miles that day (22 miles for Birdie and Wilson). Birdie calculated that they were beyond 85° South and over 6,000ft above the Barrier – and within a day's stiff climb of the great plateau. That evening Scott broke the news to Cherry, Atkinson, Silas Wright and Keohane that they would be returning to Cape Evans at the end of the following day's march.[4]

The next morning Birdie's team matched Scott's stiff pace (despite Teddy Evans and Atkinson falling down crevasses the length of their harnesses) and by the evening they had made 11 miles and climbed a further 1,000ft or so. As his tent-mates slept, Birdie prepared stores for the Upper Glacier depot and food packages for those returning to Cape Evans. He also bundled up more journal pages, a roll of film, messages for people at Cape Evans and 'just a line' to Edie to assure her he was 'as fit as could be' and keen to remain in the running for the final stage of the journey:

> Naturally none of us like to turn back ... in another 16 days or so another four will have to turn back. I am expecting to be in charge of that detachment. But one never knows. However I am here to do what I am told & I am all for Capt Scott anyhow ...[5]

On 22 December, Midsummer's Day, Birdie woke up to a cool, windless 0°F ('charming conditions'); he and those who would be continuing cached provisions, glacier climbing equipment and personal effects so their sledge-weights, including food and fuel, would be no more than 190lb per man. Birdie found himself quite moved by Cherry, Atkinson and Silas Wright's farewells and by Cherry's parting gifts of a pair of finnesko he no longer needed and part of a cotton handkerchief he hoped Birdie might find useful. Scott kept Wilson, Oates and Taff Evans on his sledge; Teddy Evans and Lashly joined Birdie and Crean on theirs. After a stiff climb of 10 miles they camped for the night and Birdie took photographs of the Dominion Range, which Shackleton had named in honour of New Zealand. The next morning Birdie rose at 5.45 a.m. to prepare breakfast, following which they built two cairns and pulled the sledges up to a ridge. There they found crevasses which Birdie estimated could have accommodated the *Terra Nova* with ease; luckily most were well bridged with firm snow and despite frequent slips and near-misses everyone made it across safely.

That night Scott, keen to increase their pace, announced they would now rise before 6 a.m. for a 7.45 a.m. start, stop for lunch between 1 p.m. and 2.30 p.m., then march until 6.30 p.m. The new regime made Birdie feel as if all his muscles were being 'tuned up' but they made 14 miles on Christmas Eve across a 'chaos of crevasses'. On 25 December – Christmas Day and Lashly's 44th birthday – they began a 'strange & strenuous' day with a modestly celebratory breakfast of pony meat. As they marched, the headwind 'fairly ripped' at their faces and left Birdie's body feeling numb; it was impossible to shed or add clothes without holding everyone up so he settled for going 'the whole hog' and sometimes being too hot. In the midst of a crevasse-field Lashly suddenly dropped 50ft into a chasm; thanks to his harness holding, the 'undefeated old sportsman' clambered out safely, but his response to cries of 'Happy Christmas' and 'Many Happy Returns of the Day' were unprintable.[6] At lunchtime they celebrated Christmas again with some chocolate and a few raisins (mysteriously produced by Birdie); once they left the crevasses behind, Scott 'got fairly wound up & went on & on' urging his companions forward with cries of '15 miles for Christmas day'. When they finally pitched camp Birdie checked his hypsometer; they had now climbed to 8,000ft, at which altitude he served up Christmas dinner:

We had a great feed which I had kept hidden & out of the official weights since our departure from Winter Quarters. ... a good fat hoosh with pony meat & ground biscuit, a chocolate hoosh made of water, cocoa, sugar, biscuit, raisins & thickened with ... arrowroot (this is the most satisfying stuff imaginable). Then came 2½ sq. inches of plum duff each & a good mug of cocoa … [and] 4 caramels each & 4 squares of crystallised ginger. I positively could not eat all mine & turned in feeling I had made a beast of myself. I wrote up my journal. In fact I should have liked somebody to put me to bed.

As Lashly and Crean dozed, Birdie suggested to Teddy Evans that they should meet up again in England one Christmas and find some poor children and 'just stuff them full of nice things'.[7]

When he awoke on Boxing Day, Birdie felt that the last thing he wanted to do was to strap a harness around his 'poor tummy' and march into a head-wind that would sting his scabbed face, lips and nose. As they climbed Birdie knew he could no longer calculate altitudes using his hypsometer as, since their previous camp, he had inadvertently broken the thermometer element of his instrument. He had hoped and expected to find a spare in the general equip-ment box; having found none he reported the incident to Scott:

> I … got an unusual outburst of wrath … my name is mud just at present – it is rather sad to get into the dirt tub with one's leader at this juncture but accidents will happen & this was not carelessness as I look after my instru-ments with the utmost care. That hypsometer was one of my chief delights & nobody could have been more disgusted than myself at the breakage.

The day went from bad to worse:

> There is something the matter with our sledge … I asked Dr Bill & he said their sledge ran very easily. Ours is nothing but a desperate drag with con-stant rallies to keep up. We certainly manage to do so but I am sure we cannot keep this up for long. We are all pretty well done up tonight after doing 13.3 miles. Our salvation is on the summits of the ridges where we … make up lost ground easily. In soft snow the other team draw steadily ahead & it is fairly heartbreaking to know that you are pulling your life out hour after hour while they go along with little apparent effort.

On the evening of 28 December Birdie settled down to write his journal entry for the day:

> The last few days have been absolutely cloudless with unbroken sunshine for 24 hours – it sounds very nice but the temp never comes above zero … [the] unceasing wind of the great plateau … whistles round the tents – all day it

blows in one's face. … it will be great for sailing the sledges back before it … I should like to know what there is beneath us – mountains & valleys etc. simply levelled off to the top with ice. We constantly come across wind disturbances which I can only imagine are caused by the peaks of ice covered mountains … However they are getting less & less and are now nothing but featureless rises with apparently no crevasses. Our first 2 hours pulling today …

Birdie suddenly stopped writing.

From the start his sledge fell behind Scott's and when Birdie's team eventually caught up, Scott had come over to them and swapped places with Teddy Evans. Scott initially found Birdie's sledge heavy to pull but Birdie's new team managed to keep up with the others despite Scott's feeling that Birdie, Lashly and Crean did not 'swing' with him as the team on his own sledge did.[8] Scott returned to his own sledge but sent Taff Evans over to swap places with Lashly – which appeared to improve the situation until they encountered hard sastrugi. When they stopped for lunch, Scott convened a full-scale conference on possible reasons for Birdie's sledge falling behind: were members of Birdie's team tired? Was their technique less effective as that of Scott's team? Was there (as Birdie suspected) something wrong with their sledge?

That afternoon they reverted to their original teams but swapped sledges. Scott's team initially found no problem with Birdie's sledge but began to struggle as soon as they hit soft snow and could only watch as Birdie's team – pulling Scott's sledge – overhauled them. Following further examination of Birdie's sledge and close questioning of Birdie's team, Scott declared that any problems were due to the team's failure to load and maintain their sledge properly, following which the sledge's structure was now distorted. He told Birdie and his team that he expected them to resolve the problem themselves.[9]

Instead of filling his main journal pages with this sad and lengthy tale, Birdie turned to the back pages of his journal notebook and, just under where he had noted on Christmas Day that there appeared to be 'a difference' with Scott's sledge, simply noted: 'PM lecture on sledges etc.'

Over the following two days Birdie added further short notes to the back pages of his journal:

29th: AM fix up sledge … Kept up in forenoon. Afternoon behind – came in at finish – bad surface.
30th: Adrift from first – stop to re-string sledge. Camped for lunch ½ mile back from others. Another crack in afternoon arrived camp ¾ hours late very hard surface.

On the evening of 30 December Edward Wilson came to Birdie's tent and they had a long talk about the situation. The timing was clearly unfortunate given that Scott would, within the next few days, make his final decision as to who would continue on to the South Pole.[10] On 31 December, in an apparent effort to reduce Birdie's sledge-load, Scott told Birdie and his team to depot surplus gear, including their ski equipment (four pairs of skis, sticks and boots, together weighing some 70lb), which had recently been little-used due to bumpy surfaces. That evening, Taff Evans and Crean worked on the sledges in one tent while Scott hosted a general repair and maintenance session in his tent. On New Year's Day the refurbished sledges ran well, although Birdie's team found it hard marching at an altitude of 9,500ft while the others skied on suddenly improved surfaces. Birdie was in visibly low spirits despite Scott making a point of talking to him and sticks of chocolate being passed round to celebrate New Year.[11] The following day his mood improved following a 13-mile march over comparatively good surfaces – and a sighting of a skua further inland than anyone had ever seen one. That night they camped less than 150 miles from the Pole.

On the morning of 3 January Scott announced that he, Wilson and Taff Evans would definitely be in the South Pole party and that Teddy Evans, Lashly and Crean would definitely be turning back. That left Birdie and Oates, of whom one had wanted to go to the Antarctic since he was 7 years old and the other was keen to reach the Pole for the sake of his regiment.[12]

It seemed that Scott felt both were worthy of their places in the South Pole party, which would now number five. That night Birdie kept his journal notes short: 'Owner came in morning – decision about return of support etc. Last march at 12 miles photographs of party coming in … Squaring up etc.'

He then wrote to Emily from 87° 32' South:

My dearest Mother

I am now sending you a note from what is perhaps the bleakest most unutterable spot in this round world. We have arrived here on our flat feet & dragging our means of livelihood etc as usual. … but you will be pleased to hear that Captain Scott has selected your offspring to accompany him to the Pole or as near it as we are destined to go. … It is terribly hard work this marching in harness for over 9 hours a day through yielding snow. To add to it the wind blows incessantly against us as if to bar us to the confines of the apex of the Earth, & we are going up & up. … we are about 10,000 feet high now[13] & God alone know how high the Pole will be.[14]

While five men might be 'squeezed up' in a four-man tent, Birdie felt the party represented the Royal Navy (Scott and Taff Evans), army (Oates), Royal Indian Marine (himself) and the scientific community (Wilson). Geographically it covered England (Wilson and Scott), Scotland (himself – and Scott via some 'Scotch origin'), Wales (Taff Evans), Ireland (Oates' regiment) and British India (where he and Oates had served). In terms of rank there were captains (Scott and Oates), a lieutenant (Birdie) and a petty officer (Taff Evans). Birdie felt that they were up to the task:

> We are certainly all fit & strong – if thin and often weary at the end of a day's march – This altitude is against us of course – as far as physical effort is con-cerned – but every day reduces the weight we have to pull as also does every depôt we make. The Pole should (D.V.) be pulled off in a fortnights time & then we should be able to get this wind behind our backs & streak for home.

Although he knew that, even with everything in their favour, he was unlikely to be on the ship leaving Cape Evans in early March 1912, he tried to leave Emily with some hope of his early return:

> We cannot possibly get back before some time in March when the ship may or may not have left. However with such splendid companions & every-thing so carefully arranged in the food line (by myself) we ought to journey through this lifeless land without mishap & be safe in our Winter Quarters again in due course. … Things are very hopeful but nothing is absolutely cer-tain in a land of such extremes. I think we are going to reach the Pole. I think the British flag will be the only one to fly there. I shall … thank God that our country has the honour it deserves. … I am no party to record breakers but I realize that the polar business must be cleared up – once & for all – & may the Lord grant that I shall be one of those to see it done. I am hoping that the dogs may meet us returning on the Barrier in which case they will run back with the news if we are too late to catch the ship. I shall be able to send you word & the remainder of my journal then.

Birdie assured Emily that he and his companions felt close to 'those from whom they derive their hope & strength' and that he looked forward to receiving her letters when he returned to Hut Point.

On 4 January Birdie carefully recalculated and rewrapped rations for teams of five and three men and helped repack the sledges. He breakfasted with Crean, Lashly and Teddy Evans. Birdie had initially expected Teddy, as second in command, to be in the South Pole party; although he had recently felt this was less of a foregone conclusion, he still felt sorry for his friend and fellow 'Old Worcester'. Teddy, who had sacrificed his own polar ambitions to accommodate those of Scott, was understandably 'frightfully cut up'. He had also wanted to reach the Pole for his wife Hilda's sake and before leaving he handed Birdie a little silk ensign she had given him to fly at the Pole.[15] Birdie entrusted his 'notes, messages, letters, etc.' to Teddy and bade his erstwhile sledging team farewell. He had slept little the previous night and was rather dreading the journey (particularly because he was now the only one without skis), so was grateful when Teddy Evans, Lashly and a visibly emotional Tom Crean accompanied them southwards for a mile or so and waved them off with a rousing '3 cheers'.

For nine hours Birdie plodded between, but just behind, Scott and Wilson, trying to keep up with his four companions without disturbing their rhythm:

> ... it is a long slog with a well-loaded sledge & more tiring for me than the others as I have no ski – however, as long as I can do my share all day and keep fit it doesn't matter much one way or the other. ... We had our first Nly wind on the plateau today & a deposit of snow crystals made the surface like sand.

By the time they camped the sun had come out so Birdie spread his gear out to dry. Now, in Teddy Evans' absence, he was in sole charge of taking 'sights' as well as recording meteorological data, keeping track of provisions and fuel and taking photographs.[16] For the next few days he found sufficient time and energy to jot down a few words about his march:

> 5th, On ski – sights – Getting on to heavier sastrugi 12.5 [miles].
> 6, ... very heavy sastrugi – afternoon dropped bag walked back. 10.6 miles.
> 7, Depoted ski etc – an hour later surface improved – party returned for them. ... Heavy surface 9.1 [miles] Drift etc in pm camped 7 pm.[17]

On the evening of 7 January Taff Evans asked Wilson to look at a cut he had suffered on his hand while sledge-making on New Year's Eve and which was not healing up; Wilson cleaned and dressed it securely so Taff could continue with his duties of pitching the tent and looking after equipment.

Over the next few days Birdie recorded good and bad news:

> 8th, Bliz – no march. ... drifts over tent ... Air very thick.
> 9th, Bliz. No march forenoon. My watch dropping 26 mins ... bad light fuzzy weather – Furthest South. Fine in evening. Long sights, etc. Good surface.

Now they had passed Shackleton's famous 'Furthest South' landmark of 88° 23' South, they were within 100 miles of the Pole. The fact that one of the two carefully calibrated watches that Birdie used as compasses (to take navigational readings) had dropped time was worrying.[18] There was no third watch to check against the possibility that the second watch might have gained twenty-six minutes, as Wilson had given his watch to Atkinson when the latter had turned back. Although Birdie sometimes needed to touch the hands of his watch when taking readings, he always worked with bare fingers to avoid any accidents; now, although he could still check latitudes, longitudes would be more difficult to verify.

At lunchtime on 10 January they camped at 88° 29' South and constructed 1½ Degree depot (named for its approximate distance from the Pole); they lightened their sledge by depoting 30lb of biscuits, a week's provisions for five men, oil and some surplus gear. They were now averaging about 11 miles a day and soon crossed 89° South. By the morning of 14 January they were only 60 miles from the Pole but were now facing a chill southerly wind wearing balding finnesko which had lost their insulating qualities. Oates was feeling the cold the most but Birdie and the others were suffering too: 'cold fingers and feet ... Bills eyes, Evans hand. Face freezing up.' On 15 January they made a provisions depot with everything bar nine days' rations to see them to the Pole and back; by the time Birdie took sightings and wrote them up he was too tired to make a journal entry.

On 16 January they lunched at 89° 42' South, 18 miles from the Pole, and resumed their march in good spirits, confident of reaching their destination the following day. Suddenly, Birdie's sailor's eyes noticed a strange bump on the horizon. His initial reaction was that it was a cairn, but in a spirit of optimism he decided it could equally be large sastrugi. When he noticed a black spot beside the object he knew it was not simply a snow feature. As they approached they saw sledge and ski tracks and the pawmarks of many dogs, and knew that they were looking at a black depot flag and the remains of a camp. The sight of more tracks heading south across virgin snow told them that Amundsen's party must – barring a catastrophic accident – have already reached the South Pole. Over the next few hours they talked much but nothing changed the facts: Amundsen's party had, thanks to using dogs rather than ponies, been able to leave earlier than they had; they had found the route they needed through the Transantarctic Mountains to the plateau and had been able to ski and sledge across the plateau towards the South Pole. Wilson sat down to sketch Amundsen's flag and the remains of the Norwegian camp. They decided to pitch their own tent a few miles closer to the Pole, away from reminders that they were now extremely unlikely to be first to the Pole.

On the morning of 17 January, after a restless night, they rose and followed the Norwegians' tracks into a strong headwind. After some 3 miles and two marker-cairns, the tracks veered off in a direction which Birdie reckoned was too far west if they wanted to reach the Pole as quickly as possible. They struck out on their own course and by 12.30 p.m. had covered another 4 miles. Evans' hands were getting cold so they camped for lunch and ate a morale-boosting 'week-end' hoosh. In the afternoon they made a further 7 miles and camped early so Birdie could take a full set of readings and sightings. When he finished he joined the others for another good hoosh followed by sticks of chocolate all round and cigarettes for the smokers. He then retired to his sleeping bag to do his calculations and to write to Emily:

> South Pole 17 Jan '12
> My dearest Mother
> A line from the spot might not be out of place though I am pretty busy with observations & must turn out again at 1 a.m. so as to get the sun from all angles. I dont suppose you ever thought your son would be at the apex of the Earth. Well here I really am & very glad to be here too. It is a bleak spot – what a place to strive so hard to reach – I am nearer to you here than at Winter Quarters, in fact a rapid flight up the Greenwich Meridian would be my shortest way home. Now the great journey is done it only remains for us to get back. Fortunately we are all fit & well & should with luck catch the ship in time for the news. Every day will now bring me nearer to your letters & all I want to hear & know. It is sad that we have been forestalled by the Norwegians but I am glad that we have done it by good British manhaulage. That is the traditional British sledging method & this is the greatest journey done by man unaided since we left our transport at the foot of the Glacier – We have now nearly 800 miles to tramp home with our sledge. I could not have better companions – we are a most congenial party & five is a pleasant little crowd when one is so far from home.[19]

On the morning of 18 January Birdie went through his calculations with Scott and they agreed they were about 3½ miles off the Pole itself – 1 mile beyond it and 3 to the right. As they marched Birdie spotted what he thought might be another cairn. It was Roald Amundsen's tent, where they found a note confirming that he and four companions had reached the South Pole on 16 December 1911. Amundsen had also left two letters, one addressed to King Haakon of Norway, the other to Scott, requesting him to ensure the letter to the king was posted in due course.[20] The Norwegians had also abandoned some mitts (which Birdie sequestered), sleeping socks and navigational aids, including a hypsometer – of which, like Birdie's, the thermometer was broken. Scott wrote a note to leave in Amundsen's tent (confirming their presence at the Pole), Wilson made some sketches and Birdie took photographs of his dejected companions beside the tent.

When they reached Birdie's South Pole fixing, they made camp, built a small cairn and erected their Union Jack and sledge-flags.[21] Birdie planted his camera in the snow, checked the exposure, adjusted the focus, then ran back, sat down and with his bare fingers pulled the string attached to the shutter. They swapped positions and took several more photographs. That night Birdie, confident he had now 'fixed' the South Pole, completed his records and mapped a 5-mile radius around the Pole, showing their morning camp, Amundsen's tent and South Pole markings and, at the centre, their own cairn and flag, duly labelled 'South Pole 17th & 18th January 1912'.[22] That done, he wrote to his sisters:

Dearest May

We have found the exact spot of the South Pole today & left the British flag there – I had the honour to be the observer – in fact I have navigated the party here & done all the observations since Teddy Evans returned. Amunsden's [*sic*] people left a tent … [t]hey were here exactly a month ago – I am awfully sorry for Capt. Scott who has taken the blow very well indeed. They had 5 people also. … They must have found an easy route up … They had been running on ski alongside their dog sledges. I was glad of a pair of their reindeer mits having lost my own dogskins some days back. We now head for home & all it means – news from my own home is my first thought – Then news from the outer world, to see everybody we left in the good old ship again & last but not least the fleshly considerations of unlimited rest and food. You will be glad to hear I have been to this spot I am sure.

Dearest Edie

… Long ere you read this you will have heard that I had the honour to be included among the 5 British representatives at the South Pole. … A better party one could not wish to be among. I am glad to say I am fit & strong having walked for 380 miles with a pony & pulled a heavy sledge for 400 miles more chiefly at an altitude of 10,000 feet. Of course none of us are as strong as we were & one feels inexpressibly weary at the end of a long march if the surface has been heavy – a good meal & a nights rest however & you are as fit as ever. Our ration is an excellent one, but we could all eat far more needless to say — 34 ozs a day is however enough for us to work well on. As you will have heard the Norwegian's dogs brought them here long before our feet could bring us. In fact they were actually here while we were struggling on the Glacier. They probably found an easy way up & had a very fast journey. Well, we have got here too & if ever a journey has been accomplished by honest sweat ours has. We will have manhauled over 1200 miles before we reach home again.[23]

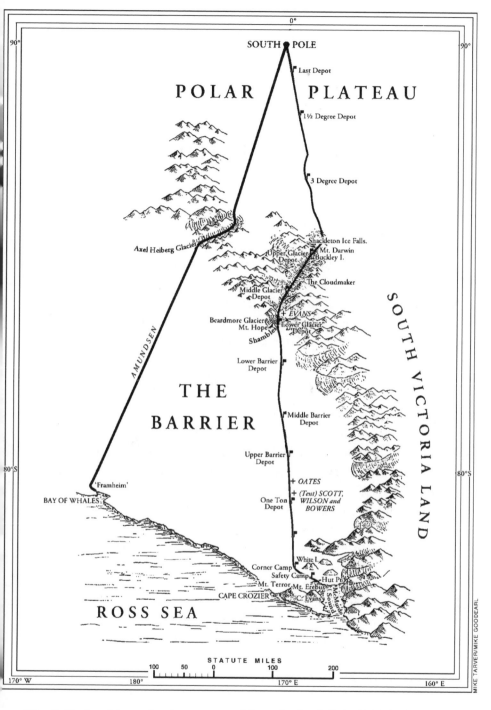

Map 8 Scott and Amundsen's routes to and from the South Pole. © *Michael Tarver, Mike Goodearl*

16

THE LONG HAUL BACK

On Friday 19 January 1912 Scott, Wilson, Birdie, Oates and Taff Evans set out to march almost 800 miles back to Hut Point. The only chance of their news reaching the *Terra Nova* before she left McMurdo Sound was if they maintained a good daily average mileage and if someone from Hut Point or Cape Evans met them on the Barrier with a dog team and sped back to the ship with a message.

Following their first day's march Birdie resumed his journal:

> During breakfast time I sewed a flap attachment on to the hood of my green hat so as to prevent the wind from blowing down my neck on the march. We got up the mast & sail on the sledge & headed North picking up Amundsen's cairn & our outgoing tracks shortly afterwards ... with much relief [we] left all traces of the Norwegians behind ... In the afternoon we ... fairly slithered along before a fresh breeze. It was heavy travelling for me not being on ski but one does not mind being tired if a good march is made. We did 16 [miles] altogether for the day & so should pick up our ... Depot tomorrow afternoon.

The next day, thanks to their makeshift mast and groundsheet sail, and another 'good sailing breeze', they reached their first return depot and picked up four days' food, fuel and personal gear. By evening they had covered about 18 miles but, as a blizzard set in, Oates looked tired and was clearly feeling the cold. The next morning the blizzard trapped them in their tent, but in the afternoon, with sail hoisted, they made 5½ miles. They had been climbing steadily since leaving the Pole and now, at an altitude of 10,000ft, were finding marching even with a light sledge exhausting. When they camped on 22 January they were within 30 miles of 1½ Degree depot, and the fuel and ten days' provisions which would see them through to Three Degree depot.

On 23 January the sledge ran 'like a bird' for 15 miles, so much so that Birdie had to act as brakeman as well as navigator; by the time they stopped everyone's hands were so cold they could hardly pitch their tent. Evans' fingers were badly blistered, his nose was white, hard and congested from frostbite and he clearly felt frustrated at his condition; Oates was suffering badly from cold feet and Wilson was afflicted by snow-blindness.[1] Birdie and Scott were still in reasonable condition but were feeling perpetually hungry.

The next day the southerly gale was so strong that the sledge overran (despite the sail being at half mast and Oates and Birdie braking at the rear); they camped after 7 exhausting miles with a further 7 miles to go to 1½ Degree depot. The following morning another raging blizzard confined them to their tent – Birdie was now seriously worried that their enforced stops and slow progress would soon put them 'in queer street' in terms of rations, but when the wind dropped in the afternoon they sailed into 1½ Degree depot where fuel, food and depoted personal gear awaited them. That night, Oates' feet were still chilled from acting as brakeman and Wilson was dousing his snow-blinded eyes with zinc sulphate and cocaine.[2]

On 26 January Birdie noted that it was now a year since they had set out on the depot journey – a year that had turned him into 'an old hand at Polar travelling' who was now returning from the South Pole. Wilson's snow-blindness was gradually improving but Evans' frostbitten fingers were getting worse and Oates' big toe was turning blue-black.[3] They were all losing weight (particularly Evans) and would, as they marched, console and torture themselves with long discussions about wonderful meals, past and future. Birdie had again stopped making his nightly journal entries but was cheered to find beside the track his dogskin mitts, which like Evans' night-boots and Oates' pipe (now also retrieved) had been dropped on the way south. A 16-mile march on 28 January and a longer one the following day encouraged Birdie to restart his journal:

… we picked up the memorable camp where I transferred to the advance party. How glad I was to change over – The camp was much drifted up & immense sastrugi were everywhere … We did 10.4 miles before lunch … it was beastly cold & my hands were perished. In the afternoon I put on my dogskin mits & was far more comfortable. A stiff breeze with drifts … temp -25°. … We completed 19.6 miles this evening & so are only 24 miles from our precious Depôt. It will be bad luck indeed if we dont get there in a march & a half anyhow.

Birdie found out later that Wilson – who had been skiing with Scott and Birdie while Oates and Evans walked – had damaged his *tibialis anterior* tendon.[4] The next morning, nursing a bruised and swollen shin, Wilson walked beside the sledge while Birdie used his skis. Despite this they managed almost 20 miles. That evening Wilson tended Oates' foot and dressed Evans' fingers which were now, following the loss of several nails, raw and sore. On 30 January heavy surfaces and hunger slowed them to 13½ miles, but the following day they picked up more rations at Three Degree depot and Birdie retrieved his depoted skis after almost 600 miles of marching.

On 2 February, following two good skiing days, Scott tumbled down a steep slope and damaged his shoulder. Birdie was now the only fully fit person out of five, but they were now within about four days of the top of the Beardmore and had seven days' food to cover 65 miles to Upper Glacier depot.[5]

Birdie recorded that 3 February was a day of mixed fortunes: 'Splendid day – little wind – Bills leg still bad also Evans' fingers & Capt. S's shoulder. ... Good going on old tracks ... missed tracks later, decided to head N irrespective of old tracks – 16 miles.' The next day, just before their lunch stop, Scott and Evans tumbled into a hidden crevasse, but they still managed to complete an excellent day's march of just over 18 miles. That evening, Birdie did most of the camp-making in temperatures some 20°F below those they had experienced at similar latitudes on the outward journey.[6] In the tent, Wilson examined and tended Oates' blackening toes; the soldier's face was also turning a worrying shade of yellow and Evans' frostbitten nose was now in almost as sorry a state as his blistered, frozen fingers.[7] That night Birdie turned in without making a journal entry.[8]

On 5 February a field of wide crevasses forced them into zigzagging for 18 miles against a biting wind. The following day, temperatures plunged to the extent that even the hardy Wilson was feeling the cold. By 7 February food was running low and when Birdie checked what remained, he was horrified to find that a tin of biscuits – a full day's supply of one of their staples – was unaccountably missing; he was distraught as he had checked and rechecked everything as they went along and knew they were not eating more than their daily allowances.[9] When they finally reached the depot they found a note from Teddy Evans saying that he, Lashly and Crean had passed through safely about three weeks previously. In another few miles all twelve men would be safely off the plateau, but Birdie by now had fallen out of the habit of recording news (however good or bad) in his journal.

On 8 February, at a height of just over 5,000ft, they stepped from their tent onto rock rather than snow and ice for the first time in fourteen weeks. Their morning march, in a searing southerly wind, was miserable but when they camped for lunch the temperature rose and they spread out their sodden sleeping bags and wet clothing to dry. That afternoon they 'geologised' and collected samples of dolerite, limestone and weathered coal peppered with fossils and vegetable traces; the following morning, in a relatively balmy 10°F, Wilson sketched while Birdie collected more rock specimens.[10] Refreshed and rested, they were now ready for the 100-mile descent of the Beardmore Glacier.

During their first afternoon the temperature suddenly rose to 12°F and they found themselves plunged into unfathomable murk which curtailed their march. The following day visibility was still poor and, with less than two days' rations in hand, they stumbled into the most jumbled field of crevasses Scott had ever seen. For three hours they tacked hither and thither and when they eventually broke out of the icy chaos they were confronted by a series of huge, closely packed chasms. When they finally camped at 10 p.m. they had been marching for twelve energy-sapping hours, but felt they should restrict themselves to short rations rather than risk running out of food.

On 12 February they breakfasted on tea, thin hoosh and biscuit. That morning they passed one of their outward camps but a bad steering decision in the afternoon landed them in another maze of cracks and crevasses;[11] by 9 p.m., following several differences of opinion and shifts of tack, they were in the midst of even worse ice-turmoil.[12] They camped and ate another meagre dinner, following which Birdie calculated they now had one meal each left. Despite their anxieties they slept well but woke to find Cloudmaker Mountain swathed in mist.

As the gloom lifted they breakfasted on a biscuit each, strapped on crampons and headed downhill. Evans' alleged sighting of Middle Glacier depot proved to be a false alarm, but it was not long afterwards that Wilson spotted the depot flag. They stopped, read notes from Atkinson and Evans (both of whose parties had passed through safely), ate a good meal and gratefully loaded three and a half days' provisions onto their sledge. On 15 February they made 14 miles but progress was painful. Wilson's leg still troubled him, he and Birdie were both suffering badly from snow-blindness, and Taff Evans had, in addition to his other ailments, developed a bad foot-blister and was so debilitated by the end of the day that he was unable to help make camp. After a dinner of thin pemmican hoosh and biscuit they all went to bed hungry.

They covered 7½ miles during the morning of 16 February, but by the afternoon Taff was giddy and feeling sick; after he collapsed in the snow they managed to raise him but he could only shuffle beside the sledge. At night-camp Wilson suggested that Taff's not inconsiderable physical problems – the infected cut on his hand, frostbitten fingers and face, foot-blister, perpetual hunger and possible after-effects of crevasse falls – were exacerbated by his distress at being unable to carry out camp-making and other duties. That night they again went to bed hungry. The next morning, 17 February, Taff looked the better for a good sleep and declared, as he invariably did, that he felt well and ready for their march. They helped him onto his skis but had not gone far before his ski-shoes fell off; when they continued to do so after several adjustments they undid his harness so he could walk behind the sledge. Despite their all making slow progress over difficult surfaces, Taff fell further and further behind, so they increased the number of stops to allow him to catch up with them. When they spoke to him he seemed befuddled: on one occasion he asked Birdie for a piece of string; on another he assured Scott all was well.

As Taff drifted further astern they camped, boiled water for tea, made and ate their lunch – but whenever they looked back down the track Taff was still in the distance. They left the sledge and tent and skied back to meet him. Scott arrived first to find his long-standing friend on his knees, frostbitten hands bare and clothing awry. Taff was unsure what had happened but suggested he might have fainted. They tried to get him to his feet but after he collapsed back onto the snow, Birdie, Wilson and Scott fetched the sledge, leaving Oates (who was now also having difficulty in walking) with Taff. When Birdie, Wilson and Scott returned Taff was drifting into unconsciousness. They rolled him onto the sledge and hauled him back to the tent, where he died peacefully a few hours later.[13] Hunger and frostbite had clearly played their part in his demise but Wilson wondered if Taff's final decline had owed something to a brain injury incurred when he had banged his head during a crevasse fall.

Scott, Wilson, Oates and Birdie buried Taff's body in the snow, packed up camp and, in the small hours of 18 February, made their way to Lower Glacier depot. After five hours' sleep, they rose at 2 p.m., loaded their sledge with rations and continued to Shambles Camp, where the last few ponies had met their end. With five men's rations for a four-man team, they allowed themselves a good hoosh of pony meat before heading towards Mount Hope where Wilson wanted to collect some rock samples. After a sound night's sleep they sat in the sunshine and adjusted their sledge for the next leg of their journey – a task Taff would, until recently, have carried out with willing dexterity. At noon they began pulling their refurbished sledge loaded with provisions, retrieved personal possessions and rock samples. Although the sand-like Barrier surface restricted their progress to 5 miles, they ate another nourishing pony-meat and pemmican hoosh before retiring to sun-dried sleeping bags feeling better than they had for days.

On 20 February the temperature suddenly dropped and they struggled on poor surfaces for 7 miles to reach Desolation Camp, where, on the outward journey, they had been trapped by a blizzard for four days – and from where they now discovered some pony meat had mysteriously gone missing. The next day they managed 8½ miles on poor surfaces but they knew they needed to increase their pace still further in order to reach Hut Point before the end of March, or even complete the next stages of their journey on full rations. On 22 February, thanks to a fresh south-easterly, they made good progress but Birdie's suggestion of steering east resulted in their missing a pony-meat cairn (possibly the remains of Victor). With visibility worsening they decided against retracing their steps so camped, ate the pony meat they had with them and retired early.

The next morning Birdie rose early to take a set of angles which became the basis of a somewhat inconclusive discussion between him and Scott; by lunch-time Birdie had spotted an old double cairn which suggested they were at least parallel with their outward tracks. Wilson was still suffering from his latest bout of snow-blindness but they made 8 miles in seven hours, which made them feel their pulling power was holding up. On 24 February they arrived at Southern Barrier depot where they found, as expected, ten days' packaged rations. Disappointingly, however, there was less fuel oil than anticipated and the depoted pony meat (the remains of the unlamented Christopher) had gone off.[14] They found another three notes: Meares said they had experienced difficult surfaces, Atkinson reported that Keohane had been ill but was now recovering and Teddy Evans mentioned his party had suffered from high temperatures and poor surfaces.

That night the temperature dropped to -17°F, comparable to the levels they would have expected on the plateau. They were all in low spirits, a situation not improved when Scott criticised Birdie's skiing technique and offered suggestions for improvement. Birdie, who had through no fault of his own skied considerably less than the others during the Southern journey, was stung by Scott's words but eventually accepted his leader's assurance that he was not questioning Birdie's commitment to the task in hand. By evening they had notched up 11 miles, their first double-digit distance for some time. During the night the temperature plunged to -37°F but by the morning Wilson's snow-blindness had improved sufficiently for him to join Birdie at the front of the sledge and give Scott a break from navigating. They advanced 11½ miles for nine hours' pulling, and camped within 43 miles of Middle Barrier depot.

The next morning, in a temperature of -33°F, they struggled to don their footgear but kept their morale up during the march by discussing when and where a dog-sledge might come to meet them.[15] When they camped the temperature was -37°F but they were 12 miles nearer their depot with six days' food and three days' fuel in hand. On 28 February, following an overnight low of -40°F, they forced cold feet into frozen finnesko – a process which was by now particularly painful for Oates. They marched for 11½ miles into a biting headwind, made camp, prepared and ate a hot pony-meat hoosh and retired to their sleeping bags before the inevitable drop in temperature. That night, Wilson was too tired and cold to make an entry in his journal. Birdie, having already abandoned his journal, was struggling to keep up his full set of navigational and other records.[16]

On Wednesday 29 February – Leap Year Day – Birdie and Wilson donned fresh, comfortably dry finnesko. All day they struggled against a Force 4 north-westerly gale but camped in the knowledge that they were within a day's march of their precious depot. The next morning, following a bone-chilling overnight low of -41.5°F, they reached Middle Barrier depot in good light. By now they were virtually out of fuel so were disturbed to discover that the fuel cans contained significantly less than they expected; this was particularly worrying given that their next depot was over 70 miles away and that, in current temperatures, they needed more fuel than previously to melt snow and ice into water.

As Wilson tended Oates' feet that night, Birdie and Scott could see the damage the cold spell was doing to the stoical soldier's feet. On 2 March they rose early but only left at 8 a.m. due to Oates' struggles with his footgear; as they marched, poor visibility masked tracks and cairns, and rough surfaces offset any benefit from following winds. The next day poor surfaces brought the sledge to a grinding halt; after heaving for over four hours for a gain of only 4½ miles they conceded defeat and camped. After a good warming hoosh they climbed into their sleeping bags, hoping for better things in the morning.

On 4 March they rose well-rested and emerged from the tent into bright sunshine, but by the end of the morning they had only gained 3½ miles for four and a half hours' strenuous pulling. With some 40 miles to go to Mount Hooper depot, they had a week's food in hand but only three or four days' fuel. Oates perked up following a hearty lunch and a rise in temperature to -20°F and they made a further 5 or so miles before camping. In the tent that evening Birdie and Wilson tried to look on the bright side: temperatures could stay at the current higher levels; the returning parties might all be safely back at Hut Point; a dog team might already be on its way south to meet them.

On the morning of 5 March Oates awoke to find his left foot had swollen badly during the night. He struggled on and they camped that night within 30 miles of their depot. After another dinner of full rations they discussed what they would do when they returned home, but by now Oates could only rouse himself occasionally to join in the conversation. Before they climbed into their frozen sleeping bags, Wilson, bare-fingered, gently tended Oates' badly damaged feet. They all slept soundly and even Scott failed to wake at his usual early hour. Overnight Oates' left foot deteriorated further; he could hardly get into his footgear and now limped painfully beside the sledge; when they stopped to hunt for tracks he would sit on the sledge while the others unharnessed themselves and peered around in the snow. That day they only made 6½ miles, significantly below the 9-mile average they needed to maintain if they were not to run out of fuel.

As Wilson tended Oates' feet in the evening, Birdie and Scott worked on making a spirit lamp to use when oil for the primus stove ran out – as it surely would do if there was another fuel shortage at Mount Hooper depot. The following morning, 7 March, Oates' left foot looked considerably worse and it took him an hour or so to don his footgear. By now, Wilson was suffering from spending hours kneeling, motionless and bare-fingered, in low temperatures tending Oates' feet. That morning the sun came out again, but a morning of slow pulling advanced them only 4 miles. With Mount Hooper within striking distance they tried to cheer themselves with the thought that someone with a dog team might have already deposited more rations and – more importantly – more fuel.

On 9 March, with Oates hobbling painfully alongside the sledge, they reached Mount Hooper depot, but immediately realised that no one had been there since Meares and the returning parties had passed through and taken their alloted rations and fuel allowances. This raised the worrying possibility that something had happened to Meares or the dogs during the final leg of their journey and that, if so, One Ton depot might also not yet have been restocked. All they could do was plough on. Birdie was still navigating but now made few, if any, daily records before falling asleep.

On the morning of 10 March Oates asked Wilson for his professional opinion as to whether he had any chance of making it back. Wilson said he did not know. They were all aware, however, that as a foursome they were making slower progress than the three healthier ones would on their own. When they left the tent the weather was calm, but within an hour a howling northwesterly forced them to camp and spend the rest of the day shivering in their tent. Overnight Oates' hands became almost as bad as his feet and he could barely get dressed for the march. As they openly discussed his condition, Oates seemed to be asking for advice, but Birdie, Wilson and Scott could only urge him to continue as best he could. Unspoken words hung in the air as Scott virtually ordered Wilson to open his medicine case and give his three companions thirty opium tablets each; after he had done so Wilson closed his medicine case in which there remained one tube of morphine. The next day tracks proved elusive but Scott, Wilson and Birdie dragged the sledge for another 7 miles while Oates hobbled painfully beside it. Following their evening meal Birdie calculated they had six days' rations, which should, at their current rate of progress (around 7 miles a day), sustain them for 42 miles. They were, however, still 55 miles away from One Ton depot.

On 12 March three of them marched and Oates hobbled for another 7 miles. They woke the next day to a temperature of -37°F and a strong northerly headwind that made marching impossible; by the time the weather had cleared and they had clambered into their frozen marching gear and footwear it was 2 p.m. They made 5¼ miles before stopping for a belated lunch, but when Scott suggested they make a late afternoon march, Oates, Birdie and Wilson protested that they felt too cold to start up again. In an effort to save precious fuel they agreed they should prepare and eat their supper in the dark. On 14 March a southerly wind initially filled their sail but by mid-morning the wind swung westwards and began piercing their marching gear and mitts. By lunchtime Wilson was so cold that he could hardly get his skis off; by the time Scott and Birdie made camp the temperature had dropped to -43°F and Oates' left foot had received another dose of frostbite. Scott, Wilson and Birdie, who were now barely staving off frostbite themselves, were baffled by the unexpected ferociousness of the temperatures and winds given the time of year.

At lunchtime on 15 March Oates announced that he simply could not struggle on any further and suggested that the others should leave him in his sleeping bag to die. Birdie, Wilson and Scott could not abandon their stoical companion and helped him rise and prepare for the march, coaxing him a few miles closer to One Ton depot. After they camped that night even Edward Wilson's solicitous care could do little to relieve Oates' intense pain and suffering. As Wilson worked on his feet, Titus spoke of his devoted mother – who, like Wilson, possessed a strong Christian faith – and his regiment, whom he hoped would be proud he had reached the South Pole. He asked Wilson to forward his personal diary to his mother and to write to her on his behalf, as due to the state of his hands he had been unable to do so recently.[17] That night Oates fell asleep for what he clearly hoped would be the last time.

The next morning, all four men awoke to the familiar sound of a raging blizzard. As tent-flaps were opened for the morning weather inspection, Birdie's friend Titus, with little ado and few words, crawled outside and away from the tent into the whiteness, still wearing his night footgear.[18] Oates had, determinedly independent to the last, made his own decision as to when to leave his companions.

Scott, Wilson and Birdie were now in a position to increase their pace in the hope of reaching One Ton depot before their rations (which now included Oates' share) ran out. As the blizzard that had enveloped their friend was set in for the day, they were left sitting in their tent, pondering what had just happened and considering their own prospects. The next morning they embarked on a bone-chilling march, which ended with lunch eaten in a temperature of -40°F. By now even Scott, who was still regularly writing his journal (the basis of his reports to the Central News Agency and a planned book on the expedition), was losing track of dates and admitted to being uncertain as to whether or not it was now Saturday 17 March (which would have been Oates' 32nd birthday). They were at their fourteenth outward camp, 30 miles short of One Ton depot and at roughly the latitude the depot would have been had it not been for sick ponies and poor weather on the outward journey. All three now felt perpetually cold (other than immediately following a hot meal) and were on the verge of serious frostbite. Birdie, despite having witnessed his friend crawl out to his death, tried to keep cheerful and do what he could to ensure they reached One Ton depot as soon as possible.[19] Before leaving camp they lightened their sledge by leaving a theodolite, a camera and Oates' sleeping bags beside some pony-walls.

At lunchtime on 18 March they reckoned the depot lay 21 miles away – a distance they would, until recently, have easily covered in two or three days. They debated whether they could lighten their sledge further but all that remained was their diminishing rations and fuel, the minimum of equipment, their only tent and sleeping bags, some spare clothing, their diaries and expedition records, and the geological specimens which Wilson felt they must take back by way of scientific record. By now, Wilson's feet were in the best condition, as Scott, who had previously managed to avoid being badly frostbitten, had been forced through his own fault to cede the title of 'best feet'. This sorry state of affairs had resulted from an ill-advised attempt to enliven his pemmican with a spoonful of curry powder, which had led to indigestion, a sleepless night and such fatigue the following day that he had failed to notice his right foot 'go'. Although Birdie's feet were also beginning to suffer from frostbite, he was in better overall condition than Scott or Wilson, but there was now little to choose between them. Due to the shortage of fuel they ate their pemmican cold that night and limited themselves to a half-pannikin of cocoa heated on their homemade spirit lamp; as the welcome warmth diffused through their bodies they felt ready for a good night's sleep.

On the morning of 19 March they marched into a headwind in -40°F and camped for lunch 15½ miles from One Ton depot. At their present rate of progress they might, weather permitting, reach their next goal in three days, but they now only had two days' rations and a day's fuel left. That afternoon they made another 4½ miles and camped some 11 miles from the depot. Scott's right foot was in such a state that he could hardly walk and he was worried that with no hot food or drink the trouble would continue to spread until amputation might be necessary. On 20 March the blizzard kept them trapped in the tent. The next day was little better, but Wilson and Birdie remained ready to set out for One Ton depot whenever possible; once there, they would feed themselves, pick up provisions and fuel, and return to Scott.

Birdie and Wilson woke up on 22 March with the firm intention of setting out for One Ton depot. The journey might take two days but conditions could scarcely be worse than those they had experienced on their Cape Crozier expedition. As a doctor, Wilson might feel he should stay with his incapacitated leader, but Atkinson's experience had shown them that one man, however fit, could quickly become lost in a blizzard. Now, Birdie had no rations to account for or arrange into packages, no pony to exercise or care for, no cooking duties and no records to write up. In anticipation of leaving the tent to march to One Ton depot he wrote to Emily – as he had done before every stage of his momentous journey:

Date uncertain, about March 22nd 1912.
Blizzard Camp 11' S. of 1 Ton Depôt.
My own dearest Mother
  As this may possibly be my last letter to you I am sorry it is such a short scribble. I have written little since we left the Pole but it has not been for want of thinking of you & the dear girls. We have had a terrible journey back. – Seaman Evans died on the glacier & Oates left us the other day – we have had terribly low temperatures on the Barrier & that and our sick companions have delayed us till too late in the season which has made us very short of fuel & we are now out of food as well. Each depot has been a harder struggle to reach, but I am still strong & hope to reach this one with Dr. Wilson & get the food & fuel necessary for our lives. God alone knows what will be the outcome of the 23 miles march we have to make, but my trust is still in Him & in the abounding grace of my Lord & Saviour whom you brought me up to trust in & who has been my stay through life. In His keeping I leave you & am only glad that I am permitted to struggle on to the end. When mans extremity is reached God's help may put things right & although the end will be painless enough for myself I should so like to come through for your dear sake. It is splendid to pass however with such companions as I have & as all

5 of us have mothers & wives you will not be alone. There will be no shame however & you will know I have struggled to the end. Much and dearest love to your dear self and May and Edie – Oh how I do feel for you when you hear all – you will know that for me the end was peaceful as it is only sleep in the cold.

Your ever loving son to the end and in this life & the next when we will meet & when God shall wipe all tears from our eyes
  H R Bowers.[20]

'H R Bowers' might seem formal but anyone who found the letter would know, if the worst came to the worst, who had written it.

Wilson and Birdie did not set out for One Ton depot that day, or the next, or the next. As a blizzard closed in, all they could do was consider their stark choices: they could try to rally themselves and pull Scott on the sledge, probably at the expense of some of their equipment, journals or specimens, for eleven long, slow miles; alternatively, they could travel as a pair, lighter and faster, but would then need to retrace their steps with a food-laden sledge to find and feed Scott. Having done that, they would need to make a third march, pulling the sledge, Scott, tent, food and whatever else they could back to the depot. By that time Birdie and Wilson would have marched almost 35 miles and would still have about 150 miles to go to Hut Point. As the Antarctic winter closed in their companions would be able to do little or nothing to find or help them.

Outside the tent the snow whirled. Inside the three men eked out their final rations and fuel and tried to keep as warm as possible until it passed, or the inevitable happened.[21] As Scott wrote letters Birdie and Wilson conserved their diminishing energy. As they all became weaker, colder and sleepier there seemed little use for the pills Wilson had so reluctantly distributed.[22]

Birdie wrote no more letters, but before placing his letter to Emily in an envelope he added a footnote: 'My gear that is not on the ship is at Mrs Hatfield's Marine Hotel, Sumner, New Zealand.' Birdie liked everything to be in good order.

Wilson wrote a few letters – to his wife, to members of his family and close circle, and to Mrs Oates, to whom he described her son's self-sacrificial death. Scott wrote to Oriana Wilson, to Emily Bowers, to his wife and members of his family, to those who had supported his mission and to the public, to whom he wanted to explain the outcome of the expedition. Some letters were completed in one session, others over a number of days as he added details and postscripts and made amendments.

Within the tent, there were no recriminations. As Wilson's life ebbed away Birdie picked up one of Scott's letters and wrote on the back of it, as clearly as he could: 'Dr Wilsons note to Mrs Wilson is in the satchel in the Instrument Box with his diary & two sketch books. HRB.'[23]

Birdie, having done what he could for his friend, drew his arms back into his sleeping bag and waited for his earthly life to draw to a close. Scott continued to write until cold and exhaustion finally overcame his willpower.

By the end of March 1912 pristine white snow shrouded the small green canvas tent.

The longest silence had begun.

Map 9 Journey of the search party, October–November 1912. *Map by Patricia Wright* ©
Adrian Raeside

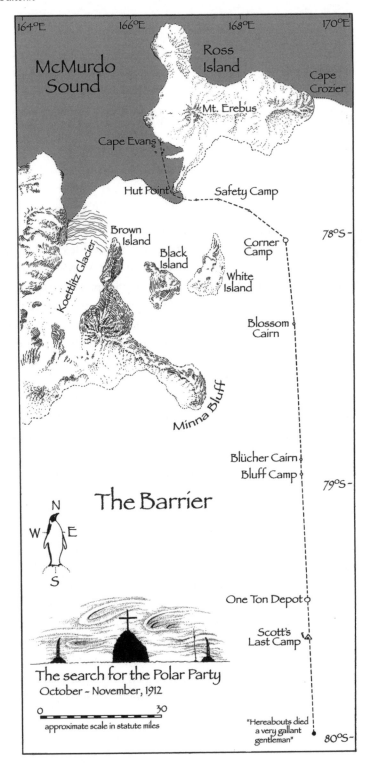

BREAKING THE SILENCE

On 28 January 1912 Cherry, Atkinson, Silas Wright and Keohane had arrived back at Cape Evans, where they found Meares and Dimitri.[1]

A few days later the *Terra Nova* sailed into McMurdo Sound with Harry Pennell at the helm. After the shore party helped unload mules, dogs and supplies for the following season, Pennell set off to pick up Griff Taylor's Western party (which he did) and Campbell's party (which he was unable to do because of ice). On 13 February Atkinson and Dimitri took two dog teams to Hut Point from where they would head south to meet up with the South Pole party and, if possible, carry their news back to the ship. For the next few days they were trapped in the hut by poor weather. Then, just as conditions began to improve, Crean staggered in with the news that Teddy Evans had collapsed on the Barrier with scurvy and that dog teams would be needed to bring him back as quickly as possible.

With Teddy Evans out of action and Scott's party still on their way back to Hut Point, Atkinson suddenly found himself in charge; he was also, as a doctor, the only person who might be able to save Teddy Evans' life. He decided he must stay with his sick colleague rather than head south immediately to meet up with Scott. After some discussion with Silas Wright at Cape Evans, it was agreed that Cherry and Dimitri should take a sledge and go to One Ton depot with further provisions and, if necessary and feasible, continue further south.

Cherry and Dimitri left on 26 February and arrived at One Ton depot on 3 March with sufficient dog food for a week plus the return journey. That day, the *Terra Nova* left McMurdo Sound with a still-ailing Teddy Evans, Meares, Ponting, 'Sunny Jim' Simpson, Griff Taylor, Day, Forde, Clissold and Anton aboard. It was agreed that Pennell would try again to pick up Campbell's party on his way north; regardless of the outcome the *Terra Nova* would continue to New Zealand, but if the ice prevented Pennell from picking up Campbell's men they would face a hard winter.[2]

Cherry knew that if there was no sign of the South Pole party at One Ton depot he was to decide, based on weather conditions, whether to continue south in the hope of meeting up with them. As night temperatures plunged to -37°F and blizzards set in he decided to stay at One Ton depot, particularly given Scott's instruction (repeated by Atkinson) that the dogs were not to be risked in view of the plans Scott already had for several expeditions with dog-sledges next season. Over the following week the weather remained poor; Dimitri began complaining of feeling cold and ill and the dogs steadily ate all their food except for what was needed for the return journey to Hut Point.

On 10 March Cherry depoted rations to last the South Pole party for a month and turned north again. After a miserable journey back he and Dimitri arrived at Hut Point on 16 March to find Atkinson and Keohane still there; they were now all cut off from Cape Evans. None of them was particularly anxious about the South Pole party, given that Scott had only expected to be back at Hut Point on or around 29 March. As the days became darker, however, Atkinson decided to make one more attempt to meet up with the South Pole party. Cherry was still exhausted from his previous journey and in no state to travel, so Atkinson and Keohane set out on 26 March with a dog team to take provisions to Corner Camp. When they found no sign of the South Pole party there, they continued for a further 8 miles south towards One Ton depot but, with the weather closing in, they knew there was little chance of the two teams seeing each other except near a depot. On 30 March they depoted enough provisions at Corner Camp to sustain the returning South Pole party until Hut Point. By now the South Pole party was definitely overdue and Atkinson was convinced something had happened to them.

Atkinson and Keohane returned to Hut Point on 1 April knowing that they, Cherry, Dimitri and the dogs needed to get back to Cape Evans before winter enveloped them in darkness.

* * *

When Harry Pennell arrived at McMurdo Sound in early February 1912 he brought with him a pile of letters and gifts from Birdie's family, including Birdie's special sledge-flag.

The pennant with the Bowers family crest had been lovingly assembled during summer 1911. In terms of the finer details, Emily and May had consulted with Oriana Wilson, who was by now a regular correspondent; when she sent helpful details about sledge-flags to Emily she mentioned how much 'Ted' admired and liked 'Birdie', how much he enjoyed the younger man's humour and how happy he thought Birdie's home life sounded.[3] In late August 1911 Emily received a postcard from the Scottish mainland confirming that the body of the pennant was almost ready for her and May to add their finishing touches; after doing so they sent it to Lyttelton for Harry Pennell to collect and take to Birdie ready for when he returned from the Southern journey.[4]

On 30 March 1912 Harry Pennell, having handed Birdie's mail and sledge-flag to the shore party, wrote a letter to Emily to enclose with Birdie's letters and journal pages from Cape Evans.[5] Based on accounts from Evans' party, Pennell could tell Emily that Birdie and his four companions had been, at the beginning of January, in good health and condition and ready for the final stage of their great journey. Pennell told Emily that Birdie had established himself as the 'heart and soul' of the party in countless ways, and that his being selected for the South Pole party was a tribute to both his outstanding physical strength and mental abilities. He assured her that while several people had envied Birdie being chosen for the Southern journey, none had grudged him his place. Pennell knew that Birdie would have regaled Emily with tales of his Cape Crozier expedition, and told her that when Captain Scott asked Dr Wilson what would have happened if Birdie had not found their tent again, Dr Wilson had replied, 'Oh, Birdie would have got us back somehow.'

❋ ❋ ❋

By early May 1912 Cherry, Atkinson, Silas Wright, Debenham, Gran, Nelson, Lashly, Crean, Keohane, Dimitri, Hooper, Williamson (previously on the ship's party) and Archer (Clissold's replacement) were all safely ensconced at Cape Evans. They all agreed that there was now little hope for the South Pole party. They were unsure, however, whether Campbell's party were on their way to New Zealand or still trapped by ice some 100 miles north of Cape Evans, probably with inadequate shelter and food.

As winter deepened at Cape Evans the old routines gradually re-established themselves: observations were taken, equipment was checked and repaired, dogs and mules were fed and exercised. Debenham was now in charge of Ponting's darkroom and developed Scott and Birdie's films of the Southern journey and those taken by the Cape Evans party. As katabatic winds whistled and blizzards swirled around the hut, they prepared and listened to lectures, grew hyacinth bulbs (a recent gift to 'Sunny Jim' Simpson), played bagatelle, enjoyed music from the gramophone and pianola, wrote items for the

Terra Nova's South Polar Times and kept themselves as fit and healthy as possible. On 22 June, their second Midwinter Day, they decorated the hut with sledge-flags and Birdie's 'Christmas tree', and enjoyed a splendid feast featuring *Croûte Erebus* and *Charlotte Russe glacée à la Beardmore*. After dinner Gran dressed as a clown and distributed presents, following which they enjoyed a magic-lantern show by Debenham and, thanks to Cherry, a new issue of the *South Polar Times*.

After the festivities had drawn to a close, Atkinson asked everyone to consider what they should do when sledging conditions improved. They could head south to try to establish what had happened to the South Pole party (which he suspected might involve their travelling as far as the crevasses of the Beardmore Glacier), or north to try to help Campbell's party (always assuming the latter were not already in New Zealand). They knew how important the records carried by the South Pole party were and decided they must first go south. Over the next few months they made plans and restocked and created food depots. On 29 October Silas Wright led off from Hut Point on skis, followed by Gran, Lashly, Crean, Keohane, Williamson, Nelson, Hooper and seven mules; two days later Cherry, Atkinson and Dimitri followed with dog teams.

Late at night on 11 November they left One Ton depot and continued south. They followed the line of the previous season's marker cairns for 11 miles; in the early hours of 12 November, Silas, who had been skiing ahead, noticed an irregular shape in the snow. He gestured to the others to stop and approach quietly. They gathered around and then cleared enough snow to give them access to the green tent.

Inside they found three frozen bodies which they eventually recognised as Scott, Wilson and Birdie. Scott was half-sitting, only partially covered by his sleeping bag, between his two companions, eyes open, one arm flung across Wilson. Birdie and Wilson, on either side of their leader, were in their sleeping bags. Birdie was curled up as if he had simply fallen into a deep sleep in the cold.[6]

After they found Scott's journal Atkinson, in accordance with Scott's instructions, read enough of it so that he could tell the others that the five men had reached the South Pole in mid-January, but that on the return journey Evans and Oates had become ill and died; Scott, Wilson and Birdie had died after a long blizzard had prevented them from reaching One Ton depot and the food and fuel they needed. They covered the bodies and Atkinson read the burial service from Corinthians. They then removed everything from the tent, collapsed it over the bodies and dug up chunks of ice with which to construct a huge cairn over the bodies. They topped it with a cross made from skis; they used Gran's skis so that he could wear Scott's skis for the remainder of the journey from the Pole to Cape Evans. They all signed a message stating that the cairn was the grave of Scott, Wilson and Bowers and a memorial to Oates and Evans, and placed it in a metal container attached to a bamboo pole near the cairn.

They continued south in the hope of finding Oates' body; they found his sleeping bag on top of some pony-walls, where Scott, Wilson and Birdie had left it, but when they realised the deep snow meant there was little chance of finding his body, they built another, smaller cairn in his memory. They decided that to try to hunt for Taff Evans' body would be fruitless, so they returned to the place they now thought of as Sorrowful Camp,[7] picked up the South Pole party's possessions and their sledge (on which they found a large number of rock specimens), and continued northwards in the hope they could still do something for Campbell's party.

When they arrived back at Hut Point on 25 November, Cherry entered the *Discovery* hut first. He emerged beaming, waving a note which Campbell and his party had left almost three weeks previously on their way back to Cape Evans.

✳ ✳ ✳

On 18 January 1913 the *Terra Nova* returned from New Zealand to McMurdo Sound. On board were Teddy Evans (restored to health and recently returned from England), Pennell, Rennick, Lillie, Wilfred Bruce, Frankie Drake and ship-wright Davies. They were carrying what they knew would be eagerly awaited letters and gifts for the shore party and had decked the wardroom for a great celebratory feast. Bottles of champagne stood ready to be opened.[8] Everyone now knew the South Pole party had been beaten by Amundsen's team, but they were encouraged to receive a hearty 'three cheers' from the shore party – and Pennell in particular was much relieved to see Campbell and his party alive and looking well. When those on shore shouted to them that Scott, Wilson, Birdie, Oates and Taff Evans had died on the return journey the ship fell silent.

The anchor was dropped, flags were lowered and the wardroom table was quietly unset. Over the next few days, as others packed up, 'Chippy' Davies hewed a huge wooden cross, on which – following some discussion among the shore party – he chiselled out the closing line of Tennyson's *Ulysses*: 'To strive, to seek, to find, and not to yield.' On 20 January 1913 Davies, Cherry, Atkinson, Silas Wright, Debenham, Crean and Keohane carried the cross across to Hut Point and erected it on Observation Hill, 900ft above the *Discovery* hut.

On 26 January 1913, following her shortest stay yet in McMurdo Sound, the *Terra Nova* left for New Zealand.

✳ ✳ ✳

Almost a year earlier, in early March 1912, Amundsen had announced to the world that he had reached the South Pole on 14 December 1911.

On 1 April 1912, following the *Terra Nova*'s arrival in New Zealand under Pennell's command, information on the progress of Scott's expedition was cabled, first to the Central News Agency in London, then around the world. On 2 April 1912 *The Scotsman* ran a long report about the expedition, including details of Birdie's narrow escape from the sea-ice during the depot journey and his appointment to the South Pole party.[9] Over the next few weeks pictures and articles appeared in newspapers and magazines all over the world. There was much press speculation as to whether Scott and his party had already reached the South Pole, but by mid-April the front pages were filled with news of the sinking of the *Titanic*, with the loss of over 1,500 lives.

By May 1912 Emily Bowers had received Birdie's own accounts of his time in Antarctica, with details of his Cape Crozier adventure and information on all but the final stages of the Southern journey. She also received Captain Scott's letter, which assured her that Birdie appeared to be completely in his element, was in wonderful fitness and health and was proving to be a lynchpin of the expedition.[10] In his covering letter to Emily, Harry Pennell suggested that she would probably hear little more until the *Terra Nova* returned to New Zealand in early 1913 and that the ship would probably not be back in England before September 1913.

Given this information, Emily knew she had time for another visit to 'the Continent'.[11]

❋ ❋ ❋

In the early hours of 10 February 1913 Teddy Evans steered the *Terra Nova* into the harbour at Oamaru, some 150 miles south of Christchurch.

Those on board were anxious not to jeopardise Scott's agreement with the Central News Agency and to ensure that their news reached London before any local or other newspaper reporters in New Zealand broke the story. Under cover of darkness, Tom Crean rowed Pennell and Atkinson ashore; as soon as he returned to the ship the *Terra Nova* slipped away and continued up the coast. Pennell and Atkinson found the nightwatchman and, without giving their names, asked him to summon the harbourmaster. Captain Ramsay rose from his bed and came to meet them; after Pennell and Atkinson swore him to secrecy he took them back to his house. Following a few hours' sleep, they went to Oamaru's telegraph hut from where – again under conditions of secrecy – they dispatched a coded telegram which they, Evans, Bruce and

Drake had prepared on the way north.[12] Their mission fulfilled, they sat in a secluded field to wait for the eleven o'clock express train to Christchurch; on the train some eager reporters, noticing their unusual attire, approached them but they politely deflected questions. In Christchurch a further cable was dispatched from Joseph Kinsey's office with a few more facts about the tragedy and a 3,000-word message Scott had prepared before setting out for the Pole.[13]

Over the next twenty-four hours the news was dispatched around the world by the Central News Agency. Back in New Zealand, the Oamaru evening paper of 10 February had only been able to report that two mysterious Englishmen (suspected of being members of Scott's party) had passed through the town; a Christchurch reporter described encounters with two polite but taciturn Englishmen on the express train and a less-than-forthcoming Joseph Kinsey. With the benefit of time differences, some London newspapers broke the news of the tragedy in their late 10 February editions, while several American newspapers ran relatively lengthy reports that day.[14]

Pennell and Atkinson spent the night of 10 February at Sumner's Marine Hotel, where Birdie had left the personal effects mentioned to Emily in the postscript to his last letter.[15] Following the expiry of the Central News Agency's twenty-four-hour exclusivity period, the *Terra Nova* entered Lyttelton harbour with her flags at half mast. Pennell and Atkinson walked over the hills from Sumner to Lyttelton, as Birdie had so often done, and caught a tug out to meet the ship. Teddy Evans dispatched further telegrams to London, including one to the India Office, the official point of contact for news concerning Royal Indian Marine officers.

By 13 February Captain Scott's lengthy 'Message to the Public', written almost a year previously, had been cabled all over the world. That afternoon, Joseph Kinsey and members of the expedition party joined city officials and a large congregation for a memorial service in Christchurch cathedral.[16]

❋ ❋ ❋

On 11 February 1913 an official letter from the India Office in Whitehall, London, was posted to Emily Bowers in Bute:

Madam

I am directed to inform you that Lieutenant E.R.G. Evans, R.N., Commander of the Terra Nova has telegraphed to this Office stating that your son Lieutenant H.R. Bowers, Royal Indian Marine, died on the 29th March 1912; and I am desired by the Marquess of Crewe to convey to you an expression of his sympathy with you in your bereavement and of his deep sense of the loss which the Royal Indian Marine has sustained by the death of so able and brave an officer.[17]

Emily was not in Bute to receive the letter. She had spent Christmas with friends on the Continent and was in Rome. There, almost three years after she had received Birdie's cable about going to Antarctica, she learned of his death from news cables pinned up in the British Library. May, who had not accompanied Emily on this trip, left Bute immediately for Italy. On Friday 14 February a 'Miss Bowers' (May or Edie) attended a memorial service for Scott's party at St Paul's Cathedral, London – a service also attended, in an unprecedented breach of royal protocol, by the king himself.[18] That day, Scott's 'Message to the Public' was also read out in schools throughout Britain, including in Birdie's old school in Sidcup.[19] On Bute, although none of the Bowers were present, a memorial service was held at St Ninian's church, Port Bannatyne.

When Emily returned to Britain, friends and relations rallied round as they had done in the past and she went to Sidmouth to spend time with the Radfords. By now she had received Scott's final letter to her, assuring her that Birdie had remained cheerful and indomitable in body and spirit to the end, and had talked of her, his sisters and his happy home.[20] She sent a copy of the letter to the India Office, from where it was forwarded to Buckingham Palace; an official at the palace wrote saying that Their Majesties had been greatly touched to read Captain Scott's beautiful tribute to Lieutenant Bowers.[21] The family ordered 'In Loving Memory' cards stating that Lieutenant Henry R. Bowers, RIM, had died at the age of 28 on about 27 March 1912 and now rested 'with his brave comrades amid the Antarctic snows'.[22] In response to a letter of sympathy from Joseph Kinsey, Emily responded on black-edged mourning paper:

> You, who knew my dear boy, will partly understand how great my loss is, & he was my only one. I have read with great appreciation the various kind expressions of sympathy you have forwarded from different societies in New Zealand. My son always spoke of the kindness & hospitality he had received in the colonies & I feel very grateful to all those who helped to make the time spent there so pleasant.[23]

In Scotland, Birdie's death was widely reported in newspapers and memorial services were held in Greenock and on Bute.[24] Emily arranged for Birdie's name to be added to the Bowers' family tombstone in Greenock, immediately below that of her husband, who had also died, almost thirty years previously, thousands of miles from the town of his birth. The Sidcup *District Times* ran several articles about Birdie, including one in which a school friend recalled visiting Birdie on the *Terra Nova* in London: Birdie had told his friend that, although he had enjoyed chasing gun-runners in the Persian Gulf, the Antarctic expedition was the 'great thing of his life'.

The Royal Geographical Society's official magazine carried an obituary written by Birdie's mentor, Captain Wilson-Barker of HMS *Worcester*.[25] The captain described his protégé's childhood and upbringing, educational achievements, his many interests and hobbies (particularly nature study and photography) and Birdie's 'keenest pride and pleasure' in his appointment to Scott's expedition. Wilson-Barker concluded that Scott's men had left 'an undying memory of gallant lives well and bravely ended, of duty quietly fulfilled, and of achievement won through strenuous endeavour, heroic endurance, and at the cost of life itself'. He added that Emily Bowers had written to him saying she was glad that her son, Wilson and Scott had not abandoned their ailing companions, even though this had cost them their lives.

❊ ❊ ❊

On 14 June 1913, earlier than Harry Pennell had predicted, the *Terra Nova* sailed into Cardiff.[26]

Teddy Evans was on board but had only joined the ship in British waters; he had stayed on in New Zealand with his wife's family but on the steamship voyage back to England, Hilda Evans – Birdie's favourite of 'the wives' – had suddenly taken ill of peritonitis and died. Over the next few days, Evans and the others on board took part in a memorial service and a lavish civic dinner welcoming them back. They then signed off from the expedition and bade each other farewell.

On 21 June Teddy Evans wrote to Emily Bowers telling her he had spoken about Birdie at an 'Old Worcesters' dinner and had presented 'Birdie's little white ensign' to the king.[27] The ensign, found with Birdie's body, was the one Teddy Evans had given his friend to carry to the Pole. Teddy did not mention this latter fact but told Emily that it was now framed and hanging above the king's writing table on HM Royal Yacht *Britannia*. Teddy also told Emily that he had addressed the boys at Birdie's old school, Sidcup Hall College. For her part, Emily Bowers presented a large photograph of Birdie and other members of the expedition to Port Bannatyne School in Bute.[28]

On 7 July Emily was granted probate of her son's estate, which amounted to £219.[29] She would also receive Henry's RIM pension (£100 a year) from the

India Office, his salary for the expedition (£116) and, from the Mansion House Fund (set up in response to Scott's dying plea to 'look after our people'), a capital sum of £4,500.[30] On 8 July Emily joined Sir Clements Markham, Captain Wilson-Barker and Birdie's friends Cherry-Garrard and Teddy Evans at Greenhithe for the unveiling of a memorial plaque on HMS *Worcester*.[31] Almost 200 cadets gathered on deck to hear Sir Clements talk about 'Cadet' Bowers' career and read Captain Scott's final letter to Emily. On 26 July Emily joined members of the expedition, Kathleen Scott and Oriana Wilson at Buckingham Palace, where King George presented her with a medal and clasp to recognise Birdie's achievements.[32]

In the autumn Emily received a letter from Oamaru, informing her that, thanks to the town's Scott Memorial Fund, a memorial tablet to the South Pole party had been unveiled at Waitaki High School for Boys. Emily responded as a grieving mother and a former teacher:

> What can I say? My boy was my only son & fatherless from infancy & his loss is a great sorrow for we were more to each other than ordinary mother and son. But through it all, I feel it is better so – than that they should have saved their own lives & left their sick companions, though that was an impossibility with such men. May the courage & faithfulness of their lives & deaths be a lasting heritage for good, to the boys & young men of this present generation & may it be so to your boys.[33]

Emily also visited Sidmouth parish school where she had taught almost forty years previously and presented a large photo of Birdie and members of the expedition party.[34]

On 10 November 1913 Emily attended a meeting of the Royal Geographical Society in London (of which her late husband had been a Fellow); there, in the presence of RGS dignitaries, the Italian ambassador and Sir Clements Markham, members of the expedition and relations of those who had died received medals from the Society and its Italian counterpart.[35]

In June 1914 Emily received another letter from Oamaru telling her of the continuing work of the Scott Memorial Fund in the school and town; she responded with the hope that it would remain 'an influence for good to the youth of the future' and a donation to the fund. By then Emily and her daughters had, thanks to the capital sum from the Mansion House Fund, purchased the first home they had ever owned; it was located down the hill from Caerlaverock, on the seashore at Ardbeg and they renamed it (in Gaelic) 'the house of the sea'.[36] On Saturday 26 September they attended a service at

St Ninian's church, Port Bannatyne,[37] during which a memorial tablet commissioned by the Royal Indian Marine was unveiled by Captain H.B. Simpson, one of the few Scots in the RIM.[38] On 30 November Lord Willingdon, Governor of Bombay, unveiled an identical tablet in the north aisle of Bombay Cathedral.

In September 1914 Henry Rennick, Birdie's erstwhile cabin-mate on the *Terra Nova*, died when his ship, HMS *Hogue*, sank in the Atlantic after being hit by a German torpedo.[39] Around that time Edie Bowers, until then the least-travelled member of the Bowers family, 'joined up'. She travelled to London where George Wyatt, the *Terra Nova*'s former agent (with whom the Bowers had stayed in touch), ensured that she and her luggage made it onto the hospital ship SS *Dongola*.[40] Edie left England in a convoy heading for Salonika and the Dardanelles with 1,000 'Tommies', a few hundred officers and doctors, and a handful of other nurses. She wrote to Emily telling her that, despite sailing near a minefield in the Channel and being seasick during a violent storm in the Bay of Biscay, she was having the time of her life and predicted (happily correctly) that she was 'not one to die an untimely death'.[41]

During the Great War others were less fortunate. Harry Pennell, who wrote to Emily in December 1915 with news of his recent marriage, died on 31 May 1916 when the *Queen Mary* sank with the loss of almost 1,300 lives during the battle of Jutland.[42] That same month a memorial tablet to Scott's party was unveiled at St Paul's Cathedral in London by the prime minister, Herbert Asquith.[43]

Several of Birdie's friends, including Cherry-Garrard, Teddy Evans and Dennis Lillie, survived the war and kept in touch with Emily. In December 1917 Cherry wrote saying that he had shown George Bernard Shaw (his neighbour) Birdie's description of the sea-ice 'incident' on the depot journey and that Bernard Shaw had declared it to be a good piece of writing.[44] In 1920, under the leadership of Frank Debenham, the Scott Polar Research Institute opened in Cambridge as a lasting and living memorial to the five men who had died on the return journey from the South Pole. Two years later Cherry's story of the expedition, *The Worst Journey in the World*, was published; it covered the whole expedition and its aftermath but at its heart lay the story of the Cape Crozier journey, during which Birdie's sterling qualities – lack of false graces, kindness, unselfishness, stoicism and infectious cheerfulness – had sustained Cherry in difficult and sometimes dangerous times.

On 25 September 1924, May Bowers, aged 46, married her erstwhile neighbour Sir William Maxwell, aged 82, whose wife (a great friend of all the Bowers) had died the previous year. Emily continued to travel to London, Sidmouth and to Continental Europe, with and without her daughters. She regularly went away over Christmas, Birdie's favourite time of year. One autumn, when she and Edie were passing through London on their way to Italy, Emily lunched and went shopping (in a 'lovely large car') with Oates' mother, Caroline, and her daughter Lilian.[45] Caroline Oates had, in her grief-stricken belief that her son's death had been unnecessary, shunned many of the official ceremonies relating to the expedition, but the two women maintained contact and Emily allowed Caroline to see and copy some of Birdie's letters. A few years later, on another visit to Italy, Emily took her first trip on a funicular railway ('oh dear I never thought to see myself go up in such a thing'); despite suffering from attacks of fatigue and eye trouble during her stay, she visited friends in London and Sidmouth on her way back to Bute.[46]

On 7 August 1928 Emily died of heart failure at the family home, at the age of 81.[47] May, a widow since Sir William's death in 1925, was again living there; she and Edie bred dogs and played their part in the local community.[48] The sisters continued to cherish their brother's memory and in 1937 they met Reverend George Seaver, who had already written a biography of Birdie's friend Edward Wilson, in co-operation with Oriana Wilson.[49] Seaver spent hours with the sisters reading Birdie's letters and journals; he also wrote to Captain Wilson-Barker, Captain Hunt and Birdie's friends from different stages of his life, including James Paul of Greenock and Cherry (whom he invited to write the introduction to *'Birdie' Bowers of the Antarctic*). Seaver agreed to share royalties from the book with the sisters as he had done with Oriana Wilson.[50] While working with Seaver on the book, the sisters brought out the sledge-flag made for Birdie but still unused due to its having arrived in Antarctica after Birdie had left on the Southern journey. They also found Emily's correspond-ence with Frank Milner of Waitaki High School for Boys in Oamaru; May re-established contact with Milner and, on 19 January 1939, presented the flag to the school so it could be hung in the school's Hall of Memories, opened in 1927 in memory of former pupils killed or injured in the Great War or in the service of their country.[51]

In November 1948 May and Edie travelled to London for the Royal Command performance of Ealing Studios' *Scott of the Antarctic*, in the presence of King George VI and Queen Elizabeth.[52] They had, like many survivors of the expedition and their families, lent letters and journals to the screenplay writer, Walter Meade – a colourful character who had served in Persia with the Indian Cavalry around the time Birdie had been in the Gulf with the RIM. In the film Birdie was portrayed by Reginald Beckwith, whom the expedition members who visited the film set felt had a very strong resemblance to Birdie. Following the performance May and Edie were presented to the queen; that Christmas they also received cards from Walter Meade and Reginald Beckwith.

By this time May and Edie had been approached by a Mr Angus McMillan, a philatelist from Paisley whose special interest was stamps and special frankings from the polar regions – which Birdie had suggested almost forty years ago might become collectors' items.[53] Angus McMillan visited the sisters on Bute on Sunday 8 October 1950 and May also put him in touch with Atkinson's widow, who was now a near-neighbour.[54] When May died in 1952, aged 73, Edie became the custodian of Birdie's possessions. When Edie died in 1964, aged 85, she left much of her estate to the Aldridges, but bequeathed most of Birdie's Antarctic letters and journals to Angus McMillan.[55] In 1986 McMillan sold the bulk of the collection to the Scott Polar Research Institute where it joined their now nationally and internationally renowned archive of information on polar expeditions.

By then Scott's reputation, which had flourished through two world wars and for several decades thereafter, had somewhat waned. This was largely due to Amundsen and Shackleton being perceived as more 'modern' men and to efforts, including by Scott's detractors, to identify specific causes or errors of judgement which had resulted in the deaths of Scott and his South Pole team. The two expeditions to the South Pole were now sometimes being described as a 'race'. In 1985 *The Last Place on Earth*, a television adaptation of Roland Huntford's 1979 *Scott and Amundsen* (in which Birdie was played by Sylvester McCoy), portrayed Amundsen as a polar traveller of supreme single-mindedness and determination, but failed to give Scott any real credit for the scientific and other aspects of his expedition. Gradually, however, as interest in climate change and advanced research in the Antarctic grew, the importance of the work carried out by the scientists in Scott's party received wider recognition. Now, at the beginning of the twenty-first century, it is generally accepted that Scott and Amundsen – and indeed Shackleton – had very different backgrounds, personal qualities, leadership styles and objectives for their expeditions, and each can be recognised as a great man without detracting from the reputation of the others.

It now also seems that Scott, while not perfect (by his own admission), was unlucky in terms of weather in a way that Shackleton and Amundsen were not. Before Birdie set out on the last stage of the South Pole journey, he suggested to Edie that, while he and his companions could do their utmost, man was very 'limited' in Antarctica and that even a small thing could upset man's 'best laid plans'.[56] Since 1912 many people have died in the polar regions and it is perhaps less surprising that Birdie and his companions perished than that they had already survived, at various times, lengthy blizzards, intense cold snaps, the break-up of sea-ice, falls into huge crevasses, long journeys in twenty-four-hour sunshine and total darkness, illness, injuries, frostbite, dehydration and hunger.[57] Birdie, long before going to Antarctica, believed that 'unseen arrangement' and chance guided his life. If he had not been the son of an adventurous sea captain and an intrepid missionary teacher, he might not have joined HMS *Worcester*, met Captain Wilson-Barker and Sir Clements Markham, been offered a place on Scott's expedition and then selected to go to the Pole. Had Birdie not died on the return from the Pole, he might well have died during the Great War, like his friends Pennell and Rennick (both of similar ages and ranks).

Birdie once told Emily that he felt fame might detract from the happy anonymity of his life on Bute. While he never received the same wide level of recognition as Scott or Oates, he continued to make his quiet mark. In 1973 a modest plaque was placed on the gatepost of his Greenock birthplace. In 1999 Charles Lagerbom's *The Fifth Man* made the case that Birdie's death was one of the true tragedies of the expedition. Birdie has appeared as a character in plays, both on television (played by Lee Ingleby) and on radio (by Peter Callaghan); he can also be seen in the original and digitally remastered versions of Ponting's film *The Great White Silence*.[58] In 2009 the RIM memorial tablet to Birdie was moved from a now-redundant St Ninian's church to Bute Museum, where it joined his compass, sledge-frame and photographs. In 2010 and 2011 'Birdie's little white ensign' was displayed in the Royal Collection's exhibition, 'The Heart of the Great Alone', in Edinburgh, Christchurch (New Zealand) and London.

The HMS *Worcester* memorial plaque to Birdie is now at the Scott Polar Research Institute, near the bell of the *Terra Nova*. On the other side of the world Birdie's sledge-flag still hangs at Waitaki High School for Boys, where it is seen regularly by hundreds of boys, their parents and visitors. In 2011, on the Firth of Clyde, the Royal West of Scotland Amateur Boat Club launched a new rowing skiff which they named in Birdie's honour. The *Birdie Bowers* now regularly plies the choppy waters that Birdie loved, with crews that have included a 7-year-old boy.

It was at the age of 7 that young Henry Bowers, over 120 years ago, wrote a letter suggesting that one day he might visit the distant and unexplored land of Antarctica.

EPILOGUE

Relatively few people, even today, are fortunate enough to visit McMurdo Sound, Cape Evans or the South Pole.

In late 2011 millions watched the BBC's *The Frozen Planet* series, in which Sir David Attenborough visited and described the Antarctic scenery and wildlife, which had so fascinated Birdie and his companions. Viewers also saw the inside of Scott's hut with its wonderfully conserved wardroom table, shelves of provisions and artefacts, and the Tenements, where Birdie slept and worked at his improvised desk.

The Scott Polar Research Institute has exhibited pages and published a transcript of Birdie's polar journal, thus allowing people to read and enjoy his vivid descriptions of his environment and his travels in Antarctica. Photographs of Birdie and his companions and the Antarctic landscape can be seen in archives, museums, books, auction house catalogues and on websites. While Birdie and his companions did not survive to understand all they achieved, they live on in the names of institutes and geographical features, in street names, on memorials, in photographs and films, on collectors' cigarette cards, on badges and in the pages of books.

During the centenary year of Scott's party reaching the South Pole, tributes are being paid to their achievements and to their endurance and sheer bravery. Sir David Attenborough speaks warmly of the lasting contribution to both exploration and science made by all of the South Pole team, including Bowers, Wilson and Scott, who dragged to their final resting place geological specimens which proved that the world's coldest, driest, windiest continent was once temperate and joined to Africa, India and Australia.

Birdie understood that Antarctica is a mysterious, wonderful and sometimes dangerous place. That is still true today. Man can explore it and investigate it but, for now at least, thanks to the Antarctic Treaty, no one country can dominate it. We are privileged to be able to visit it, wonder at it and admire it – but, as Sir David Attenborough exhorts us, we must also respect and cherish it.

APPENDIX A

EXPEDITION PERSONNEL

Shore Party Officers & Scientists (officers RN unless stated)

Dr Edward Atkinson (RN), 1881–1929, *surgeon/parasitologist* (nicknames: Atch, Jane)
Lieutenant Henry Bowers (RIM), 1883–1912 (Birdie, Henry to family)
Lieutenant Victor Campbell, 1875–1956 (The Wicked [First] Mate)
Apsley Cherry-Garrard, 1886–1959, *assistant biologist* (Cherry)
Bernard Day, 1884–1952, *motor engineer*
Frank Debenham, 1883–1965, *geologist* (Deb)
Lieutenant Edward Evans, 1881–1957 (Teddy)
Tryggve Gran (Royal Norwegian Navy), 1889–1980, *ski expert/sub-lieutenant* (Trigger)
Dr George Murray Levick (RN), 1877–1956, *surgeon*
Cecil Meares, 1877–1937, *in charge of dogs*
Edward Nelson, 1883–1923, *biologist* (Marie)
Captain Lawrence Oates (army), 1880–1912 (Titus, Soldier)
Herbert Ponting, 1870–1935, *photographer* (Ponko)
Raymond Priestley, 1886–1974, *geologist*
Captain Robert Scott, 1868–1912 (The Owner)
George Simpson, 1878–1965, *meteorologist* (Sunny Jim)
T. Griffith Taylor, 1880–1963, *senior geologist* (Griff)
Edward Wilson, 1872–1912, *chief scientist, doctor, zoologist, artist* (Uncle Bill and variants, Ted to family)
Charles Wright, 1887–1975, *physicist* (Silas)

Shore Party Crew

Petty Officer (PO) George Abbott, 1880–1923
William Archer, 1871–1944, *cook (second season)*
PO Frank Browning, 1882–1930
Thomas Clissold, 1886–1964, *cook (first season)*
PO Tom Crean, 1876–1938
Able Seaman Harry Dickason, 1885–1944

PO Edgar Evans, 1876–1912 (Taff)
PO Robert Forde, 1877–1959
Dimitri Gerof, 1888–1932, *dog driver*
Frederick Hooper, 1889–1955, *steward*
PO Patrick Keohane, 1879–1950
Chief Stoker William Lashly, 1867–1940
Anton Omelchenko, 1883–1932, *groom*
PO Thomas Williamson, 1877–1940 *(second season only)*

Terra Nova Officers & Scientists (only those referred to in text)

Lieutenant Wilfred Bruce, 1874–1953
Francis Drake, 1878–1936, *paymaster/expedition secretary* (Frankie)
Dennis Lillie, 1884–1963, *biologist*
Lieutenant Harry Pennell, 1882–1916 (Penelope)
Lieutenant Henry Rennick, 1881–1914
Francis Davies, b. 1885, *leading shipwright* (Chippy)

Expedition Agents

Joseph Kinsey, 1852–1936, *New Zealand agent*
George Wyatt (dates unknown), *London agent*

APPENDIX B

GLOSSARY

Barrier, the (Great Ice Barrier): Sheet of ice (*c.* 400 miles wide) linking Ross Island to the Beardmore Glacier; aka Ross Ice Shelf.

cracks and crevasses: Gaps in ice, varying greatly in width and depth. Cracked sea-ice and tide-cracks (between land-ice and sea-ice) move with tides and sea-swell. Crevasses, up to hundreds of yards deep, are sometimes 'bridged' with snow of varying degrees of thickness (and safety).

finnesko: Boots made entirely from fur (usually reindeer) used for marching (including with crampons) and skiing; originally worn by the inhabitants of Arctic regions, they were adopted by polar explorers, worn with multiple socks and dried grass for additional insulation.

hoosh: Stew made from pemmican (q.v.), pony or other meat and melted snow, usually cooked on a primus stove (invented by Arctic explorer Fritjof Nansen).

hypsometer: Instrument for estimating altitudes using a thermometer and boiling water.

icebergs: Large chunks of ice broken off ice-shelves or glacier tongues. When a large iceberg splits it is said to 'calve'; when it breaks down completely it becomes 'brash' ice. The word 'floe' can be used for icebergs or for smaller 'pancakes' of sea-ice.

katabatic winds: Ferocious winds occurring when cold air from high-altitude ice-fields is drawn to the coast by gravity (from the Greek *katabatikos*, going downhill); a strong katabatic can knock a man down.

pemmican: Cooked dried meat with added fat (Scott used 60 per cent extra fat), usually eaten as hoosh (q.v.).

pram: Norwegian-style high-bowed skiff.

sastrugi: Frozen furrows caused by the action of wind on snow.

theodolite: An instrument (usually mounted on a tripod) used to measure elevation and, following mathematical calculations, to work out longitude and latitude.

APPENDIX C

NOTES ON MEASUREMENTS

(Detailed conversion tables can be found in diaries, websites, etc.)

Distances: A 'mile' indicates, unless otherwise stated, a geographical mile (equivalent to a nautical mile or knot) which equals *c.* 1.15 statute miles or 1.85 kilometres. Yards, feet and inches are also used.

Weights: Shown in pounds (lb), stones (14lb), and tons.

Temperatures: Shown in degrees Fahrenheit (32°F = 0° Centigrade; 0°F = -18°C); no account is taken of wind–chill factors.

Winds: Shown in miles per hour (mph) or based on the Beaufort scale, e.g. Force 8 = strong gale, *c.* 42mph.

Money: shown in pounds (£), shillings (*s* or /-) and pence (*d*); present-day equivalents can be roughly estimated using published or web-based tables/calculators.

NOTES AND SOURCES

All archive documents are, unless otherwise stated, held by the Scott Polar Research Institute (SPRI), to which organisation many thanks are due for permission to quote from material in the Bowers' papers and other archives. Letters and documents are, unless stated otherwise, written by Bowers (HRB) or addressed to him. Every effort has been made to trace and obtain permission from owners and/or copyright holders of documents or images; I apologise for any inadvertent omissions and will be pleased to incorporate additional acknowledgements in any future editions.

Prologue

1   Details of events (e.g. the fall into the hold) not recorded by HRB are from diaries and other writings by members of Scott's team (as listed in Selected Bibliography).

1. Family Roots

1   Abram Lyle (1820–91) was one of Greenock's most prosperous sugar-refiners; in 1883, the year of HRB's birth, one of Lyle's refineries launched their Golden Syrup (which was later used on the *Terra Nova* expedition).
2   The *Geelong*, owned by John Willes & Co., was a sister ship of the *Cutty Sark*.
3   It is not known if Jane's first husband died at sea or at home; William sometimes stayed with his grandparents (e.g. 1861 census day) when his mother travelled.
4   *The Straits Times* (27 October 1875).
5   Burma (now Myanmar) was eventually completely annexed by Britain following a series of Anglo-Burmese wars; it and adjoining territories (including Malaya/Malaysia and Singapore) were collectively referred to as 'Further India'. The Irrawaddy Flotilla Company (headquartered in Rangoon/Yangon and in which Todd, Finlay & Co. and other Scottish shipping companies were shareholders) had recently obtained a contract to transport British troops and government officials on the Irrawaddy.

6 Information from Captain Bowers' 'Report on the Practicality of Re-opening the Trade Route between Burma and Western China' (copy in National Library of Scotland), *Irrawaddy Flotilla* and material in the Royal Geographical Society and SPRI archives (including SPRI/MS1505/4).

7 The Burma-China border area was controlled by Panthays, a Chinese-Muslim minority. Upper Burma was not yet part of the British Empire.

8 From a list of goods destroyed in the fire of 6 March 1870 (SPRI/MS1505/4/3/5).

9 Census of 2 April 1871 (when Captain Bowers was at home in Greenock).

10 The Captain was nominated for a Fellowship by a fellow Scot, immediate past-president Sir Roderick Murchison (patron of missionary-explorer David Livingstone). Clements Markham, a veteran of the Royal Navy and the India Office, was then RGS secretary.

11 Mary Bowers married Henry Robertson in Greenock on 14 November 1871.

12 In a series of complex financial operations the new company raised funds from investors (including Henderson's) with which it purchased Henderson's Burmese fleet; Henderson's was then appointed Managing Agents of the fleet.

13 *The Straits Times* (May 1876).

14 Perak became part of 'Further India' following a civil war between its Malay and Chinese inhabitants; the annexation was never ratified by the British government, which refused to intervene when the British Resident, Mr Birch, was murdered while attempting to collect taxes from local residents.

15 *Penang Gazette* (SPRI/MS1505/4/4/1), in which a friend describes the Captain as having been previously 'fat and jovial'.

16 George Seaver does not mention Emily Bowers' Cheltenham upbringing in *'Birdie' Bowers of the Antarctic*; given that HRB's sisters knew he had already written books on Edward Wilson from Cheltenham, this suggests they knew little of Emily's life in Cheltenham. When May filled in Emily's death certificate in 1928, she did not fill in Emily's father's first name or profession. Information on Emily Webb's family and early life is therefore from census, public or local archival sources.

17 According to the 1841 census he first lived in Leckhampton (near Cheltenham) with his maternal grandmother Hannah Jelliman.

18 Between 1800 and 1840 Cheltenham's population grew from *c.* 3,000 to over 30,000; travelling times from London fell from several days to around ten hours (Cheltenham's first railway station opened in 1840). Cheltenham's arms (granted 1877) include books (learning), pigeons (identified mineral springs by pecking salts from the ground) and a tree (parks, tree-lined street); its motto is *Salubritas et Eruditio* – health and learning. For more on Cheltenham, see books by Steven Blake and Anthea Jones' *Cheltenham, a New History*.

19 1851 census.

20 The influence of Francis Close (born Bath, 1797) on religious thought in Cheltenham in the 1840s was such that Alfred Lord Tennyson (who regularly visited the town) described Close as 'the Pope of Cheltenham'. See also Robert Trafford's *The Rev. Francis Close and the Foundation of the Training Institution at Cheltenham 1845–78* (Cheltenham: Park Published Papers).

21 The Evangelical movement in Britain began in the 1730s. Evangelicals (who unlike Methodists or Baptists remained within the Anglican Church) became associated with the missionary movement and social reform; they emphasised the importance of personal conversion and Bible learning, and their services included more hymns than did 'high' Anglican services.

22 Evangelical Anglicans felt threatened by the Catholic Emancipation Act of 1829 and the subsequent establishment of the Oxford or Tractarian movement. One of the latter's leaders, Rev. (later Cardinal) Francis Newman, suggested that the Anglican, Roman Catholic and Orthodox Churches should reunite into an overall Catholic Church which, to Evangelicals such as Close, ignored the Reformation. Close preached famously anti-Catholic sermons, including on 5 November each year, the anniversary of the 1605 Gunpowder Plot against England's new Protestant monarch.

23 The scroll, dated 3 December 1856, is in Gloucestershire Archives, Gloucester.

24 Information from Trinity School's official log (Gloucestershire Archives); the 1851 census shows Emily, aged 3, as a 'scholar' suggesting she was receiving lessons at the nearby infants' school (founded by Close) or at home from Ann Bushell, a teacher lodging with the Webbs.

25 Per the 1861 census, the Webbs lived at 29 St George's Place (now part of Jenner Walk).

26 Under the pupil-teacher system, established some twenty years previously, outstanding pupils in senior classes helped to instruct younger pupils, maintain classroom discipline and act as escort on 'outings' (which in Emily's case included viewing a 'Panorama' in Pittville Pump Room and attending the 'lying in state' of a recently deceased associate of the school). School and pupil-teacher were both remunerated and pupil-teachers were encouraged to continue to teacher training college.

27 Information from Charles More's *Training of teachers, 1847–1947* (Gloucestershire Archives) and from Emily Webb's college attendance records (University of Gloucestershire Archives).

28 Sidmouth was popular with summer visitors, particularly following the cessation of the 'Grand Tour' due to wars with France. In 1852 printmaker George Rowe (1796–1864) moved from Devon to Cheltenham, where he continued to sell prints of his *Forty-eight views of cottages and scenery at Sidmouth, Devon*. Heneage Gibbes' father was Sir George Smith-Gibbes, an Evangelical preacher and one-time Cheltenham resident.

29 Pouchet, the author, was a French natural historian who believed in 'spontaneous creation' rather than evolution; his comprehensive and lavishly illustrated book (which predated Darwin's *Origin of the Species*) had been translated into English.

30 Per 1871 and 1881 census information, Emily's brother William became a tailor and her sister Elizabeth a milliner; no references to correspondence with or visits to or from the Webbs have been found in Emily's letters.

31 *Sidmouth Herald* (29 September 1934), Sidmouth Museum.

32 Extract of marriage register (SPRI/MS1505/4/3/6).

33 The murder is mentioned in *The Straits Times* (7 November 1878), *The Chersonese with the gilding off* by Emily Innes (an eyewitness, pub. 1885) and in Isabella Bird's *The Golden Chersonese and the way thither* (pub. 1883). 'Chersonese' means peninsula.

34 *Penang Gazette* (11 June 1879) and *The Straits Times* (19 June 1879).

35 Letters from Margaret Bowers, 10 and 11 August 1880 (SPRI/MS1505/8/1 and /2).

36 According to her death certificate, Margaret Bowers died from 'ill health and natural decay'.

37 Information on Bithiah Paul and William Boag Paul is from census/public information and George Seaver, *'Birdie' Bowers of the Antarctic*, London: John Murray, 1938 (hereafter Seaver).

38 *Greenock Telegraph and Clyde Shipping Gazette* (22 February 1913); the church had long-standing connections with the East India Company (two ministers became EIC padres).

2. Learning the Ropes

1 The winters of 1883/84 to 1885/86 are recorded as being particularly snowy in Scotland; see Seaver, p. 5.

2 Information on Captain Bowers' last illness and death are from an 'In memoriam' and copies of the *Penang Gazette* (SPRI/MS1505/4).

3 The Aldridges had a family connection with the Bowers (a generation or so before the Captain) of which May later tried to trace the precise details, but full family records were not available.

4 Alexander Foucar worked in the family business in London and lived at 8 Tressillian Crescent, Brockley, Kent (1881 census). Emily stayed there, including while obtaining probate of Alexander Bowers' estate. By 1891 (although probably from earlier), Emily, her children and the Foucars lived at 13 Carlton Road, Chislehurst, Sidcup.

5 From HRB's letters and his sisters' conversations with George Seaver.

6 Moody (1837–99) and Sankey (1840–1908) were American Evangelicals whose hymns were very popular in England.

7 Per the 1891 census, the following lived at Edengrove, Dairsie: Henry Robertson, Mary Robertson (*née* Bowers), Jane Smith (*née* Bowers), Jane's son by her first marriage, William Allan (training as a lawyer) and children by her second marriage (Margaret, 19, and Alexander, 15). Emily appears to have remained closer to the Bowers than to her own family in Cheltenham.

8 Miss Lonsdale's Seminary was based at Bannockburn, Hatherley Road (SPRI/MS1505/1/1/3/22, census reports and information from Bexley Local Studies & Archive Centre).

9 *Sidcup & District Times* (February 1913) (Bexley LS&AC).

10 The Bowers lived at 19 Pathfield Road, Streatham; Emily then moved a short distance to 26 Lewin Road, the vicarage of the neighbouring baptist church, which she attended. All Emily's children stayed at school well beyond the legal leaving age (11 from 1893, 12 from 1899).

11 SPRI/MS1505/1/1/2/1: 'chink' is slang for coins (from the noise in a pocket) and 'ten bob' for 10 shillings (now around 50p).

12 Emily and HRB's copy of *The Universe*, inscribed with her name (dated 1871) and a dedication to HRB (28 June 1896), is in SPRI's special collections.

13 Information on HMS *Worcester* from Clive Bradbury, other 'Old Worcesters', the 'Old Worcesters' website and public sources.

14 Seaver, Chapter II; SPRI/MS1505/2/2.

15 John Davis was an early Polar explorer (a contemporary of Walter Raleigh); his biographer was Sir Clements Markham.

16 Sir Clements, secretary of the RGS when Captain Bowers received his Fellowship, did not (despite a reputedly prodigious memory) seem to make the connection between HRB and his father; his notes on HRB in his Antarctic diary (RGS archives) do not mention Captain Bowers' Fellowship.

17 Markham had, inter alia, explored the Northwest Passage in search of Sir John Franklin and his lost ship.

18 Mentioned, inter alia, in Singapore's *Weekly Sun* (15 March 1913).

19 Bible in SPRI's special collections (MS1505/18/5).

3. Sailing the Seven Seas

1 Information from a newspaper article (21 June 1908) on Captain Pattman (SPRI/MS1505/17/1).

2 From a long letter-cum-diary beginning on 7 December 1899 (Seaver, Chapter III).

3 Before the Suez Canal opened, Tristan da Cunha was a regular port of call for British ships. 'Mother Carey's Chickens', the sailors' name for storm petrels, comes from the Latin *Mater Cara* ('dear mother') referring to Christ's mother Mary whom sailors regard as a protector.

4 Letter of 21 February 1900 to Emily (SPRI/MS1505/1/1/3/1).

5 Captain Pattman's death in 1912 was recorded in several Australian newspapers.

6 By Rev. Robert Roberts of Huddersfield (pub. 1863).

7 Letter of 1 November 1900 to Emily (Seaver, Chapter III).

8 Canopus is one of the Southern Hemisphere's brightest stars and is used for navigation from 37° South.

9 From the 'Government Gazette Extraordinary' of 23 January 1901.

10 Story related by HRB's sisters (Seaver, Chapter IV).

11 The race was mentioned in Wilson-Barker's obituary (*The Geographical Journal*, April 1913).

12 Launched in March 1901, the *Discovery* was a sailing ship with an auxiliary engine, designed specifically for scientific work and to withstand ice.

13 Information on dinner from Seaver (p. 36); information on Evans and on Armitage (who travelled with the Jackson–Harmsworth Arctic expedition, 1894–97) from publications in Selected Bibliography.

14 HRB may have discussed his polar interests with Captain Pattman. The latter gave a broadsheet about Franklin and the Northwest Passage to cabin boy Joseph Fawcett in 1896 and another former *Loch Torridon* apprentice, William

Colbeck (1871–1930), took part in Borchgrevink's Antarctic expedition (1898–1900) and commanded the *Morning*, the relief ship for the *Discovery* expedition.

15 HRB's letter-log of 28 December 1901 (Seaver, Chapter IV).

16 Information in this section from letters to Emily (15 January 1902, SPRI/MS1505/1/2/3/2) and May (22 January 1902, SPRI/MS1505/1/1/2/3).

17 Letter of 14 June 1903 from Wilson-Barker (who gave Henry the camera) to HRB (SPRI/MS1505/1/2/3/8).

18 Letter of 15 January 1902 to Emily (SPRI/MS1505/1/1/3/2) and diary entry, 20 April 1902 (quoted in Seaver, Chapter IV).

19 The Bowers lived at Dagmar Lodge, Belmont Road, Wallington, Surrey – address on letter of 11 September 1902 to May (SPRI/MS1505/1/1/2/2).

20 1901 census information on HMS *Worcester* cadets and Bayards of Wallington.

21 Letter of 28 December 1902 to May (SPRI/MS1505/1/1/2/4).

22 Information from www.thelochlong.info and *San Francisco Call* (13 June 1903).

23 Letters of 3 and 13 June 1903 from Tryon Campbell Bayard to HRB (SPRI/MS1505/1/2/3/1-2).

24 Information from letters dated 27 March, 24 April, 22 and 29 May, 10 July, 13 August, 25 September, 9, 16 and 22 October 1903 (SPRI/MS1505/1/2/2/2-12).

25 Miss Radford and her family lived at Sidmount, Sidmouth, and remained friends with Emily for the rest of their lives; a letter regarding HRB's death in Antarctica was forwarded to Emily at Sidmount in April 1913 (SPRI/MS1505/7/3/3). Emily's investments were 'safe' but did not pay dividends (letter of 12 March 1909 from Captain Bower's nephew, William Allan in Penang, to May Bowers, SPRI/MS1505/6/1/11). The Bowers occupied the top flat at 14 Samos Road, Anerley, Crystal Palace, London.

26 Letter of 13 August 1903 from Emily (SPRI/MS1505/1/2/2/7).

27 Possibly inspired by *Punch* cartoons, these also featured in the 1910–12 *South Polar Times*.

4. Entering New Worlds

1 The sailing sloop HMS *President* (launched 1878) previously sailed as HMS *Gannet* and became the RNR's training ship in 1903 (succeeding another ship of the same name).

2 Although James Paul is referred to by Seaver as 'James Paul of Glasgow' (Seaver, p. 131), he is almost certainly the son of Bithiah Paul, Mrs Bowers' Greenock friend. The shipping line HRB joined was founded in 1903 by Alexander Park Lyle (1849–1933, son of sugar-refiner Abram); it later became part of Scottish Ship Management Ltd, which traded until 1987 (National Maritime Museum and public records).

3 It is interesting to note that within the Bowers Papers at SPRI (reference SPRI/MS1505/15/3) is a copy of the menu and table plan for a lunch on 16 September 1904 at the Great Hall, Criterion Restaurant, hosted by the Royal Geographical Society and Royal Society, for officers of the recently

returned National Antarctic expedition. HRB was in the UK at the time but his name does not appear on the table plan (although there are some blank spaces) on which five names are marked with a pencil cross: Captain R.F. Scott, Lieutenant A.B. Armitage (whom HRB had met on HMS *Worcester*), Mr S. Flemming, Mr C.P. Oates and Mr H.W. Simpson. The only possible explanations are that he was there (but did not, based on later information, meet Scott) or that Captain Wilson-Barker or Sir Clements Markham (who were there and whom HRB met more regularly on HMS *Worcester*) gave the menu and table plan to him for interest.

4   Letter of 13 October 1904 to May (SPRI/MS1505/1/1/2/5). Information on New York and other destinations from HRB's postcard of 24 October 1904 (private collection) and letters to/from Emily and May, October 1904 to March 1905 (SPRI/MS1505/1/1 and /2).

5   Roosevelt won the election; British Evangelicals were strong supporters of William Wilberforce and others campaigning against the slave trade and slavery.

6   The trust is referred to in publicly available documents relating to the house acquired by Emily and HRB's sisters in 1914; HRB is shown as then being a 3rd officer on the *Cape Breton*.

7   Postcard of 8 February 1905 (private collection).

8   Letters of 31 October and 3 November 1904 from Captain Wilson-Barker (SPRI/MS1505/1/2/3/9 and /10).

9   The Russian fleet sailed south during the Russo–Japanese war; in May 1905 the Japanese fleet, under Admiral Togo Heihachiro, destroyed two-thirds of the Russian fleet during the sea battle of Tshushima (regarded as the greatest naval battle since Trafalgar).

10 Letter of 5 April 1905 from Emily (SPRI/MS1505/1/2/2/22); letter of 30 March 1905 from Captain Wilson-Barker (SPRI/MS1505/1/2/3/11).

11 Seaver, p. 49.

12 Letter of 13 April 1905 from Emily (SPRI/MS1505/1/2/2/23).

13 Seaver, p. 47; SPRI/MS1505/1/1/3/5.

14 Seaver, p. 51; letter of 1 October 1905 to May (SPRI/MS1505/1/1/2/12).

15 Letter of 5 October 1905 to May (SPRI/MS1505/1/1/2/13).

16 Information in this section from Seaver, Chapter V, and letters of November 1905 to February 1906 from HRB to his family (SPRI/MS1505/1/1).

17 The Gymkhana Club hosted racquet-and-ball games, as well as equestrian activities.

18 While HRB found the problem difficult to pinpoint, his sisters later attributed it to his being constantly torn between the physical world, with all its fascinations, pleasures and possibilities, and that of the spirit, which to him and Emily was almost as tangible (Seaver, p. 54); the conflict is often evident in HRB's letters to Emily and May.

19 Postcards sent by HRB to members of his family (private collection).

20 Karachi was at that time in India; the 'son and heir' was the Prince of Wales, Prince George, then on a visit to India and Burma.

21 Ceylon is present-day Sri Lanka.

22 Letter of 17 December 1906 to May (SPRI/MS1505/1/1/2/28; quoted in Seaver, pp. 55–7).

5. In Captain Bowers' Footsteps

1   HRB was critical of Henley but the latter agreed that HRB's comments about him should be quoted in Seaver's biography and was very complimentary about HRB.
2   Information from RIM notebook (private collection). The king's younger brother, Arthur Duke of Connaught, was inspector-general of the British Forces.
3   Letter of 22 March 1907 to Emily (SPRI/MS1505/1/1/3/8; quoted in Seaver, pp. 61–2).
4   Letter of 31 March 1907 to Emily (SPRI/MS1505/1/1/3/9).
5   Letter of 15 April 1907 to May (Seaver, Chapter VI; SPRI/MS1505/1/1/2/33).
6   Diaglott Bibles (parallel Greek and English texts) were originally printed in America in the 1860s and later widely distributed by the Evangelical 'Watch Tower Society'.
7   Letter of 11 May 1907 to Emily (quoted in Seaver, p. 66).
8   Seaver (pp. 67–8); letter of 26 May 1907 to May (SPRI/MS1505/1/1/2/37).
9   Letter of 9 June 1907 to Emily (Seaver, p. 69; SPRI/MS1505/1/1/3/14).
10 The idea was considered as early as the late 1700s and exploratory work was carried out in the late 1800s – Lloyd George was keen on the project.
11 Letter of 19 June 1907 to May (SPRI/MS1505/1/1/2/39).
12 Letter of 30 June 1907 to Emily (SPRI/MS1505/1/1/3/17).
13 Letter of 5 July 1907 to May (SPRI/MS1505/1/1/3/40).
14 'Laskars' were Indians serving on RIM and other British ships on long-term contracts.
15 Seaver, p. 77.
16 Letter to May, date unknown (quotation in Seaver, p. 72).
17 Letter of 13 July 1907 to Emily (SPRI/MS1505/1/1/3/19).
18 Louis married Mary Oakley Pigott (1873–1921), the daughter of missionaries working in Asia and Australia, and became a missionary himself. The *Lusitania* was a luxury liner which predated its larger competitor the *Titanic*.
19 Information from letters of 24 July, 10 August, 1 and 13 September 1907 to May, and 9 August, 6 and 13 September 1907 to Emily (SPRI/MS1505/1/1/2/42-45 and /1/1/3/21-23).
20 Letter of 20 September 1907 to Emily (SPRI/MS1505/1/1/3/24).
21 Letter of 8 October 1907 to May (private collection).
22 A common practice at the time to save paper and postage costs.
23 Letters of October and November 1907 to Emily and May (SPRI/MS1505/1/1/2 and /3).
24 Letter of 14 November 1907 to May (SPRI/MS1505/1/1/2/49).
25 Letters of 29 November 1907 to May (SPRI/MS1505/1/1/2/50) and Emily (SPRI/MS1505/1/1/3/30).
26 Seaver, p. 84.
27 Letter of 5 January 1908 to Emily (SPRI/MS1505/1/1/3/31).

28 Letters of 17 and 23 January and 7 February 1908 to Emily (SPRI/MS1505/1/1/3/32-34).
29 Letters of 23 February and 7 March 1908 to May (SPRI/MS1505/1/1/2/51 and /52) and 2 March 1908 to Emily (SPRI/MS1505/1/1/3/37).
30 Letter of 7 March 1908 to May (SPRI/MS1505/1/1/2/52).
31 Letters of 1 and 6 April 1908 to Emily (SPRI/MS1505/1/1/3/38 and /39).
32 Letter of 23 February 1908 to May (SPRI/MS1505/1/1/2/51).
33 Letter of 31 May 1908 to Emily (SPRI/MS1505/1/1/3/40).
34 Letter of 6 July 1908 to Emily (SPRI MS1505/1/1/3/43).

6. Scotland, Dangerous Waters and a Beautiful Island

1 As no family diaries have been traced for the period, information comes from May and Edie Bowers' recollections (Seaver, Chapter VIII) and the author's research and first-hand knowledge of the area.
2 Caerlaverock is on Ardmory Road on the lower slopes of Ardbeg Hill, near Port Bannatyne.
3 Emily's neighbours were Sir William Maxwell (1841–1925), a veteran of the Co-operative movement, and his second wife Agnes (1852–1923) who moved to Bute in 1904. Caerlaverock (specially built for Sir William's retirement) is also the name of the family seat of Lord Maxwell of Bute, suggesting that Sir William, a lifelong socialist (whose views were initially not popular on Bute), had a dry sense of humour.
4 Letter of 28 December 1909 to May (SPRI/MS1505/1/1/2/80).
5 Postcards to Emily, May and Edie (private collection).
6 Letter of 20–22 January 1909 to May (SPRI/MS1505/1/1/2/57).
7 Letter to Emily (Seaver, p. 99; SPRI/MS1505/1/1/3/44).
8 Captain Allen Thomas Hunt (1866–1943) rose to the rank of admiral and was knighted.
9 A 'ripper' (used by HRB to describe men and women) is slang for an excellent person, a good example of their type.
10 From HRB's letters home, January to March 1909 (quoted in Seaver) and letters of 18 to 27 March 1909 to Emily and May (SPRI/MS1505/1/1/3/49-50 and /1/1/2/59).
11 *Dhows* are traditional Arab single- or double-sailed vessels used to carry heavy items in and around the Arabian Peninsula; crews usually range between twelve and thirty hands: information from *HMS Fox in East Indies*, 1908–10 (A.H. Shirley, OUP, 1910), Seaver (Chapter IX) and public sources. Britain and Russia had, with little or no reference to local rulers and tribes, agreed spheres of influence in Persia, Afghanistan and Tibet; the North-West Frontier Province had become a separate administrative unit from the Punjab in 1907.
12 Letter of 27 March 1909 to Emily (SPRI/MS1505/1/1/3/50).
13 Letters of 1 April 1909 to Emily (SPRI/MS1505/1/1/3/51) and 7 April 1909 to May (SPRI/MS1505/1/1/2/61).
14 Letter of 8 April 1909 to Emily (Seaver, pp. 104–5; SPRI/MS1505/1/1/3/52).

15 Seaver, p. 111.
16 Letter of 14 April 1909 to Emily (Seaver, p. 106; SPRI/MS1505/1/1/3/53).
17 Letters of 14 and 23 April 1909 to May (SPRI/MS1505/1/1/2/62-63).
18 From letters of 14 to 20 May to Emily and May (Seaver, Chapter IX; SPRI/MS1505/1/1/3/57-58 and /1/1/2/65).
19 Letter of 2 June 1909 to May (Seaver, Chapter X; SPRI/MS1505/1/1/2/68).
20 Emily used the expression 'spicy breezes' in her letter of 5 April 1905 (SPRI/MS1505/1/2/2/22); the phrase is from a hymn by Reginald Heber (1783–1826), author of *From Greenland's icy mountains* and *Holy, holy, holy*). HRB's description of Trincomalee is from a letter of 9 June 1909 to Emily (Seaver, Chapter X; SPRI/MS1505/1/1/3/60).
21 Letter of 12 July 1909 to Emily (SPRI/MS1505/1/1/3/64).
22 Letter of 27 June 1909 to May (SPRI/MS1505/1/1/2/70). *War in the Air* (pub. 1908) envisions a global war involving aerial battles, the rise of Eastern powers against the British Empire and America, and a broken, brutal and barbaric post-war society.
23 Letter of 27 June 1909 to Emily (Seaver, Chapter X; SPRI/MS1505/1/1/3/62).
24 Letters of 4 July 1909 to Emily (SPRI/MS1505/1/1/3/63) and 13 July 1909 to May (SPRI/MS1505/1/1/2/72).
25 HRB's bicycle trips in Ceylon are described from letters quoted in Seaver, Chapter X.
26 Dagobas or stupas, found all over Ceylon/Sri Lanka, are among the largest brick structures of the pre-modern world.
27 Letter of 15 August 1909 to Emily (SPRI/MS1505/1/1/3/66).
28 HRB described cycling in Ceylon as the most strenuous exercise he had ever had. He lost 2 stone (from 12 stone to 10 stone) but when, two months later, he had regained over a stone but was still the same girth, the staff surgeon suggested he had replaced fat with muscle.

7. Uncertain Times and a New Beginning

1 HRB described events in hindsight in a letter of 9 April 1910 to Emily (SPRI/MS1505/1/1/3/82).
2 Letter of 15 August 1909 to Emily (SPRI/MS1505/1/1/3/66).
3 Letter of 27 August 1909 to Emily (SPRI/MS1505/1/1/3/67).
4 The Laccadive Islands lie off Kerala, south-west India.
5 Probably Lieutenant (later Commander) Wilfrid Ward Hunt (1883–1970), who was decorated during the First World War; his grandfather, George Ward Hunt, was a Tory chancellor under Disraeli.
6 Letter of 29 October 1909 to Emily (SPRI/MS1505/1/1/3/70).
7 Letter of 10 November 1909 to May (SPRI/MS1505/1/1/2/77). Clarens was popular with musicians, writers and Russian exiles (of the latter May met several). Hotel Beau-Site (now a health centre) was used as a prisoner-of-war detention centre in the First World War, then reverted to a hotel until the 1950s.
8 Letter of 23 November 1909 to Emily (SPRI/MS1505/1/1/3/72).

9   In Sir Edward R.G.R. Evans, *South with Scott*, London: Collins/White Circle Series, 1921 (hereafter Evans), Chapter I.

10 Letter of 15 December 1909 to Emily (SPRI/MS1505/1/1/3/75).

11 Seaver, Chapter XI; HRB's charts were used by other RIM vessels and lodged by Captain Hunt with the Hydrographic Office in London as definitive versions.

12 Information from letters to Emily, Christmas Day 1909 and 29 January 1910 (SPRI/MS1505/1/1/3/76 and SPRI/MS1505/1/1/3/78), and to May, 28 December 1909, one undated and 7 to 10 January 1910 (SPRI/MS1505/1/1/2/80, SPRI/MS1505/1/1/2/81 and SPRI/MS1505/1/1/2/82).

13 Peary and Cook both claimed to have reached the North Pole first (although Cook withdrew his claim in late 1910); Norwegian explorer Roald Amundsen had also been planning an assault on the North Pole around this time.

14 *The Dollar Princess* was adapted from a German operetta and opened in autumn 1909. The title refers to the daughters of rich American businessmen who (the daughters) married into European families.

15 Letter of 31 January 1910 to May (SPRI/MS1505/1/1/2/84).

16 Letter of 10 February 1910 to Emily (SPRI/MS1505/1/1/2/80).

17 Letter of 22 February 1910 to May (SPRI/MS1505/1/1/2/86).

18 The unusual weather was attributed to the after-effects of a huge comet which passed over both hemispheres in early January 1910.

19 Letter of 1 March 1910 to May (SPRI/MS1505/1/1/2/87).

20 Letter of 20 March 1910 to May (SPRI/MS1505/1/1/2/88).

21 Information on May and Emily's holiday and time in London with HRB is taken from May's 1910 diary (private collection).

22 Letters of 30 March 1910 to Emily (SPRI/MS1505/1/1/3/81) and 3 April 1910 to May (SPRI/MS1505/1/1/2/90).

23 Letter of 11 September 1910 to Emily (SPRI/MS1/1/3/95).

24 For definitions of pemmican and finnesko, see Glossary.

25 Seaver, Chapter XI.

26 Henry's telegram is quoted in May's 1910 diary. He probably sent more than one cable as he did not know whether Emily and May were in Switzerland, Italy, France, London or Bute.

27 Letter of 9 April 1910 to Emily (SPRI/MS1505/1/1/3/82).

28 French government-owned steamship service, which sailed between France and the Middle/Far East.

29 Letter of *c.* 9 April 1910 to Captain Wilson-Barker and reminiscences by May and Edie (Seaver, Chapter XI).

30 Letters of 18 and 23 April 1910 to Emily (SPRI/MS1505/1/1/3/83 and /84).

31 D.V. stands for *Deo volente* – God willing.

32 May's 1910 diary (private collection).

33 Captain Harry McKay of the *Terra Nova* rammed and blasted the ice to free the *Discovery*.

34 The smell is mentioned in, inter alia, Evans, Chapter I.

35 Seaver, Chapter XII.

36 Sir Clements Markham's diary entry of 18 May 1910 (RGS archives: CRM 53) mentions a long talk with HRB.

37 Following a lying-in-state in Westminster Hall the coffin was taken to Paddington Station and transported by royal train to Windsor for the funeral.

38 Evans, Chapter I; HRB's fall is also mentioned in a letter from a school friend of HRB (*Sidcup & District Times*, 1913).

39 May's diary and a letter of HRB refer to a brief meeting with Sir Clements Markham that weekend, but no further details have been traced.

40 Letter of 7 June 1910 to Edie (SPRI/MS1505/1/1/1/1).

8. Heading South

1 The latter expression, used in several letters to Emily, is from the book of Revelations, in which St John describes a new heaven where Christ rules and loved ones, parted by death, are reunited forever.

2 Letters of 6 and 9 June 1910 to Emily (SPRI/MS1505/1/1/3/85 and /86).

3 Copy of menu in National Library of Scotland (GB/A.4175(6)).

4 Letters of 19 June 1910 to Edie (SPRI/MS1505/1/1/1/2) and 26 June 1910 to May (SPRI/MS1505/1/1/2/95).

5 Quotations in these pages are from letters to Emily and May, June to September 1910 (SPRI/MS1505/1/1/3/89-95 and 1/1/2/97-99); see also Seaver, Chapter XII.

6 Titus Oates (1649–1705) was an English Protestant at the time of King Charles II. Captain Lawrence Oates had owned the *Saunterer* (built 1900, recently restored) since 1905.

7 The Oates family regularly holidayed in Sidmouth where Emily Bowers had taught; it is not known whether the two men or their mothers discovered the coincidence.

8 The fact Scott did not 'send' Oates to Siberia to assist Meares in selecting ponies has been widely debated (given the poor condition of the ponies). Oates only arrived from India in late April/early May 1910, by which time Meares had left for Russia. Oates was famously straightforward, outspoken and determined – and had paid £1,000 to join the expedition – so Scott would have found it difficult to send him to Asia against his will. Oates appears to have no motive for telling HRB anything other than the truth regarding his preference for being on the ship.

9 Letter of 28 November 1910 to May (SPRI/MS1505/1/1/2/104).

10 Wilson described HRB (in a letter to his wife) as a 'short, red-headed, thick-set little man with a very large nose' who was a 'perfect treasure', 'a real good sort' and a 'perfect marvel of efficiency', who possessed 'the most unselfish character I have ever seen in a man anywhere' (Seaver, Chapter XII).

11 Reid's Palace Hotel was built by Scotsman William Reid (1822–88), a former cabin-boy who made a fortune in the wine trade; he died before the hotel opened but his sons ran it until 1925.

12 Letter of 26 June 1910 to Emily (SPRI/MS1505/1/1/3/90). In the Doldrums (5°N to 5°S) winds from the northern and southern hemispheres meet and sailing ships often become becalmed.

13   For definition of pram, see Glossary.

14   Wright walked from Cambridge to London to persuade Scott to accept him for the expedition; Gran had been introduced to Scott by Nansen during Scott's visit to Norway in March 1910.

15   In Silas Wright, *Silas, the Antarctic Diaries and Memoir of Charles S. Wright*, ed. Colin Bull & Pat F. Wright, Ohio: Ohio State University Press, 1993 (hereafter Silas), p. 14.

16   Letter to May, probably August 1910 (SPRI/MS1505/1/1/2/97).

17   Oates refers to hating the pianola in his letter of 14 August 1910 to his mother (SPRI/MS1016/335/1). HRB quotes the 'sister' lyrics in his letter of 28 August 1910 to Emily (SPRI/MS1505/1/1/3/93); scientist Raymond Priestley referred to the song in his 1962 RGS Scott Memorial Lecture (*The Geographical Journal*, June 1962).

18   This and other rowdy incidents are related in, inter alia, Elspeth Huxley's *Scott of the Antarctic*, Scribner, 1978.

19   The letters arrived in Bute on 5 September 1910.

20   Scott and Shackleton's disagreement centred on the former's perception (shared by Markham) that he had the right to mount a second British expedition in the Ross Sea area. Shackleton felt he had an equal right as long as he did not use Scott's *Discovery* headquarters at Hut Point; in the event Shackleton was forced to use the latter due to weather conditions and Scott (during the *Terra Nova* expedition) used Shackleton's Cape Royds hut and abandoned stores there, at Hut Point and elsewhere.

21   While HRB appears to have disapproved of the idea of exploiting mineral or other resources in Antarctica, the *Bay of Plenty Times* (10 October 1910) reports Mr Allen Thompson, a companion of George Wyatt, Scott's London agent, suggesting that Scott's scientists would be searching for gold in Antarctica and that, given the lack of insuperable difficulties in mining it, the latter might eventually resemble Alaska. Wilson later discounted this idea (Lyttelton newspaper cutting, SPRI/MS1505/17/2).

22   For definition of theodolite, see Glossary; HRB described Scott's theodolite as combining 'the good points of various patterns' (SPRI/MS1505/3/5/1).

23   South African outings and activities are described in letters to May and Emily (SPRI/MS1505/1/1/2/100 and 1/1/3/92-95). HRB clearly discussed Scotland with Wilson but it is not known whether he mentioned that Emily Bowers came from Cheltenham, Wilson's home town.

24   In his letter of 14 August 1910 to William King (SPRI/MS1416/2), Oates mentions that HRB's great ambition was to explore the upper reaches of the Amazon – a trip which also appealed to Oates.

25   Oates' Boer War injury is mentioned in Apsley Cherry-Garrard, *The Worst Journey in the World*, London: Vintage Classics, originally Constable, 1922, reissued 2010 (hereafter Cherry-Garrard), p. 30, and elsewhere.

26   HRB's letters posted from South Africa on 2 September arrived on Bute on 26 September; Emily and May would not have known whether replies would reach him in Australia or New Zealand. HRB's estimated dates were fairly

accurate: the *Terra Nova* arrived in Melbourne on 12 October and left New Zealand on 29 November 1910.

27 Letter of 28 August 1910 to Emily (SPRI/MS1505/1/1/2/98). The quotation is from Kipling's *Kim* (1901).

9. To the Point of Departure

1 Information from letter-journal from September to October 1910 to Emily (SPRI/MS1505/1/1/95).

2 The Beardmore Glacier was named by Shackleton (during the *Nimrod* expedition) in honour of a Glasgow shipbuilder who had employed him following his returning home ill from the *Discovery* expedition. Shackleton climbed the glacier to reach the polar plateau on the way to his 'Furthest South'; Scott used the same route.

3 Letter of 25 September 1910 to May (SPRI/MS1505/1/1/2/101). The use of sledge-flags was a long-standing tradition of British Antarctic expeditions; Sir Clements Markham, who was interested in chivalry and genealogy, designed banners for Scott's *Discovery* expedition.

4 Melbourne newspapers (11 October 1910) announced the cancellation of an address by Captain Scott scheduled for the following day due to the 'non-arrival' of the ship.

5 Letters of 17 to 21 October 1910 to Emily and May (SPRI/MS1505/1/1/3/96 and /97 and 1/1/2/102); letter of 11 November 1910 to Emily (SPRI/MS1505/1/1/3/95).

6 Lieutenant Riley and Seaman Johnson apparently failed to meet Scott's high standards.

7 *The Whip* (Cecil Raleigh, Henry Hamilton) involved spectacular special effects (e.g. an on-stage train crash and a horse race with live animals); first performed at the Drury Lane Theatre, London (1909), it toured internationally.

8 William Henry Fitchett (1841–1928) was an English-born clergyman, writer, educator, property speculator and holder of public office; his works include *How England Saved Europe* (1899–1900) and *Deeds that Won the Empire* (1897) (information from Australian Dictionary of National Biography).

9 Scott hoped for £5,000 from the Australian government but a generous local businessman matched the £2,500 grant. The Melbourne fundraising appears to have been sufficiently successful that the *Terra Nova* bypassed Sydney and sailed straight to New Zealand; letter of 21 October 1910 to Emily (SPRI/MS1505/1/1/3/97).

10 Amundsen was a veteran of the Northwest Passage and the 1897–99 *Belgica* Antarctic expedition. He had then raised funds and borrowed Nansen's ship, the *Fram*, for an attempt on the North Pole. Competing claims by Frederick Cook (who withdrew his claim in October 1910) and Robert Peary of having reached the North Pole made him change course at Madeira and try for the still-unconquered South Pole. Peary was also planning (and wrote to Scott about) an attempt in 1911 on the South Pole (Diana Preston, *A First Rate Tragedy*, New York: Mariner Books, 1997 (hereafter Preston), p. 119, et al.).

11 Letter of 28 November 1910 to May (SPRI/MS1505/1/1/2/104).

12 The hotel was damaged in the 2011 earthquake but was until then a backpacker's hostel.

13 Information and quotations in this section from letters of 17 November to 7 December 1910 to Emily (SPRI/MS1505/1/1/3/99-103).

14 Ponting's book was published on 1 June 1910, the day the *Terra Nova* left London. The dogs collected by Wyatt had been used during Peary's attempt on the North Pole.

15 The motor-sledges were developed by Scott and Reginald Skelton (who resigned from the expedition when Teddy Evans was appointed second in command) and built by the Wolseley Tool and Motor Company. They had caterpillar tracks and were effectively forerunners of First World War tanks; Scott saw them tested during his March 1910 visit to Norway (Preston, p. 119, et al.).

16 Rum and other alcoholic drinks were a long-standing component of naval rations and taken for granted on expeditions, as this effectively was. HRB noted that several people had overindulged in Cardiff.

17 Letter of 28 November 1910 to Emily (SPRI/MS1505/1/1/3/102).

18 Letter of 26 November 1910 to Emily (SPRI/MS1505/1/1/3/101).

19 Letter of 28 November 1910 to May (SPRI/MS1505/1/1/2/104). Although uncertain as to the crest's provenance, HRB was sure it was not simply 'Father's fancy' and probably referred to ancestors whose profession as archers (or bow-ers) gave the family its name.

20 Letters of 29 November 1910 to Edie and May (SPRI/MS1505/1/1/1/4, 1/1/2/104 and /106).

10. Down to the Ice

1 Quotations from letter of 10–20 December 1910 to May (SPRI/MS1505/1/1/2/106).

2 Campbell Island (then British, now New Zealand) lies at 52° South (a similar latitude to Cape Horn).

3 Scott's report appears measured but he described 2 December as a day of disaster and the outlook as being grim. Cherry-Garrard was among the least experienced sailors on board and greatly admired the efforts of HRB and others under such conditions.

4 The *Balaenoptera Sibbaldi* (Sibbald's rorqual) is believed to be the world's largest mammal; it is named after Scottish physician and antiquary Sir Robert Sibbald (1641–1722).

5 See Michael Tarver, *The S.S. Terra Nova*, Brixham: Pendragon Maritime Publications, 2006, Chapter 6; the *Terra Nova*'s progress through the pack ice was considerably slower than that of the *Discovery*.

6 Silas, p. 55; Cherry-Garrard, Chapter 3.

7 Gran described the skis to a reporter in Lyttelton (cutting in SPRI/MS1505/17/2); HRB can be seen skiing in *The Great White Silence*.

8 Letter of 18 December 1910 to Edie (SPRI/MS1505/1/1/1/5).

9 Letter of 25 December 1910 to Emily (SPRI/MS1505/1/1/3/104).

10 Scott appears to have put on a good face but complained in his journals about the lack of progress.

11 The seamen had already eaten similar fare washed down with beer and whisky; 'wardroom' dinner and entertainments are described in Scott's and other accounts.

12 Letter of 1 January 1911 (misdated 1910) to May (SPRI/MS1505/1/2/107).

13 The practice is described by both Ponting and Scott.

14 Scott decided not to announce the names of those going on the Southern and Pole journeys until relatively near the time (Shackleton felt he had announced his choices too early).

15 Based on Shackleton's experience, the ponies might have made it part-way up the Beardmore Glacier but would have been unlikely to reach the plateau.

16 Mount Erebus, the highest mountain on Ross Island and the world's most southerly active volcano, is almost 12,500ft (c. 3,800m) high.

17 Described in, inter alia, Robert Falcon Scott, *Journals: Captain Scott's Last Expedition*, ed. Max Jones, Oxford: Oxford World's Classics; originally London: John Murray, 1910–12, 2005 (hereafter Scott), and Herbert Ponting, *The Great White South*, London: Gerald Duckworth & Sons, 1921 *et seq.*

18 Described in, inter alia, HRB's journal written for Emily, May–June 1911 (SPRI/MS1505/3/5/5).

19 Some regard Scott's decision to divide the hut's living space based on rank as indicating elitism or snobbery on his part. Such a set-up would have been the norm on Royal Navy ships (which the *Terra Nova* effectively was); HRB noted that, while he sometimes mixed with his crew in the RIM, he would not have done so in the Royal Navy. Although Shackleton, a merchant naval officer, is sometimes regarded as a more democratic leader than Scott because his Cape Royds hut had a single living area, a diagram of its layout shows he had his own cabin (Scott shared his sleeping and living area with Wilson and Teddy Evans).

20 A name given by Scott to what was previously known as New Land.

21 Letter of 23 January 1911 to Emily (SPRI/MS1505/1/1/3/107).

11. The Depot Journey

1 Information of the depot journey is drawn from, inter alia, a journal written by Birdie for Emily, May–June 1911 (SPRI/MS1505/3/5/5); Seaver, Chapter XIII, and Cherry-Garrard, Chapter 5.

2 Letter of 24 January 1911 to Emily (Spink sale, 14 July 2010).

3 When he revisited the *Discovery* hut, Scott was annoyed because Shackleton appeared to have left open a window, through which snow had entered (Scott).

4 Letters of 25, 26 January and 1 February 1911 to Emily (SPRI/MS1505/1/1/3/108-9 and /3/5/3).

5 Scott (13 February 1911).

6 Bowers' letter-journals to his family; also cited in Seaver, Chapter XIII and Cherry-Garrard, Chapter 5.

7 The incident occurred around the time the sea-ice broke up under HRB's party, suggesting similar conditions may have led to both occurrences.

8   HRB's formal report to Scott is, at the time of writing, in private hands and unable to be viewed. Both alternative endings are with the document, which also bears annotations by Scott: 'Crean & the Curry Powder, Cherry & the Emperor Penguin' (source: Christie's website). This, and Scott's evident relief (in his journal as well as in talking to HRB) that no one was lost or injured, suggests he did not regard those involved as being to blame; Scott and HRB both knew, however, that the loss of so many ponies on the depot journey had significant implications for the expedition's transportation plans.

9   From HRB's journal (SPRI/MS1505/3/5/9).

10 From T. Griffith Taylor, *With Scott: the Silver Lining* (London: Smith, Elder &Co., 1916).

12. Deepest Winter

1   By coincidence (probably unknown to HRB), Victor had been sponsored by The Lydney Institute in Gloucestershire, Emily's home county.

2   Measurements taken in the hut that year show HRB to be, at 5ft 4in, the smallest officer by almost 3 inches; his weight (12 stones) and measurements (waist: approximately 33in; chest: 40in; calf: 16in) were, however, equal to or greater than those of most of his taller companions.

3   A football match can be seen in *The Great White Silence*.

4   From a journal written for Emily (SPRI/MS1505/3/5/5).

5   Information from the manuscript of Scott's lecture notes (Canterbury Museum, Christchurch, New Zealand: Scott, R.F., 'Southern Journey 1911–1912', lecture; 2010.102.1).

6   Scott's lecture notes show he never expected the South Pole party to be back before the *Terra Nova* left McMurdo Sound; he was well aware from his *Discovery* experience of the risk of ships becoming trapped in the ice.

7   Since HRB asked his question, huge sea-spiders have been found frozen in the ice and seen on the Antarctic seabed (including in BBC's *Frozen Planet* series).

8   The Midwinter dinner is described in, inter alia, Scott and Cherry-Garrard.

9   The *Terra Nova's South Polar Times* (edited by Cherry) was the successor to the *Discovery South Polar Times* (edited by Shackleton). In the former, Griff Taylor and HRB were frequent contributors, Wilson was the main illustrator and Dennis Lillie's cartoons make regular appearances.

10 Snapdragon, a popular Victorian Christmas parlour game, involved a bowl filled with flaming brandy and raisins from which, as other lights were extinguished, participants tried to extract the raisins (source: Ivan Day).

11 Letter of 26 June 1911 to Emily (SPRI/MS1505/1/1/3/111).

12 Details of the Cape Crozier journey are drawn from a letter dated October 1910 [should be 1911] to May (SPRI/MS1505/1/1/2/110), which is extensively quoted in Cherry-Garrard and Seaver.

13 Relaying involves dragging one sledge forward before returning for the second one, thus walking 3 miles to progress one.

14 HRB recorded winds of Force 10 or 11 and temperatures of -77°F.

15 Scott had (per Cherry-Garrard) tried to dissuade Wilson from making the Cape Crozier journey, but agreed on condition Wilson brought HRB and Cherry back safely.

16 Conversation described in Cherry-Garrard, Chapter 17 (p. 537 in Vintage edition).

17 The ice had doubled the weight of their tent, sleeping bags and clothing.

13. Getting Ready

1 Letter of 15 September 1911 to Emily (SPRI/MS1505/1/1/3/112).

2 Letters of 16 and 18 October 1911 to Harry Pennell (RGS archives: RGS/ HLP/2/6 and /7).

3 Letter of 27 October 1911 (written as 1910) to Edie (SPRI/MS1505/1/1/1/8).

4 He also wrote to her before leaving on the depot journey (SPRI/MS1488/2); HRB was not particularly fond of Kathleen Scott but may have written because he knew Scott was writing to Emily Bowers at those times.

5 A cinematograph (a late nineteenth-century invention) combines the functions of a camera, projector and developer. The filming session is mentioned in Scott; Edward Wilson's *Diary of the Terra Nova Expedition*, ed. H.R.G. King, USA: Humanities Press, 1910–12 & 1972 (hereafter Wilson/King) and Michael Smith's *An Unsung Hero: Tom Crean – Antarctic Survivor*, Cork: Collins Press, 2000 & 2009; the results of it can be seen in *The Great White Silence*.

6 For definition of hoosh, see Glossary.

7 Letter of 1 November 1911 to Emily (SPRI/MS1505/1/1/3/113).

14. Across the Barrier to the Beardmore

1 SPRI holds HRB's 'sledging journal' (SPRI/MS1505/3/5/9, which includes letters to his family), navigational log (copy, SPRI/MS795/2) and sightings records (SPRI/MS796). Quotations in Chapters 14–16 are from these or letters as referenced – with some small variations from SPRI published journal transcripts (not available at the time of writing) for clarity. Details of events HRB does not describe but would have known about are drawn from Scott, Wilson/King and other sources as referenced. Dates can be uncertain when the party marched overnight or was marooned for days in blizzards.

2 Those leading slower ponies left first so that everyone arrived at camp at roughly the same time.

3 Oates regularly and forcibly expressed his opinions on the ponies' poor general health and fitness, but did everything possible to look after them well and build them up for long journeys.

4 Parhelia are optical phenomena that occur at low temperatures when light refracts off ice crystals; Edward Wilson sketched and painted them during the *Discovery* and *Terra Nova* expeditions.

5 Referred to in Evans, Chapter XII.

6 Note of 23 November 1911 from HRB to Ponting, British Antarctic Expedition Correspondence Files (SPRI/MS280/28/7a).

7   Letter of 24 November 1911 to Emily (SPRI/MS1505/3/5/9).
8   For definition of hypsometer, see Glossary.
9   To sailors 'a Jonah' (biblical character swallowed by a whale) is a sailor or passenger whose presence brings bad luck and endangers the ship or enterprise. See David M. Wilson's *The Lost Photographs of Captain Scott*, London: Little Brown, 2011, for discussion of the cameras as 'Jonahs'.
10 Scott makes a similar point (Scott, 4 December 1911) and expressed an interest in exploring the eastern end of the Transantarctic range during 1912.
11 'Fiends of darkness' (opposing forces to angels) try to drag souls into Hell while angels try to raise them to Heaven.
12 *By Order of the Company* by American writer Mary Johnson (1870–1936) was published in Britain in 1900. Keohane's poem is quoted in Scott, 5 December 1911.
13 'Short commons' is slang for 'short rations'.
14 Letter of 8 December 1911 to May (SPRI/MS1505/3/5/9).

15. To the Pole

1   A williwaw is a type of katabatic wind (see Glossary).
2   Undated letter to Emily (SPRI/MS1505/1/1/3/114 and quoted in Seaver); from the context it can only have been sent back around this time.
3   The Scenic Railway was an early form of roller-coaster (developed in America in 1886) which ran through a scenery-painted tunnel.
4   According to Scott and Cherry's journals, this was a process Scott and Wilson found extremely hard.
5   Letter of 21 December 1911 to Edie (SPRI/MS1505/3/5/9).
6   Evans, Chapter XIV.
7   Ibid.
8   HRB's team now had two new members who had been manhauling for considerably longer than the others; Scott's team had been with him for several weeks and included two men with whom he had sledge-hauled during the *Discovery* expedition.
9   Scott (28 December 1911).
10 Wilson/King (30 December 1911) refers to the talk taking place but gives no further details.
11 Scott (1 January 1912) records that HRB's party was not in high spirits and suggests they had not organised themselves well. Both Scott and Wilson/King mention the chocolate.
12 Oates refers to this in a letter to his mother from Cape Evans (SPRI/MS1317/1/3).
13 The South Pole lies at around 9,200ft, approximately 800ft below the altitude at which they then were.
14 Letter of 3 January 1912 to Emily (SPRI/MS1505/3/5/9).
15 The little flag is now in the Royal Collection (RCIN60068).
16 Scott (8 January 1912) praises HRB's skill, hard work and efficiency in dealing with increased duties, and comments that he appeared to be enjoying himself, to not feel the cold and to need very little sleep.

17 Many of these short entries are written on separate lines; punctuation has been added where necessary to make the text understandable.

18 Orientation can be determined without a compass by using a precisely calibrated analogue watch set to local time; the method is more accurate at high latitudes and during long daylight hours. HRB's notes show he knew exactly how much time each watch generally dropped each day (down to seconds). The time was dropped by the watch which usually lost less time; HRB remained baffled as to what had happened and it appears the mystery was never solved.

19 Letter of 17 January 1912 to Emily (SPRI/MS1505/3/5/9).

20 Amundsen made his request to safeguard against his team's dying on the return journey.

21 As they may or may not have remembered, it was Norwegian Gran who had retrieved the forgotten Union Jack for Scott.

22 HRB's navigational log (copy, SPRI/MS795/2).

23 Letters of 18 January 1912 (SPRI/MS1505/3/5/9).

16. The Long Haul Back

1 Wilson/King (23 January 1912).

2 Wilson/King (25 January 1912); cocaine tablets were and are a standard remedy for snow-blindness.

3 Wilson/King (28 January 1912).

4 Wilson/King (29, 30 January 1912).

5 Wilson/King (3 February 1912).

6 Per Scott (4 February 1912), the temperature was 20°F lower than it had been at the same stage on the outward journey, Evans was deteriorating, they were eating good rations but getting hungrier, but HRB was still full of energy and bustling around all the time.

7 Wilson/King (4 February 1912).

8 HRB made his last journal entry on 3 February but he continued to complete navigational and other records for a while.

9 Scott (7 February 1912) describes the discovery of the shortage as causing something of a panic and resulting in HRB being very upset.

10 Wilson/King (9 February 1912).

11 Scott (12 February 1912) cites one wrong steering decision as a 'fatal' chance.

12 Scott (12 February) does not name individuals involved in navigational differences of opinion, but given he and HRB were the most experienced navigators it is likely to have been them.

13 Scott says Evans died at 12.30 a.m. on 18 February, Wilson suggests about 10 p.m. on 17 February.

14 Recorded in Oates' diary (referred to in Sue Limb & Patrick Cordingley, *Captain Oates: Soldier and Explorer*, Barnsley, Yorkshire: Pen and Sword Books, 1982 & 2009).

15 Scott had regularly requested that the dogs should be well looked after following their return so they could be used again the following season. He also asked

several people to ensure a dog team was brought to One Ton depot or further if necessary to meet them in the hope that this would allow the news to be taken to the *Terra Nova* and thus to New Zealand (rather than as a rescue mission).

16 The last entry in HRB's log book (SPRI/MS795/2) is on 12 March 1912 but he stopped making records in his navigation book (SPRI/MS796) on 27 February 1912.

17 Oates' diary contains criticism of Scott but he would have trusted Wilson not to betray any confidences.

18 Oates' hands were by then so frostbitten that he could not have opened the tent-flap ties himself; HRB regularly went outside the tent late and/or early to check the weather or (before this stage) to take readings. Scott quotes Oates as saying, 'I am just going outside and may be some time', but neither HRB nor Wilson refer to this.

19 Scott ('probably' 17 March) describes HRB and Wilson as ceaselessly cheerful but suggests that they, like him, no longer believed they would make it back.

20 Letter of about 22 March 1912 to Emily Bowers (SPRI/MS1505/3/5/9).

21 While Antarctic blizzards often blow themselves out after two days, Frank Wild (1873–1966) a veteran of the *Discovery* expedition, three expeditions with Shackleton (including *Nimrod*) and one with Mawson, records he had been in blizzards of six to nine days and that other members of Mawson's expedition had experienced one of seventeen days (Angie Butler, *The Quest for Frank Wild*, Radway, Warwick: Jackleberry Press, 2011, p. 90). In his last diary entry (29 March), Scott refers to continuous gales (since 21 March) and whirling drift outside the tent; he had earlier referred to blizzards so the poor visibility and conditions may have been due to a mixture of both.

22 Scott refers in his journal and one of his last letters to Kathleen Scott to it being agreed that they would not end their lives artificially (also suggested by Wilson's and HRB's last letters).

23 This letter (undated) was addressed by Scott to Sir George Egerton, an Arctic veteran (1875–6), Scott's commanding officer on the *Victorious* (1906), later second sea lord and chief of naval personnel.

17. Breaking the Silence

1 Information in this chapter comes from, inter alia: Scott, Vol. II; Cherry-Garrard; Evans; a lecture by Teddy Evans (*The Geographical Journal*, Vol. 42); and Max Jones, *The Last Great Quest*, Oxford: Oxford University Press, 2003 (hereafter Jones).

2 In the event the attempt failed and the *Terra Nova* left for New Zealand on 7 March 1912.

3 Letter of 22 May 1911 from Oriana Wilson to Emily Bowers (SPRI/MS1505/7/2/20).

4 The postcard, with a photograph of a Weddell seal, is part of a set from the Scottish National Antarctic Expedition (1902–04, leader William Speirs Bruce).

5 Letter of 30 March 1912 from Harry Pennell to Emily Bowers (SPRI/MS1505/7/2/13); Scott's letter to Emily before leaving for the Southern journey is quoted in Seaver (also SPRI/MS1505/7/2/15).

6 Accounts vary regarding the exact positions of the bodies; this version draws from several published accounts and from a newspaper interview given by Gran (cutting in SPRI/MS1505/17/2).

7 The name Sorrowful Camp is mentioned in Williamson's account (*Polar Record*, Vol. 14, No. 88, 1968).

8 Description from Evans, Chapter XIX.

9 Page 7 of *The Scotsman* is in the Bowers' file of cuttings about the expedition (SPRI/MS1505/17/2), suggesting that it was purchased by Emily Bowers at the time.

10 Scott's letter (October 1911) is quoted in Seaver (original SPRI/MS1505/7/2/15).

11 *The Daily Mirror* (12 February 1913) reported that Emily Bowers travelled 'continually' while Birdie was away from home.

12 Drawn from, inter alia: Pennell's diary (Canterbury Museum, MS433, A183-9); Oamaru's *Evening Post* (10 February 1913); www.nzhistory.net.nz (NZ government website); and Scott. It is still uncertain whether Pennell and Atkinson telegraphed the Central News Agency in London direct or sent a message to Kinsey for onward transmission; Pennell's diary suggests the latter and Kinsey's office also sent information to the Central News Agency later that day.

13 The message (codenamed Hereward) had been prepared by Scott with the intention that Scott or others would supplement it with details of the South Pole journey to bring it to the 6,000 words required by the Central News Agency contract. When the Agency received a shorter message they cabled Kinsey, but he declined to provide them with further information before speaking to Teddy Evans and others still on the *Terra Nova* (then in Akaroa harbour).

14 New Zealand and Australian newspapers could only run the full official story the following day.

15 Oates also left personal effects there (letter to mother, 23 November 1910, SPRI/MS1016/337).

16 Oriana Wilson may have been at the service as she had already been staying with friends in New Zealand at the time. Kathleen Scott and her son were still on their way to New Zealand.

17 Letter of 11 February 1913 to Emily Bowers from T.W. Holderness (SPRI/MS1505/7/3/2).

18 The king had not attended the service following the sinking of the *Titanic*; the order of service is in SPRI/MS1505/14/4/1. Sir Clements Markham did not attend; he was in Portugal, where he organised a similar memorial service locally (RGS archives: CM55).

19 *Sidcup & District Times* (February 1913, Bexley Libraries).

20 Letter quoted in Seaver and elsewhere; SPRI/MS1505/7/2/17.

21 Letter dated 23 April 1913 from India Office (SPRI/MS1505/7/3/3).

22 The card (copy at SPRI) includes three Bible quotations: 'Till the day break and the shadows flee away' (Solomon, iv, 6); 'They that dwell under His shadow shall return' (Hosea, xiv, 7); 'I am the resurrection and the life; he that believeth in me, though he were dead, yet shall he live' (John, xi, 25).

23 Letter of 17 April 1913 from Emily to Joseph Kinsey (MS-Papers-0022-35ve, collection of (Sir) Joseph James Kinsey, National Library, Wellington, New Zealand).

24 *Greenock Telegraph and Clyde Shipping Gazette* (February 1913). Cheltenham papers covered Edward Wilson's death but did not seem to make the connection between Emily's family, the Webbs, and Bowers.

25 *The Geographical Journal* (April 1913) carried obituaries of Wilson and Oates (but not of Edgar Evans). The March issue (largely black-edged) included over twenty pages on the expedition, including Scott's obituary and Lord Curzon's statement: 'Nor must we forget the commissariat officer, Lieut. Bowers, who came from that splendid little service the Royal Indian Marine, and who must have possessed rare merits to be selected by Captain Scott out of all the eager candidates for the last march to the Pole.'

26 A memorial service was held in St John's Church, Cardiff, on 16 February 1913.

27 Letter of 21 June 1913 from Teddy Evans to Emily Bowers (SPRI/MS1505/7/2/9); David Hempleman-Adams, Sophie Gordon & Emma Stuart, *The Heart of the Great Alone: Scott, Shackleton and Antarctic Photography*, London: Royal Collection Enterprises Ltd, 2009 & 2011, catalogue 94 (p. 199).

28 The photograph is in Bute Museum.

29 National Probate calendar (mis-describing Emily as Henry's widow).

30 Jones, p. 108.

31 Sir Clements Markham's diary entry for 8 July 1913 (RGS archives: CM55).

32 Details kindly provided by the Royal Collection and Royal Archives.

33 From letters from Emily Bowers to Frank Milner (4 September 1913; 17 and 25 June 1914) (Canterbury Museum, Christchurch, New Zealand: MS68, A176.152, 437/76). Members of the Wilson family, Kathleen Scott and Caroline Oates were also in touch with the school.

34 *Sidmouth Herald* (29 September 1934).

35 *The Geographical Journal* (December 1913).

36 Details from property documents relating to the acquisition of the property.

37 Order of service (SPRI/MS1505/14/4/3).

38 *The Geographical Journal* (September 1914); Royal Indian Marine annual report (1914).

39 From public sources.

40 Letters of October/November 1914 from Edie to Emily Bowers (SPRI/MS1505/5/1-3).

41 By 1918 Edie was working at a war hospital in Croydon; see photograph of 12 March 1918 (SPRI/MS1505/P87/1/3/8).

42 Letter of 17 December 1915 from Harry Pennell to Emily Bowers (Spink sale, 14 July 2010).

43 The Bowers had a copy of the order of service (5 May 1916, SPRI/MS1505/14/4/2) which suggests that one of them attended.

44 Letter of 14 December 1917 from Cherry-Garrard to Emily (SPRI/MS1505/7/2/7).

45 Letter of 19 October 1924(?) from Emily Bowers to Lady Maxwell (SPRI/MS1505/7/1/2).

46 Letter of 2 May 1928(?) from Emily Bowers to Lady Maxwell (SPRI/MS1505/7/1/7).

47 Information from death certificate.

48 May sold Caerlaverock in 1931 (SPRI/MS1505/6/1/12).

49 Seaver wrote *Edward Wilson: Nature Lover, The Faith of Edward Wilson of the Antarctic, 'Birdie' Bowers of the Antarctic* and a biography of Scott.

50 The book was reviewed, inter alia, in *The Scotsman* (SPRI/MS1505/17/2); the reviewer described HRB as 'a great man'.

51 Letters from Frank Milner to Lady Maxwell (May) of 27 November and 28 November 1928 (SPRI/MS1505/6/1/9-10). The presentation date is on a plaque beside the flag but it is not known whether May presented it in person. Oriana Wilson (who visited New Zealand regularly) and Mrs Campbell (Scott's sister) both gave Scott Memorial lectures at the school, of which alumni include Murray Ellis (1955–858 Commonwealth Transantarctic expedition) and David Harrowfield (Antarctic scientist and lecturer).

52 Letters, etc. on film and premiere (SPRI/MS1505/6/1/3); Christmas cards from Beckwith and Meade (SPRI/MS1505/11/2).

53 Letters from May to Angus McMillan (SPRI/MS1505/6.1.6-7), a widely recognised authority on polar philately (Scottish Book of Philatelists, 1981). Birdie refers to potential interest in frankings, etc. in his letter of 10 December 1910 to May (SPRI/MS1505/1/1/2/106).

54 Letter/card of 24 October 1948 and 28 September 1950 (SPRI/MS1505/6/1/6-7). Atkinson's first wife died in 1928; he remarried soon afterwards but died at sea in 1929. His widow came to live in Bute, across the road from Caerlaverock, but it is believed she and the Bowers sisters were not particularly close.

55 See catalogue of Bowers' papers (SPRI: H.G.R. King, 1990). McMillan gave HRB's RIM uniforms to Paisley Museum.

56 Letter of 27 October 1911 (written as 1910) to Edie (SPRI/MS1505/1/1/1/8).

57 Men died at the Ross Sea end of Shackleton's Transantarctic expedition, the new Antarctic memorial in St Paul's Cathedral (2011) commemorates almost thirty British people who have died while working in Antarctica, and three people died in a storm in the Ross Sea in early 2011. It is sometimes also forgotten that Amundsen's party nearly came to grief early in their attempt on the South Pole.

58 The plays, both called *The Worst Journey in the World*, covered different aspects of the expedition and its aftermath. The digital version of *The Great White Silence* was premiered at the 2010 London Film Festival and received an award for its restoration, with a new score incorporating the sound of the *Terra Nova* bell.

SELECTED BIBLIOGRAPHY

There are a large number of books available on Scott's journey and other Antarctic expeditions and related matter; I have listed those to which I have referred and those I found enlightening in different ways.

Avery, Tom (2004), *Pole Dance*, London: Orion

Barczewski, Stephanie (2007), *Antarctic Destinies*, London and New York: Hambledon/Continuum

Bowers, Henry R., Lane, Heather, Boneham, Naomi & Smith, Robert D. (eds) (2011), *The South Pole Journals*, Introduction by Anne Strathie, Cambridge: Scott Polar Research Institute

Butler, Angie (2011), *The Quest for Frank Wild*, Radway, Warwick: Jackleberry Press

Cherry-Garrard, Apsley (1922, reissued 2010), *The Worst Journey in the World*, London: Vintage Classics; originally Constable ('Cherry-Garrard')

Cracknell, James & Fogle, Ben (2009), *Race to the Pole*, London: Macmillan

Crane, David (2005), *Scott of the Antarctic*, London: HarperCollins

Evans, Sir Edward R.G.R. (1921), *South with Scott*, London: Collins/White Circle Series ('Evans')

Fiennes, Ranulph (2003), *Captain Scott*, London: Hodder and Stoughton

Hempleman-Adams, David, Gordon, Sophie & Stuart, Emma (2009, 2011), *The Heart of the Great Alone: Scott, Shackleton and Antarctic Photography*, London: Royal Collection Enterprises Ltd

Hooper, Meredith (2010), *The Longest Winter*, London: John Murray

Huntford, Roland (2010), *The Race for the South Pole: in their own words*, London: Continuum Books

Huntford, Roland & Theroux, Paul (2000), *The Last Place on Earth*, London: Abacus

Jones, Max (2003), *The Last Great Quest*, Oxford: Oxford University Press ('Jones')

Lagerbom, Charles H. (1999), *The Fifth Man – Henry R. Bowers*, Whitby: Caedmon of Whitby

Larson, Edward J. (2011), *An Empire of Ice*, New Haven & London: Yale University Press

Limb, Sue & Cordingley, Patrick (1982, 2009), *Captain Oates: Soldier and Explorer*, Barnsley, Yorkshire: Pen and Sword Books

McCrae, Alister & Prentice, Alan (1978), *Irrawaddy Flotilla*, Paisley: James Paton Ltd

Ponting, Herbert (1921 *et seq*), *The Great White South*, London: Gerald Duckworth & Sons

Preston, Diana (1997), *A First Rate Tragedy*, New York: Mariner Books and other editions ('Preston')

Raeside, Adrian (2009), *Return to Antarctica*, Mississauga, Ontario: John Wiley & Sons Canada Ltd

Riffenburgh, Beau (2011), *Terra Nova, Scott's Last Expedition*, Cambridge: Scott Polar Research Institute

Scott, Robert Falcon (1910–12, 2005), *Journals: Captain Scott's Last Expedition*, ed. Max Jones, Oxford: Oxford World's Classics; originally London: John Murray ('Scott')

—— (1905, 2009), *The Voyage of the Discovery*, London: Wordsworth Editions Ltd

Seaver, George (1938), *'Birdie' Bowers of the Antarctic*, London: John Murray ('Seaver')

—— (1933), *Edward Wilson of the Antarctic: Naturalist and Friend*, London: John Murray

—— (1940), *Scott of the Antarctic*, London: John Murray

Shackleton, Ernest (1909, 2007), *The Heart of the Antarctic*, London: Wordsworth Editions Ltd

Smith, Michael (2002), *I Am Just Going Out*, Staplehurst: Spellmount Ltd

—— (2000, 2009), *An Unsung Hero: Tom Crean – Antarctic Survivor*, Cork: Collins Press

Solomon, Susan (2001), *The Coldest March*, New Haven and London: Yale University Press

Spufford, Francis (1996), *I May Be Some Time: Ice and the English Imagination*, London: Faber and Faber

Tarver, Michael (2006), *The S.S. Terra Nova*, Brixham: Pendragon Maritime Publications

Wheeler, Sara (2001), *Cherry: A Life of Apsley Cherry-Garrard*, London: Vintage/ Random House

Wheeler, Sara (1997), *Terra Incognita*, London: Vintage/Random House

Williams, Isobel (2008), *With Scott in the Antarctic: Edward Wilson*, Stroud: The History Press

—— (2012) *Captain Scott's Invaluable Assistant: Edgar Evans*, Stroud: The History Press

Wilson, David M. (2011), *The Lost Photographs of Captain Scott*, London: Little Brown

Wilson, D.M. & C.J. (2011), *Edward Wilson's Antarctic Notebooks*, Cheltenham: Reardon Publishing

Wilson, D.M. & Elder, D.B. (2000), *Cheltenham in Antarctica*, Cheltenham: Reardon Publishing

Wilson, Edward (1910–12, 1972), *Diary of the Terra Nova Expedition*, ed. H.R.G. King, USA: Humanities Press ('Wilson/King')

Wright, Silas (1993), *Silas, the Antarctic Diaries and Memoir of Charles S. Wright*, ed. Colin Bull & Pat F. Wright, Ohio: Ohio State University Press ('Silas')

Works of Fiction

Bainbridge, Beryl (1991, 2009), *The Birthday Boys*, London: Abacus
Ryan, Robert (2009), *Death on the Ice*, London: Headline Review/Publishing

Films & Television Programmes

The Great White Silence, Ponting, BFI (1924, remastered 2010)
90 Degrees South, Ponting (1933)
Scott of the Antarctic (1948)
Life in the Freezer (2005), David Attenborough and others, BBC
The Frozen Planet (2011), David Attenborough and others, BBC
The Secrets of Scott's Hut (2011), Ben Fogle and others, BBC

INDEX

The names of individuals, e.g. Cherry-Garrard, Scott and Wilson, may also appear in narratives of expedition journeys made with Bowers. Appendix A is referenced as it contains the dates ranks, etc., of members of the Terra Nova expedition; endnotes have not been indexed but may contain significant further information on individuals or indexed topics.